MW01278603

Advance Pr[aise]

"Behind every astonishing door, there is another. Even this heinous hospital murder is revealed to be one in a serial line of many...
MET THE END is an extraordinary journey for the reader, the
author, and her teen-age self. It teaches us that coming of age
can happen at any age, that knowledge is always power, and that
cyanide does not stay in the bloodstream for long—as opposed
to MET THE END, which gets in your blood and stays there. It
succeeds resoundingly in defying assumption, even as to its literary
genre. It is an unflinchingly honest autobiography and also a true-
crime novel; it is both memoir and medical thriller, journalism and
self-help. Alternately soulful and hard-driving, poetic and witty,
acerbic and poignant, in MET THE END, you never see the end
'til you get there."

— **Lissa Levin**, *playwright, screenwriter and television
producer (MAD ABOUT YOU, CHEERS)*

"This is a story of family, love, loss, tragedy, murder, resilience, and
ultimately a story of survival. You may have heard of the notorious
"Angel of Death," but this is not a tale about him; it is an intimate
introduction to the family of the man whose death unveiled a serial
killer. You meet the family before tragedy strikes and stay with
them through a roller coaster ride to recovery. MET THE END is
heartbreaking, and at the same time, hopeful."

— **Dustin O'Regan**, *editor-at-large,* Sheridan Road *magazine*

"MET THE END turned my expectations sideways. I highly rec-
ommend it as a thriller concealed in intelligent and poetic history,
both geographic and personal. It is deeply personal. It is not indul-
gent; it is brave and uncompromisingly honest. And it is true."

— **D. Lynn Meyers,** *of D. Lynn Meyers casting, Producing Artistic
Director, Ensemble Theatre of Cincinnati*

"Author Brians Ragusa illustrates how tragedy and trauma plague people, families and communities, and how we rise from the ashes. A horrific tragedy that is both unique, yet all too familiar, this memoir exposes the truth of trauma and what happens when institutions and systems that are designed to protect people and bring justice fail."

—*Yvette R. Simpson*, Esq., *former Cincinnati City Councilmember; CEO, Democracy for America; ABC Commentator;* author of *On Purpose: The Power of Authenticity and Intention*

"Holly Brians Ragusa has given those of us who lived this story a summary of where we were and what we saw—a young blended family, so normal in the '70s and '80s—and nothing was normal. She shows such self-insight (and she earned it), from her youth to the present. We are all proud of her and her skill in helping us put our roles in perspective. Holly speaks the truth on so many levels."

—*Fran Suesz, longtime friend of John Powell and his family*

"When murder happens within a family, it is difficult to deal with the amounts of anger, grief and pain that are brought on. It can be especially hard on teenagers, who have ordinary difficulties with their emotions and circumstances, to find the tools and resources needed when confronted by murder. Writing this story had to be such a healing experience for Holly. It is very important after a homicide to seek and find the unique support of other families who also have experienced a murder. I was very pleased and grateful to read in *MET THE END* that there was a Parents of Murdered Children (POMC) chapter for the Powell family to attend and talk with other families about their feelings dealing with the murder. This type of healing is exactly what our organization is about, and we hope this book will encourage others to seek our support.

—*Beverly Warnock, Executive Director, Parents of Murdered Children*

Met the End

An Investigation of the Past; a Daughter's Duty to Herself

Holly Brians Ragusa

Amused Moon

Published Amused Moon 2022

Copyright © HBR Writes LLC Holly Brians Ragusa 2020

Library of Congress Control Number:

2022916818

All rights reserved

ISBN 979-8-9869156-5-4

Printing 2. 2023

Printed in The United States of America

All rights reserved. Except for brief passages quoted in media or interviews, no part of this book may be reproduced in any form or by any means, electronic or mechanical, included photocopying or recording, or by any information sharing and retrieval system, without permission in writing from the author and publisher.

Book jacket design by Nicole Roberts
Cover photos by Patricia Powell (family snapshot), Bruno Ticianelli (road)
Author photo by Michelle Abernathy
Book design by Julie Coppens

In memory of Dad, in honor of Mom

If nothing saves us from death,

may love at least save us from life.

Pablo Neruda

Whoever saves one life, saves the world entire.

Thomas Keneally

Acknowledgements

F OR MY FAVORITE love stories: Damon, Nillin and Deej;
with fierce adoration, I believe in you, too. All my love, Mom,
Heather and John—your faith and perspectives have shaped this
story, and me. Special recognition to Fran and Joe Suesz for your
enduring support and lifelong friendship. Robert Wasserman for
asking for my sources. Lori and Jeff Vetter for your memory. Dr.
Lori Gresham—For Good. To Julie Coppens, my brilliant, inimi-
table editor, your discernment and insight brought this manuscript
to life. Anne Delano Steinert, Ph.D., the bounty of your historical
work is essential, and thank you for leaving me speechless. Holly
Earley, thank you for meeting me with love at all points in my life.
To see you dancing in the purple rain, Karena Garriques. For public
and private belief in my story, thank you to Yvette Simpson, Dustin
O'Regan and also to Lissa Levin, for an editorial that drew me out.
Beverly Warnock (POMC), your work is essential, I appreciate the
support. Thank you especially to D. Lynn Meyers, for all that you
are, for what you bring to Cincinnati, for your abiding faith in this
story and in me. Sincerest thanks to Glenn Whitaker, Esq. for your
time and kindness. Great thanks to Hamilton County Prosecutor
Joe Deters and his staff for kind offers, sensitive information and
accommodation. Pat Minarcin for uncovering truths and for the
exchanges. Terry Gaines, Esq. for your sensitivity and memory.
Thank you to the Cincinnati Police Department and Homicide Division, and Capt. Lisa Davis, District 1, and Diane Arnold. Craig
Delaval at Shed Media, I appreciate your consideration. Tim Cagle,
thanks my friend, for the connection. Patricia Tennison for next
steps. Michelle Abernathy for photography that captured the me

I see. Thankful for the artistry of Nillin Rae Melodii for Amused Moon artwork. Creative thanks to Deej Ragusa, Julie Coppens and Amy Hunter for cover design conceptualization—and to Nicole Roberts for professional cover work and graphic design. Helpful perspectives, structural and line edits Zoé Davidson. Thanks for the assistance Greg Hand, Ruta and Mazie at University of Georgia research special collections library, Tunu and Jamila at the City of Cincinnati Public and Health Records, Tyrone and Missy in the Cincinnati Clerk of Courts and Dianne Nelson CPD Public Records, and Steve Kramer, historian at Greater Cincinnati Police Museum. Heartfelt thanks to Yalie Saweda Kamara, Ph.D., Dr. Kimberly Hamlin, Molly Wellmann, Annette J. Wick, Rick Pender, and a slew of inspiring Ohio poets and fellow writers, with a singular fealty for the Mercantile Library.

To those distant, thank you for abounding lessons.

To those ever present, thank you for abiding love and faith.

Contents

Epigraph   vi
Acknowledgements   vii
Foreword   xi
Preface   xv
Introduction   xvii

Chapters

1: Beginning   1
2: Family   11
3: Home   21
4: Dad   32
5: Upend   49
6: Hindsight   58
7: Caregiver   73
8: Record   80
9: Recover   89
10: Descent   96
11: Suspect   111
12: Arrest   124
13: Investigate   128
14: Grasp   141
15: Hearing   151
16: Aftermath   164
17: Help   198
18: Grit   208

19: Support   223
20: Retrospection   228
21: Bound   236
22: Casualty   242
23: Obligated   253
24: Absorb   260
25: Stakeholder   271
26: Indicate   277
27: Survive   297

Gallery   307
Afterword   321
In Gratitude   323
Endnotes/References   326

Foreword

By Anne Delano Steinert, Ph.D.

Each one of us has stories and memories we carry with us.
They are the chronicle of our lives—the record of what has
made us who we are. They are unique and human and define
our individual lives in countless ways. These are our personal
histories.

We are also each part of culture, a nation, and a global community that have larger histories, made up of some combination of
individual lives and experiences crafted together to form patterns.
These are the stories we tell each other together to form and rein-
force cultural, national, and global narratives that define and guide
us together as a people. These are our collective histories.

As an historian, my job is to interpret whatever facts and details
I can uncover about the past—to interrogate them, and to place
them within a larger context to build that shared narrative. It is
hard work. It can be frustrating, it can be electrifying, it can be terrifying, but it is less immediately personal than if I were to research
and write directly about my own personal history. That work would
be almost impossibly hard, and yet that is the work Holly Brians
Rugusa has taken on.

It is rare that a personal history and a collective history con-
verge and can be told so completely together as in Holly's story.
Only when our personal histories intersect with a news headline
might we find ourselves in a position to tell our own story and to

make significant contributions to the larger national story at the same time. Holly's story, the story of one of the victims of a serial killer and the surviving family of that victim, is important because it deepens our understanding of this particular tragedy, and to the seemingly inexplicable phenomenon of serial killers; but it is also important because it shifts our focus.

The story here is not about who the killer was. It is about who Holly Brians Ragusa was, and who this killer forced her to become. It is about the ways she carried this story in her body through her entire life, how it influenced her decisions, and how it made her who she is. True crime is a frighteningly popular genre for books, movies, and TV because people are fascinated by the violence and the gore and the pathology on display. One of the things that gets lost when we read or see true crime stories in the media is, almost always, the stories of the victims. They are gone. Their voices are silenced and the rich complexity of their lives is reduced down to one terrible event.

The other thing lost in the retelling of true crime stories is the seismic shifts they create in the lives of victims' families. In this story, Holly tells us not just about her father's murder, but also the story of the next thirty-five years and the echoes of the crime rippling through her entire life. She has courageously taken on the work of collecting, exposing, and interrogating her own personal history to add to our collective history.

All the history we know, be it personal or collective, is made up of layers of facts and interpretation and memory all filtered through the lens of the storyteller. It is, by its nature, incomplete but it expands our personal and collective understandings and builds a foundation for the next person who needs this story.

I first learned of Holly's father's murder when she took me out for coffee to ask me if I would write this foreword. I was stunned that someone I knew to be filled with so much joy and generosity had experienced such heart-wrenching tragedy. She told me the story over drinks, and we both cried a little. It is clearly still a hard story for her to tell, but she does it, because it matters to her and to our collective history. In this moment of "alternative facts," when anti-Critical Race Theory bills threaten our ability to teach children about racism, and we seem to have forgotten what desperate pregnant women did to end pregnancies before Roe v. Wade, it is more important than ever to build a record of the hard and uncomfortable parts of our collective past. If we want to be better than we have been in the past, we have to tell the truth about history, we have to face the truth, and we have to repair the damage.

Truth-telling is hard. Holly is brave.

Anne Delano Steinert, Ph.D. is a Cincinnati-based historian whose work focuses on late-nineteenth and early- twentieth century American cities. She is an Assistant Professor of History at the University of Cincinnati where she also directs the Center for the City and the undergraduate Urban Studies major. Steinert is also a founder of Cincinnati's Over-the-Rhine Museum, and was a recipient of the 2022 H. Allen Brooks Traveling Fellowship from the Society of Architectural Historians.

Preface

March 7, 2018 afternoon

Dad,

Thirty-one years ago today you moved beyond what life and others had in store for you. Though elsewhere, still here you hang on my wall and in my heart and mind. So today I think about what it might have been like to have you at tonight's dinner table and birthday celebrations, graduations and gatherings. I wonder how you might have gotten along with my children as individuals and if over time I'd have outgrown my teenage angst and what kind of relationship you and I might have replaced it with. It's interesting to me to think how John and you might have evolved as a grown father and son, similar in so many ways. Annually, this day is when I mourn the loss of a companion at Mom's side and a day more clearly than others on the calendar when I remember the hardships experienced after you'd gone. One day a year is allowed to wash over me with the maybes, the could-haves and what ifs.

Now though, after three decades, when I speak to you in a dream or quietly in my mind, mostly I know how proud you'd be of us all to have come so far, to have held onto each other, to have known we carried on your family and that we are here to remember you.

Holly

So put me on a highway

And show me a sign

And take it to the limit one more time

The Eagles, "Take it to the Limit"

One of These Nights

Asylum Records 1975

Introduction

THIS ACCOUNT COMES with the realization that we cannot escape the sensation of how Dad was killed, even as I insist on the decency to notice that he lived.

On the pages that follow are the memories, relationships and research of a time that left an indelible impression on my life. Memoir is what we, the memory-makers and recorders, make of it. This unyielding account serves up the complexities of life, written outside the lines, despite the pressure to stay inside them.

Thank you, reader, for being here.

Met the End

1

beginning [bih-gin-ing] *noun, plural noun: beginnings*
  1. the point in time or space at which something starts
  2. the background or origins of anything

T RAGEDY VISITED OUR FAMILY one summer and overstayed its
welcome. That unwanted guest ransomed our peace. It's a debt
we're still paying.

Wheels were put in motion that sun-scorched day in July, when
a devastating accident eclipsed Dad's light, confining him within a
coma. We too, felt pressed within his dark dream. When he finally
woke, our joy was made miserable to find that his terror had only
begun. With any nightmare, horror lingers.

Dad could not avoid the first collision that slammed us into
the course of events driving toward his end. If death paints a dark
portrait over reality, then murder blurs the contours, intensifying
negative spaces. Our family has sought the light withheld.

I've taken pains to describe here what our life was like before
and after the trauma of Dad's murder. Extensive research, interviews, journals and letters from that time confirmed my own memories about how our family lived, memories made in the innocence
I held as a child, my perspectives as a teenager, fantastic realities
now warped by time, like old vinyl.

My history is as complicated and messy as the next person's.

Generally stuck inside my head I likely struggled more than I needed to. Don't we all? The uniquely human processing of life and loss varies. I own mine. Having both a Dad and a Father challenged my young mind. Loyalty and abandonment make strange playmates. Youth is a trickle, then a tributary flowing into the river of our adult selves. We dry and swell, we meander. My river has deepened, cutting into my landscape, slicing away the painfully slow turns. I'm not the first to have taken decades to rise to the surface of their story. To climb the overlook and notice that indeed, currents have direction. Now I am ready to tell this story. My story. Beginnings and endings are made in the moments we react.

Events that follow, mundane or unbelievable as they may appear, remain unreal to me. Searching beyond this iceberg's tip, I want to accurately convey the monstrous mass below. Writing has revealed the enormity of survival lurking beneath first impact.

This wasn't a personal journey so much as a quest to know, a need to draw a fixed line with points plotted: how murder impacted my family. To convey the human toll, to understand the lengths to which people can and will go, to share guideposts that may alter directions or light dark passages—these were my original goals. Reconciliation with my past, knowledge of my family, restored memories and honest healing were my rewards for digging so deep. A daughter's duty to herself. This remains an attempt to connect others to my family's survival, to weather together our small or monumental stories, lashed to one another.

Despite the thousands of experiences that distinguish us, the miles that separate our joys, our sorrows and idiosyncrasies, a multitude of similarities draw you and me together. I'm hooked on the human condition, fascinated by what we share.

People live or die by their trauma, carrying those badges or burying them in the cycle of battles fought within ourselves. Telling this story, not just the living of it, became my personal war over whose legacy should survive a murder.

The killer? Or the killed?

One who takes a life? Or souls left to apprehend the magnitude of that action?

To prevail in this war as a writer, I would have to make my life, my dad's life, more compelling than that of a murderer. My dad wasn't famous. He didn't live an extraordinary life by any modern definition. His humble upbringing, his Midwestern reserve and hardworking habits, would appear common in comparison to the person who took it all away. Simple humanity, apparently, bores most of us to death. Society craves aberration and our hunger will be fed.

Dad was made mentionable for dying at the hands of a serial killer.

Less noted is the fact that his death also stopped one.

Memory and research flowed steadily in the writing of this account, only to stun me into droughts so profound, months passed without one word added to a page. Then floods of moments long sunk, nearly forgotten, would surface in my mind. A writer is often at the whim of their words.

Mired with the heft of evidence in Dad's case were a lot of unanswered questions, and new information, difficult to absorb. Over the first two years of the project, there were times I needed to step away for my own well-being. Other pieces of life inevitably needed to be added to this puzzle. Three decades had passed before the words came, with another five years spent to arrive here, to have achieved this place on these pages. I've done my level best to accurately and fairly relate events here.

THERE'S NO END of possible starts to any story. Manifold truth entrenches, each mind the point of origin. Complicated stories take time to tell. Stay with me as I reflect on how we survived ours.

My beginning finds us where we all start, knee-deep in family, recognizing that this foundation is far stronger for some than for others. You'll find me wading in a wide pool of relationship dynamics. Along with grandparents, aunts and uncles, my full family is represented by relatives on all sides of marriage and divorce.

Sprouting stepchildren, half-siblings, step-siblings, estranged parents and closely distant cousins, our family tree has grown into more of a beautifully tangled and determined groundcover.

My sister and I have the unique privilege, or curse, of not sharing blood or a last name with our dad. My brother has the unique privilege, or curse, of sharing Dad's name and manner to exactness.

I MET MY DAD when I was four years old—that's when his potent reticence stepped into our lives. William "John" Powell, born January 9, 1943, was named for his father. His childhood home was a difficult family situation set in a working-class enclave called Sedamsville, four miles west of downtown Cincinnati. Founded in 1795 by Colonel Cornelius Sedam, hard on the banks of the Ohio River, the town built up around the German Catholic church, which was overseen by the Fransciscans of Over-the-Rhine. In 1880s the parishioners moved Our Lady of Perpetual Help to higher ground, due to perpetual flooding; they added a parochial school and other community services.

Sedamsville was annexed by the City of Cincinnati in 1870, and at least for earlier generations, the rails and river brought decent jobs: a Fleischmann's Yeast factory and other industries employed area residents for decades, only to shutter during the Great Depression. There was hardly time to recover from these losses before the historic Ohio River flood of 1937 wiped out homes and businesses across the city, leaving one in eight Cincinnatians without shelter in winter. Families in Sedamsville, where the freezing waters were slow to recede, struggled more than most. Many just left for good.

In 1955, John was twelve when River Road widened to four lanes, cutting directly through what remained of Sedamsville's commercial district and hastening the town's population decline. Since 1989, Our Lady of Perpetual Help has stood permanently closed, a red brick Gothic relic of more prosperous times.

Dad would not show us where he grew up. There were no Saturday morning drives past an idyllic childhood neighborhood.

John Powell and his younger sister shared a mother and possessed little else.

Barbara was shortened to "Babe" before she became John Powell's mother. Her second child, a daughter and namesake, held tightly onto her brother's hand when their father ran off, leaving a depressed mind and body in the shell of their mother. Accidentally overmedicated during one of her recoveries at St. Mary's Hospital, Babe took a serious fall left her permanently injured, requiring tremendous amounts of care from her eldest child.

Forgoing the carefree fun his school buddies might be having, John raised his younger sister when their mother simply couldn't. Babe convalesced in hospital for such lengths of time, that for one year John and Barb, had no choice but to move in with their older cousin Joyce. Their mother couldn't work, and with no means to provide for them in her state of health, if Joyce hadn't taken them in, the siblings would have been placed in foster care and separated.

Even if he'd had the time or freedom to, John couldn't easily grab burgers and milkshakes with friends after school, cursed as he was with empty pockets. The family became exceedingly poor. For school dances or occasions John Powell was dressed in borrowed clothes. Graduation waited for later days and less fanfare, when work called him out of high school. This sort of scarcity and struggle is common, often unremedied, and goes unspoken.

"JP," as John was often called by friends, grew into a quiet man who maintained a childlike curiosity and keen focus. Handsome and able-bodied, with smiling brown eyes and (during my youth) a dark mustache, he faced a world that didn't play fair and walked into it with a determined set to his shoulders. Haunted by his absent father, who abandoned the family after a term of military service, John had a formal name change to remove William, denying even the ghost of his father to appear in his name.

With a face free of disdain, John bore his burdens privately. He did not discuss his troubles or draw attention to himself. Poverty taught him to make do, learning skills to improve his sparse situation. Where pride protected him, even his closest friends weren't made privy to his sadness at home. John would sooner have a good time than grumble, though he certainly didn't condone foolishness. Men, in those days, valued steadiness, and did not confuse stoicism for disinterest. John's guarded nature ensured he was not made ridiculous with complaint, and it shaped him into a dependable listener. He readily lent an ear to friends as they shared a few drinks and laughs over darts and watered-down bourbon.

In the early 1960's, John had married local girl Lorraine and was pulling himself into a life of his own, training as a pipefitter. He met Teddy Suesz, another Sedamsville boy, whose older brother needed a good plumber for a kitchen expansion project. Teddy recommended John, who by 1966, had two daughters at home. He welcomed the extra work to make ends meet.

When Joe Suesz met John Powell, his intuition hired him. Stopping by the jobsite regularly, the men would get to talking, and Joe liked what he heard. "Me and your dad might have shared a few beers while we worked the plumbing," Joe told me in his unmistakable low bass, a smirk on his lips and a glint of mischief dancing in his eyes.

Seeing each other out and about at local bars, Joe noticed that John was a good listener—a valued trait. Similar in mind and manner, the friends became close. They both loved motorcycles, and had been riding others' bikes for a while before deciding at the time to buy choppers of their own. Cemented by shared interest, in 1968 they started a biker club named The Pleasure Seekers. (Go ahead and giggle—I did. The club was named after a bad movie at the time. Dad also played on a men's volleyball team, the Court Jesters, a name which, according to Joe, accurately implies more laughs were had than wins.)

Exuding intellect along with an air of authority, John was elected president of the Pleasure Seekers, having cobbled together some bylaws and read Robert's Rules. Joe was named club treasurer. That first year the club organized a Poker Run, the equivalent to running a 5K race, except seated and steering on a bike. Saloon scavenger hunters rode from bar to bar, the goal to obtain a poker card from each "checkpoint" in time to win the competition, with a high-scoring hand. Games, bikes, sports, the outdoors—John also enjoyed hunting—all were welcome escapes from the responsibilities of work and marriage.

Motorcycles become a lifestyle. Bikers like Dad and Joe are bound to an identity, a culture that surrounds riders and defines their relationships to people and places. But life's winding road drives through all weather, and soon after starting the club, Joe steered through the process of a nasty divorce. As a new single, he was occasionally invited to join John and Lorraine for dinner. Joe's brother Teddy, along with his wife Annette and their two daughters, lived for a while in the same apartment building as John. Times were hard on all of them, but they worked to scrape together enough pay from week to week. When bills got tight and the electric couldn't get paid, Teddy would run an extension cord the length of his apartment and across the hallway over to John's. The three men looked out for each other in those early years, and they continued to have each other's backs well after moving out into their own homes. Staying close, John and Teddy built their families, and Joe, also a father, figured it out on his own. For years, frugality had them sharing work on each other's home projects and splitting cases of J.T.S. Brown Bourbon.

Later, when John's own marriage broke down, he and Joe bonded further over the drain and hassle of those times. John then had three children with Lorraine: two teenage daughters, Lorri and Tina, and John's youngest, a baby boy named for him. The couple's separation was tough on everyone.

Joe keenly remembers an agreement between him and John that after the divorces were behind them, they would ride all over the country on their bikes, better winds blowing them free from troubles. I like to picture these dreams, the two friends wrapped in endless sunsets, their motorcycles receding to specks in the distance.

Reality set in as the bikes only took them to and from work. Children grew, bills got paid, and as it happens, plans changed. Joe met Fran, who, catching his eye, eventually hooked his heart. Tall and self-possessed, Fran has a beautiful blend of humor, strength and sass that sits nicely next to Joe's steadiness—but back then,

John couldn't see it. When Fran met my Dad, she told me, there was no love lost between Joe's new sweetheart and his longtime friend.

"I didn't think John always appreciated what I had to say," Fran said with a coy smile, speaking her mind as usual while reminiscing with Joe and me over doughnuts in their kitchen on Suesz hill. Women and men, products of their environment—and in the 1970s, in southwestern Ohio, outspoken women were in shorter supply and looked upon without admiration for the shape of their minds.

Joe, too, remembers John's visible disappointment when he shared his decision to marry Fran. Fading from Dad's view must have been that mental picture, riding carefree across the country with a good buddy at his side. Dreams lift many of us beyond the harsh realities of daily life, and that bubble had burst for John.

By 1975, his own painful divorce finally resolved, John was also feeling sorely disconnected from his two teenage daughters when he decided to pursue full custody of his very young son. Moving out of the house John's family shared, he set out to start a new life in a no-frills apartment a few miles away.

This is where our shared story starts. John met our mom, Pat, both just getting past their divorces in the winter of 1976, at a "wine and words"-themed dinner. She liked his smile, and the feeling was mutual. When Mom introduced my sister Heather and me to "Big John," we also met his son, "Little John." Little John had just turned four; I had six months on him, and Heather was almost six years old.

Our parents were both attending Parents Without Partners (PWP) gatherings, sharing the burden of what was becoming a new and growing number of single mothers and fathers in the United States. Big PWP barbeque parties allowed us kids to run wild around a yard so that our parents could drink, flirt, and make connections. I remember quite a few backyards that weren't mine holding parts of my childhood. Cookouts, wasp stings and volleyball nets laced that summer as John and Pat started dating, and by stipulation, dated their children as well.

CINCINNATI IS OUR hometown, the place where my mom, my dad, my siblings and I grew up. Though I left Ohio and learned to live and find love elsewhere, I returned here to raise my own family. Suburbia kept my husband and me on the outskirts for a while, but we found the urban core, its walkability and culture, more to our tastes. Different parts of this city have held me for four of my five decades, and being an active and engaged Cincinnatian has become a big part of my life. I live in Over-the-Rhine, a distinct part of downtown whose history is very much present.

The Miami & Erie Canal had been completed in 1828, making Cincinnati the seat of trade in the region. Corn fed our pork and whiskey; the citizenry quickly grew, with an influx of Germans in the 1830s, then Irish escaping the Potato Famine of the 1840s, followed by waves of other ethnic groups. By 1860 Cincinnati was quickly expanding north of the canal, with row upon row of tightly packed tenements where first- and second-generation immigrants (like my German maternal ancestors) strived to create a sense of home. Beer gardens and other hallmarks of Germanic culture defined the area, along with boxy, Italianate architecture that made the most of every available square foot. In order to access this newer part of town, the busy canal had to be crossed by a number of walking or carriage bridges. Folks called it "the Little Rhine River," though the bustling man-made waterway bore little resemblance to its German namesake—and residents of those immigrant enclaves who worked in the city proper went "over the Rhine" to get home. The name stuck.

Similar to other American cities, Cincinnati is decisively split into halves, with plenty of haves and have-nots, depending on your currency. In Cincinnati, in addition to the European populations claiming space in the mid- to late-1800's, other dividing lines have been deeply carved through the 20th and 21st centuries. Just barely north of the Confederacy, my hometown's divisions have become synonymous with Cincinnati. Strategically and categorically, skin pigment and ignorance have a history of dividing us over a river and on either side of a highway through a city that was, at times, less interested in community than the promise of profit in "urban renewal."

Considering calculated moves in both mine and my city's stories, certain parallels could not be missed as I researched our city, as I discovered truth buried under more dominant narratives. No matter how many times we pave over a truth, harmful intention threatens to sink us all.

Interstate 75 bifurcates this city, repeatedly driving through this story with forward progress only for some. The enduring love I have for my hometown (and for my country, too) does not derive from glossing over or decidedly ignoring its flaws. My devotion comes from understanding Cincinnati's possibilities, and has only deepened by understanding its weaknesses and missteps. My love is informed, it has been tested, and I have chosen to stay, chosen to hope, chosen to be a part of bringing about a better side.

Cincinnati is our start and our setting, not without experience in unmaking the stories of others.

2

family [fam-uh-lee, fam-lee] *noun*

1. a group of one or more parents and their children living together as a unit

Growing up on the west side of I-75, in Cincinnati, makes me a West Sider. No matter a family's means, we West Siders are generational, known for staying close to home, living near friends with whom we graduated high school and for claiming that same high school on professional résumés. West Siders are known for our work ethic and strong sense of community. A lot of trade labor and vocational schools are found on the West Side. Loyal, cautious and less inclined to international travel, West Siders are more likely to find the world in faith, neighborhoods and work. At 51 years old I'm not a common West Sider, having not lived there since I was 19. Still, I am a West Sider, stamped for life wherever we wind up.

Westwood, where my sister Heather and I spent our earliest years, and Delhi, where Little John and eventually all of us grew up, are both West Side communities.

When Mom and Big John met, they too, were West Siders, discovering new, greener pastures in each other. Delhi Pike curbed up to a small walk-up apartment, not far from St. Dominic's Church, where Big and Little John lived together at the time we all met. John, raised Catholic, had his first marriage annulled in the eyes of God, and father and son regularly attended Mass at St. Dominic's. Visitation continued with his two daughters, Lorri and Tina, and eventually John was granted primary custody of Little

John. Shortly afterwards, he negotiated a buyout of ownership for the house that he and his first wife had shared, leaving the efficiency apartment behind. The half-moon driveway on Samoht Ridge Road welcomed Big John and his son back home, and soon all three of our bikes, Big Wheels or Green Machine vehicles running roundabout the front. Late afternoon sun glinted off the polished chrome of the Harley Davidson chopper that lounged in that drive, the iconic feature of John's reclaimed bachelorhood and bravado. Playing pretend on plastic, we wished we could be so cool.

New love and rowdy kids don't easily mix. The couple attempted to find private time as we rode our Big Wheels around the block. TV was our only screen and *The Newlywed Game,* started in 1966, was still a popular TV show in the mid- to late-1970s. Host Bob Eubanks, using the approved euphemisms for sex on network television in those days, would discuss bedroom matters with the couples. Playing outside, we kids would giggle in innocence that our parents were probably, as Bob Eubanks would say, "making whoopee."

Dinners, cookouts and trips to the park became more common, and Little John, Heather and I ran the circuit with our parents. Nibbling corncobs at parties and slipping on slides at the homes of their motorcycle-riding friends—the condensation of amaretto sours and bourbon slush drips around those edges of memory. Mom wasn't much of a drinker; John took a little water in his bourbon, and we kids were allowed to sample a taste here and there, as was the case then before everyone took things so seriously.

John, a technically skilled talent, became a union plumber, welder and pipefitter with Local 392. Tinkerer too, he polished silver and gemstones, welding them into beautiful jewelry, making us personalized belt buckles, heart-shaped necklaces and silverwork bracelets. Twisting metal around blue glass, a statue of Mother Mary that Dad created now sits on a shelf in my family room. A self-defined monogram rests his initials, JP, back-to-back on leather knife sheaths, tools, work gear, and sweaters, all adorned with the brand he fixed for himself. Work clothes, or jeans and sneakers, tanks and tees would traipse the house with Dad. Plaid buttoned down his front regularly unless a blazer, slacks and sweaters suited him for a family event or holiday. Some days Dad's grey suit vest fits my mood.

Having a man around who could handle himself made all of us feel secure. Dad could also be funny. "Got-your-nose" and "What's-that-on-your-shirt?" jokes were his bread and butter. Assuredly Dad is the reason "tickle torture" was so named: He was a master, and I remember truly struggling to breathe from laughing so hard, play-wrestling as a kid. Dad was serious about his horseshoe toss and generous with an ice cream scoop. At times hard to read, though, he could be snide, or quiet. When Dad got really mad, his silence held tremendous power. Big John was a sensitive sort, walled beneath a tough exterior shell. Eventually our mother's kindness broke through to his heart, and they loved each other, even when parenting presented its challenges.

Spending much of his time on the seat of a bike, or beside it with tools, Dad fiddled around metal spokes in mesh tanks and cut-offs. Daily, hands covered in grease would meet with the Lava soap stuck to the porcelain at his sink. Weekends the garage door would yawn wide, pushing Don Henley on Eagles' wings onto the driveway where we played. Dad's motorcycle became an outlet, a freedom he had declared for himself. On sunny days, Mom would ride with him in her terry cloth tube tops, high-waisted jeans, permed hair and oversized sunglasses. They were an idyllic poster couple for the late 1970s.

Surrounded by friends who also loved the life of motorcycles, an overnight ride to Red River Gorge camped them in Kentucky or Gatlinburg, Tennessee, for a weekend, with a longer annual trip to Florida for the Daytona Bike Show. I remember the driveway full of motorcycles tied to trailers ready to haul the friends south. Supper, Scouting events, grill-outs and get-togethers at each other's homes were standard weekend plans, and as we grew older, Mom and Dad would head out on date nights with their regulars, Teddy and Annette, Fran and Joe, Bowie and Mike, Gail and Charlie, Jeannette and Carroll—they all ran around together.

Fran and Joe Suesz were most like family, and over the years we spent a lot of time with them on their hilltop home in Price Hill. Gravel used to spin under wheels on the steep bent drive until Joe pulled in friends like John, who went to work paving it.

Big and Little John, in their brown-banded van, would pick up us girls from our home in Westwood. Mom sat up front, with us three eager ragamuffins likely unbelted on the backseat bench. The sky spared one cornflower patch over the top of Suesz hill. Anticipating swims and skinned toes in their circular concrete pool with the slide, no fences held us as we freely played around the house and outbuildings on that large grassy property. I always felt welcomed on Suesz hill and knew there'd be other kids to run with. We had the kind of fun kids used to have in those days, making the most of daylight and our imaginations. Fran, Joe and Teddy were the core, such good friends to JP, reliably good-natured and helpful to us. The wider group of friends remained in touch throughout the early years without Dad, reaching out here and there to Mom. Others broke apart or fell away for their own reasons.

We took our time becoming a family. Both Pat and John were working full-time jobs, navigating inevitable complications with ex-spouses, arranging irregular visitations to the other parent. They worked their relationship around the hurdles. A union welder, John had to travel for out-of-town jobs, sometimes for weeks or even months at a time, and we would occasionally visit him when he was working somewhere close enough to home, such as Cleveland.

Troubles of John's first marriage didn't leave his memory easily. Having felt burned delayed his decision to remarry. Dad's smirk sticks in my mind after Heather and I, young and silly, sat on his lap and asked when he was going to ask our mom to marry him. I cannot for the life of me remember what he said; those mischievous eyes, though, are still shining, his mustache grinning.

On August 23, 1979, he finally answered that question, slowly, yet affirmatively. At eight years old, my freckled nose and I stood inside a warm, wood-paneled church. White lace socks, black patent leather shoes and my two sun-bleached pigtails stood next to my sister and new brother at Mom and John's wedding. Mom wore a sky-blue spaghetti-strapped dress and matching bolero jacket.

Her hair was pulled up, soft swirls curving around her forehead and neck—I am not sure I need photos to remember. She was lovely and smiling, making it all work out as she does. My children have her exact color of hair, a warm honey blonde threatening to bake strawberry brown.

We held the wedding reception back at our home on Shaffer Avenue, not far from Westwood Elementary. A three-tiered cake laced in the same bridal blue was served from the kitchen, and my grandparents, smiling at Mom's happiness, shook their son-in-law's hand in welcome.

❖

10-8-86   6:15 P.M.

John:
You had your eyes open all the while we were here. You also were moving your leg frequently.
You are in our thoughts & prayers.

Al & Kay

OUR MOTHER, PATRICIA ANN MYERS, was born to Al and Kay Myers in 1941, not eight months after the Pearl Harbor attack and the United States' entry into World War II. Albert, a conscientious young man from Forrest City, Arkansas, came to Cincinnati as an aspiring engineer. Raised with more wits than wealth, young Al and his family farmed a small plot, living on his father's income from work with the C&O Railroad. Having grown up during the Great Depression, Al learned to pinch pennies. He valued account-ability, aligning with fiscal conservatism and a place in the pew on Sundays. He crossed the Mason-Dixon line, moving north to Cincinnati, where at the University of Cincinnati he met the lovely

Katherine Brown at a fraternity dance.

When I was little I liked to play with Grandpa's age-speckled hands, wiggling the blue ribbons of veins running under his papery skin. One of these times, my small self folded into his side with his hand in mine, I asked about him meeting my grandmother. Looking across the room to her and then down at me, he said, "I thought she looked so soft. I just knew I wanted to marry her." Indeed, he wed the beautiful Kay, times were simpler then, and they stayed and settled in Cincinnati to plant their roots. My Grandfather meant the world to me, and his cheerful blue eyes ringed with gold have never left me. "How you, Holly?," he'd holler over to me, with a tinge of Arkansas sass. "How *you*?!"

Without trying, he taught me what kind of man I wanted in my life, in the little ways that matter. Grandpa's golf played on the television set as a sun-streaked Jack Nicklaus in bright colors crossed the greens. Later he taught me to swing my first club. On a family trip, when I told him I wanted to fish in the ocean, Grandpa taught me to bait the hook. He'd make a mean pimento cheese spread, fidget with gadgets in his garage workshop and show me how to run his potato clock. He knew to have one martini a day, prop the hymnal behind his aching back during sermons, and swim daily laps at the YMCA. Though not an overly sentimental man, he cared for his family and lived his life thoughtfully, with efficiency. Chest pockets were protected for pens; Swiss army knives and jingling change were always ready at his sides. An early-balding scalp freckled over a kind face rimmed with dark glasses. Not given to excess, his proportions lived within belts and collars, dressed in his preferred pressed short-sleeved button-down. He gave his career to Cincinnati Gas & Electric Company and upon retirement they gave him a lousy pocket watch held on a plastic chain under a clear dome. Grandpa enjoyed sensible people, sensible shoes and a Sunday family dinner.

Albert was the clear head of the family, the one to carve the Thanksgiving turkey. Happily sitting at his footstool with a deck of cards, I could look up into his attentive eyes unless they were closed into a widemouthed nap after a meal. As I grew, and especially after Dad's death, lacking a proper father figure, I looked to Grandpa, and he would look back at me. Meaty conversations were often digested over an Arby's sandwich. We'd talk about things that mattered, like why NASA hadn't gotten to Mars yet, what an annuity was, to focus on savings and not to trust everything heard in the media. I'll always wish I had acted sooner on his financial advice. Grandpa was simply a fair-minded, intelligent, uncomplaining and responsible man, much like the one I chose to marry.

My grandmother Katherine, known to all as Kay, was a true lady of her age—certainly as soft and lovely as Grandpa described, but also full of advice and stories if you sat still enough to listen. Born in Cincinnati in 1918, she often visited her aunt and uncle's candy store in Over-the-Rhine before the Great Depression forced the confectionery's sale. Frugal and faithful (her family attended church in Westwood), she kept those lessons with her every day of her life. Young Kay was a wondrous vocal talent who often performed. She also played the piano, passing these gifts on to my mother and my own children, it would seem. Yellowed programs list her as a soloist.

Mom would drop us off on her way to work, and my grandmother's oatmeal warmed the mornings in a dulled silver saucepan on a low burning stove. Thick, with a thwack off her wooden spoon, it landed in a bowl (always more than we wanted) without a jiggle. We were allowed a heaping spoonful of Brown sugar and raisins, if we chose. A small pitcher of whole milk waited to thin the mixture that would otherwise stick in my throat. As unappetizing as it first appeared, I came to enjoy the sugar and cream on my tongue and was rarely hungry before lunchtime.

Grandma took Sweet'N Low in her tea or coffee and kept the squeeze bottle of clear liquid saccharine in the center of her table with the salt and pepper. When she wasn't looking, I'd tip the bottle and shake out a few droplets onto the soft print of my pointer finger. The taste, an unnatural sickening sweetness, stuck there all day. Every time I'd suck on that digit, I'd have a treat to distract me from class, a reminder of grandma's table.

Church and friends were equally important, and Kay fully

involved herself with both. Presbyterian, yet open, she studied Catholicism and Judaism as they entered our family. She shared many special things with me: I have Great Grandma Brown's aged cookbook, with her random thoughts jotted in the margins and Club pins were placed in my palm from societies she joined, ceremonies performed and Kay also handed out backhanded beauty advice, freely voicing how I could do with a little more makeup. The times were changing quickly, and Grandma's ideas of feminine etiquette and poise didn't always match my experimental styles of the '80s: broad-shouldered blazers, black boots and boy jeans.

I can see her, after they downsized to the condominium on Montana Avenue, in profile sitting at the piano, straight-backed on the bench, caressing the keys of her sweet honey-brown Kimball spinet, playing "What Is a Youth" so beautifully for me after I had watched the film *Romeo and Juliet* in my early teens. That tune stays with me, the way only music can, and brings her back to me.

Grandma's thoughtfulness and tight cursive handwriting were treasures; no holiday or birthday passed without a card or letter. Thankfully I kept all of those stationery sentiments to look back on, her perfect longhand an art form all but lost to my children's generation. Blubbering like a baby I spoke at her funeral, wearing turquoise, Kay's favorite, around my neck.

My mother was Al and Kay Myers' firstborn, of five: Patricia Ann, a.k.a. Pat, or Patsy as she was known as a youngster. Twenty years separate Mom and her youngest sister, my Aunt Lori, but the siblings were all close, a large part of the vivid and cherished memories Mom keeps of her childhood. For years her maternal grandparents shared their family home, generational love passed down.

Saturday morning drives to Heather's allergist took us past Mom's childhood home on Cheviot Avenue. Hearing about the halcyon days of her youth spent outdoors, I could picture Patsy weaving her skinny legs through the yards of her neighborhood. Mom would point out, from behind the wheel, new colors painting clapboards of her old neighboring family's homes. She'd fondly recite the surnames and playmates associated with each house—kids Mom and her brothers would romp around with into the dimming hours of evening. Dick and Stan, second and third in the Myers lineup, rollicked with their big sister, thick as thieves. (Debra and Lori would come later, uniting the siblings in different ways.) Pat skittered around on knobby knees with her brothers, eating pickled watermelon rind and fresh butter on bread. Boys who came calling in the late 1940s and early '50s sat awkwardly in the front room, after tying their horses to the lamppost.

The Myers all piled into rumble seats for road trips down south, to visit with grandparents, aunts, uncles and cousins in Arkansas. As Mom still recalls exactly the height of her Grandmother Edna's meringue, the scent of home-baked breads and the sizzle of wringed chickens frying for dinner, I've gotten to share in those feasts that she will feed on for the rest of her life.

My mother will be the first to tell you she adored her childhood, which at times seems clearer to her than what she had for breakfast yesterday. I believe those strong recollections stem from her love of innocence. Fair-minded, kind parents raised Mom, guarding her heart. Care and dignity were naturally given to all those her family knew or met. Church was still the center of many communities in 1940s America, and Pat grew into that fold. Fellowship was a bedrock of the Presbyterian church, which the Myers attended without fail.

In July of 1953, at age twelve, my mother was taken to Cincinnati Children's Hospital, delirious with a 105-degree fever. Tests eventually revealed a flareup of juvenile rheumatoid arthritis. Bedridden for seven weeks at Children's, and for four months afterward at home, Pat learned patience that summer and all through the fall and winter. The family had only known television for a year then. Without much programming to entertain for long, Mom occupied her mind with classic books such as Heidi, visits from her brothers and the paint-by-number sets and games that the Rotary and Ruth Lyons Clubs gave to hospitalized children. A valued friend of the family, Bessie Cox was a real comfort to Mom during these months; brothers Dick and Stan became her champions; her parents worked tirelessly to provide support, and all pulled her in a red wagon wherever she needed to go. Always a magnet for any

stray dog, Mom also found a friend in Taffy, a neighborhood roam-
er who became part of the family during her sickness.

Needle treatment, a medical regimen in those days, attempted
to remove the arthritis from my mom's young knees, and through
the pain of recovery Patsy taught herself to walk again. Encouraging weakened muscles to strengthen under her, she was tutored at
home for her seventh-grade year until she returned to school off
crutches, that February of '54. Bedsore scars are the only physical
reminders of her infirmity; bitterness and complaint took up no
space in her heart. Only strength lives in the kindness that pumps
through her veins.

Whether or not it actually was, life felt safer and friendlier
then. Parents worried about polio and other threats, but there was
no 24/7 news access to torment or plant fear. Raised by a loving
family in a stable neighborhood, Patsy had streets she could run
without danger, before and after her months recovering in bed.
Those childhood memories remain for her an uncomplicated view
of the world. Mom eventually grew to understand that this precious time in her own life wasn't simple or remotely fair for everyone, and her heart suffers those injustices.

The loss of both her mother, Kay, in October of 2002, and her
father, Al, in February 2003, has left a deep void. Sadly, Mom's
middle sibling, my Uncle Stan, passed too soon, in 2014. The loss
has been hard on the four left behind, who've always devoted
themselves to the responsibilities of kinship. There are many opinions and beliefs amongst us. Agreement is not a prerequisite to
family.

I need to credit the Myers clan for folding us together as an
extended family, one that I've been fortunate to grow up into.
The Myers always put family first, building a quiet strength in my
mother. This fortitude would be tested time and again in her life,
but with the support of her parents and siblings, a strong faith in
her God, belief in the goodness in others, and love in her heart, she
has bravely marched through it all.

3

home [hohm] *noun*

1. a house, apartment, or other shelter that is the usual residence of a person, family, or household
2. the place in which one's domestic affections are centered

MOM RAISED LITTLE HEATHER and me, in a two-story parged cement house on Shaffer Avenue in Westwood. Evergreen paint trimmed the eaves, and the front porch boasted a chain-link swing whose wooden slats, along with Smokey, our grey outdoor cat, comforted me there regularly. Sloped behind the house was a single detached garage that Mom rarely parked a car in. The kitchen door opened onto a rickety wooden stairway down to the walkout basement, where a small concrete slab melted my Crayola colors in the sun. A tangle of honeysuckle hid the unsightly wire running along the back fence, where the neighborhood bully Roger Snodgrass would take up space and call us names. Heather and I shared toys and Mr. Bubble baths, as well as the old and out-of-tune piano that came with the house, in the dank basement near the laundry. We stayed out of the street because cars often came whipping up over the ridge below.

Mom's bedroom faced that street, with her queen-sized bed, big enough to know loneliness, set opposite a warm wood dresser and mirror, reflecting a fresh start in the clean white chenille coverlet. A lace doily was centered under a milk glass lamp on her nightstand, alongside a glass of water and, often, a bottle of Bayer aspirin. Her bed was where we went when we didn't feel well, when Heather and I had already taken our baths, were dressed for bed and wanted to cuddle.

Jack, my father by birth, isn't in these memories that I hold of Heather and me on that bed, talking with Mom in our long nightgowns. He wasn't there when we sat on the shag carpet, legs bent under us, in front of Mom's black-and-white TV, resting on a wheeled metal cart and plugged into the corner. My memory places Jack in the kitchen a couple times, in a hallway or in the driveway, but not there. To me, in memory, it will always be Mom's room.

Sisters born twenty-two months apart, our own small side-by-side bedrooms sat looking over the backyard, across the hall from Mom's. The rooms were as different as us girls: mine painted bright and earthly in golden yellow, carpeted in Kelly green; Heather's painted ethereal pink, rugged in deep scarlet. Despite our differences in temperament and tolerance, we were our best young playmates, until older neighbors changed our views of each other. Younger sisters are easily teased by new friends and made to eat mud pies. In our neighborhood, I became the object of ridicule with Heather's friends for a while, before Little John came into our life and put me in the middle, evening us up.

Even when Heather went along with her friends, I didn't mind being left alone, preferring pretend play—and besides, sisterly love overcomes Play-Doh feedings. Asthmatic and allergic health issues kept Heather in my bedtime prayers, with a wish for her to be well. I could not take things too far with her when romping around, for fear of making her sick. Elementary school days sent me to bed fully dressed, sometimes, in case we ended up in the ER for Heather's breathing treatment in the middle of the night. I would sleep on hospital waiting room chairs, cable-knit socks pulled to my knees, pressing patterns into my legs. We largely looked out for each other as young sisters and shared the few things we had.

Jack's firstborn, our older half-sister Jennifer, we happily saw now and again growing up—the father we share, about as much.

Heather and I loved time with our next-door neighbor Edna, an older woman living on her own, who cherished our visits and was a resource to Mom. We then rode bikes and visited the old white-haired man named Hap down the street, who drew children into his workshop with friendliness and puzzles cut on his jigsaw. Neighborhood children loved to watch Hap work, discomforted as we were by all the nude girlie pinups plastering his workroom. Heather and I befriended another pair of sisters, Michelle and Lisa Brown, who lived around the top corner of our street. We all became "blood sisters," slicing our hands and pressing them together to seal our bond. In other houses nearby, Heather hung out with Martha and Cathy. I made friends with Julie and Joshua. Aside from a few sister fights, we either played well or kept out of each other's way. Sunday evenings we found our way back to each other, reheated TV dinners in front of us with *CHiPs* on the television, Heather crushing on Erik Estrada and me on Larry Wilcox.

We spent my first eight years like this, attending church every week, living in a house that somehow felt more like home after Jack left. Neighbors had come with the house, and we relied heavily on ours. Mrs. Ballard watched my sister and me after school before Mom came home from work, and Mr. Ballard dressed up in Santa's clothes at Christmas for us or caught the occasional bat that got trapped in my mother's bedroom. Edna, next door, invited us into her brown brick home shaded by the Maple out front, and the kids on our block ran in and out of our days.

My youth spins on the pinwheel of memories in our house on Shaffer, with the Christmas tree standing in its corner to the right of the avocado-green-tiled fireplace, an uncontrollable matching shag carpet tying together the front room. Toys slipped out the bathroom window down to Heather waiting in the side yard on dry days, and pretend play met us there. My tears met Mom's scissors regularly in the small hall to the kitchen, as my golden locks fell to linoleum masking as red brick.

I remember soapy baths in the white-tiled bathroom, our babysitter Laurie, who lived across the street, singing "Flea Fly Flo" with us ("Kumma-lada, kumma-lada, kumma-lada vista/Nah-nah-nah, nah-nah-nah vista!"). The moon lived with me in that house, and to this day I seek the same face that found me each evening through my childhood bedroom window, the face I sat with regularly in the sill without a screen.

Televised favorites of *A Charlie Brown Christmas* and *How the Grinch Stole Christmas* or *The Wizard of Oz* held our rapt annual attention. Childhood spun the records of Herb Alpert & The Tijuana Brass, Bee Gees, Peaches & Herb, The Alan Parsons Project and Shawn Cassidy, filtering into our home, which was otherwise quiet until late evening. After being sent to bed as a young child I'd crouch down on ragged carpet, leaning elbows over the metal cage cut into my bedroom floor and listen in to the magic of human voice captured there, transporting familiar, tinny echoes through these sound tunnels. Mice squeaks lived in the vent louvers, opening and closing with small actions of my making on a lever. At times anger paced in that cage, roaring and reverberating into my room; the lever worked its power over the volume of an argument. Other times laughter would peel through the trap, at intervals, depending on Jack's mood or my mom's patience. The vocal acrobats changed, rising and falling in waves of joy or tension. A circus of new clowns and returning attractions lived in the box, caught there between fearsome acts of bravado and daring whispers. Most nights my sleep was found in the dark with those quiet conversations not of my making.

In my heart I remember Smokey, the grey cat I hold dear and sneaked indoors at night. That familiar face met me at the Ballards after school each day after looking both ways to cross the street. When later we moved from that house, Smokey couldn't be found. I mourned that cat, my truest companion, for a year before Mom admitted that she and Grandpa, in order to prevent confusion and allergy at the new house, had decided to put him down. I still struggle with their choice.

I drive by now and again, to see the changes, to see the parged facade now covered with siding, to see the green gone from the gutters, to see a wheelchair ramp fashioned up to my front porch.

That tiny home, its closets with the glass knobs that I believed were crystal, was the fanciest thing I yet knew. Those doors and windows held my first experiences with life, with living, with love, with sadness. A small house on Shaffer remains with me, as the first place I experienced joy and loss.

Raised in the Presbyterian church, we attended weekly Sunday School while Mom rehearsed in her church choir. Kids' choir rehearsals were Wednesdays before adult choir practice. Growing up with the same families in attendance each week, our friends were made for us; plenty of good influences and intentions surrounded us. Potlucks in Fellowship Hall fed us, along with quarterly pancake breakfasts and much-anticipated spaghetti dinners. Summers placed us in reasonably priced, character-building Vacation Bible School sessions. Whatever your spirituality, if you are a financially strapped single mom, a faith-based community literally saves you.

And when we were all married together, with no more sleeping apart, the Johns became a part of life as we worked through the process of becoming a family. The three of us girls had lived without men long enough that we had to relearn the habit of closing bathroom doors. We spent our last weeks on Shaffer together, right after the wedding, packing and readying for the new memories waiting to be made on Grossepointe Lane, where our new family would call a different house home. In September of 1979, we moved to Delhi Township.

Pat sidled her claret-red Monte Carlo next to John's cream-and-brown-banded Bonneville conversion van, and we went about the work of transitioning two families into one. That house and its sugar gum maple balls littering the front yard, promised adventure, a cul-du-sac to ride bikes in, new neighbor children to boss around, and a wet bar in the blue wood-paneled basement, perfect for pretend play. Changes came for all of us: Heather and I were to share a bedroom and a brother for the first time, and John now officially had four sisters. Neighborhood friends were made anew, as we slowly lost touch with those neighbors on Shaffer.

Three different elementary schools educated us until that point, with John at Delshire, Westwood Elementary for Heather, and I'd been attending Bracken Woods through Mrs. Snyder's second grade. With our move, a carpool took us to school at C.O. Harrison Elementary on Neeb Road, making commutes easier that first year. Heather began fifth grade, John (who shared a birth year but not my grade) started second, and I started third, with multiplication tables and Ms. Leis.

Most exciting, awaiting at our new home, was the two-level, pint-sized playhouse a previous owner had built of mixed plywood, stained and tucked tight against the back of the main house. The top-floor hinged window could be hoisted open, offering endless possibilities for our young imaginations. It was the tiniest of spaces, and we three filled it, living there those early days—our fort, our clubhouse. The squat mid-century house itself, now called home, was capped in dark shingles. Ready-made flower boxes rested beneath street-facing bedroom windows, a potential paradise for planting, and Mom's green thumb soon had them filled, brimming with bright geraniums and salvia interwoven with waves of dangling asparagus fern. Stacked orange brick contrasted nicely with a thick row of purple iris blossoms swaying along the side of a stone path, calling us toward the backyard. There, another garden bed soon bloomed with marigolds, ready for me to pinch when they dried, for a penny per top. Mom paid up. Black-eyed Susans shaded beneath a maple near the flare concrete patio, whose bricks and mortar held a built-in grill top that we used to launch ourselves from, risking life and limb. Sliding doors took us off the patio into the lower level of the house, where Big John's swanky bachelor blue-velour sofa and chair fit monotoned to the paneling, set off perfectly by the white trim around his amazing aphelion-style television. On that incredible tube we later viewed the first MTV music video.

10-11-86

John
You moved your leg & arm quite a bit tonight. Also you moved your head & your thumb kept rubbing my thumb.
Keep hanging in there—
I have all the faith in the world in you
Love,
Pat

MOM SAT US DOWN at the table in the cozy combined dining area and living room right after we moved in together. Building a family from scratch, she told Heather and me that we were to start calling John "Dad" now. (She remembers it differently.) At the time it really bothered me, my memory and journals were clear. I like to think eventually I would have gotten there on my own, that our bond would naturally have deepened without prompting, and I would have bestowed that title upon him willingly. I'll never know. Love leads us all places we aren't ready for. He was Dad to us from then on.

This was 1979, and despite the times, no quick Brady Bunch resolutions actually met the rigors of blended family life. Today's world has parents approaching transitions with more psychology. I understand who my Mom is, what the times were and what she meant by insisting we comply. Pat wanted John to be the clear head of the house, much as her own father, my Grandpa, had been in hers. As far as she was concerned, Dad deserved the respect of that familial title. It tightened corners, bringing the concept of kin into reality. Through older eyes, it's clear that Mom was then, and still is, herding us together, moving us all along the hard road home.

We hung posters on bedroom walls, shelved albums and books, and watched Saturday morning cartoons. *The Electric Company* and *Zoom* played after school on our new family room TV. Mom worked over the yard and Dad started renovation projects that made the house feel more like home. Pulling wagons and ourselves into the neighborhood, we skated in the Fourth of July parade. Riding banana-seat bikes from dawn to dusk, we collected summer days as thoughtlessly as lightning bugs in jars. That first Hallow-een, when we asked permission to host a haunted house in our backyard, our folks helped us create one, where we welcomed new neighbors who soon became friends.

Dad stepped fully into his role when, soon after our move, Mom unexpectedly needed a hysterectomy. Forced into every aspect of our care, Dad drove us to school, oversaw chores, allotted desserts and enforced bedtimes. Not a gourmet, though, his path of least culinary resistance was fast food, and we happily made regular stops at "K-Rogers" (Kroger) and "Skee-leenies" (Skyline Chili) and "Whitey-Cassells" (White Castle). The silly nicknames he gave our local establishments have stuck with us—Dad's way to be in on the fun.

John remained true to Catholicism, while Mom took us children to Westminster Presbyterian church each Sunday, with lunches at Wendy's or Arby's afterwards with our grandparents, aunts or uncles. As Heather grew, she began practice in bell choir, and John joined the kids' choir with me. Sunday evenings brought us together with friends our own age in the weekly Bible Study group. Some Saturday evenings we helped Grandma cube the bread for Communion, and we savored the grape juice thimbles we children were allowed at service the next morning. We spent most of Sunday at church, and parts of other weekdays too, between sock hops, charity lunches, fitness classes and recitals, children's musicals and holiday cantatas.

Faith-based communities uplift and define. The faithful accept, serve, conform, and challenge through the evolutionary process of belief. I'd often attend other churches with friends, when Saturday sleepovers woke to Sunday mornings in a pew. Presbyterian myself, I knelt at Catholic Mass but passed on their Communion. I stood in stadium-sized cathedrals swaying with ministerial energy. Hearing tongues spoken, I witnessed the spirit move folks in Pentecostal Baptist furor and saw others fall to the floor. I had hands laid on me, and raised my own in jubilation. I read from programs and hymnals across houses of God. Fervor begged me to save my young, sin-filled soul, and told me to burn my albums (I didn't). At sixteen, I attended a week-long summer conference for Presbyterian teens at Purdue University and found a new fellowship. Wherever I worshiped, I happily sang praise-filled songs.

At thirteen, I stood in a pro-life rally with a friend in Cincinnati. Her more evangelical church had become mine briefly in our 8th-grade year. Other faith homes are where young people with limited entertainment options are often gathered. For me, a Duran Duran-loving preteen without a wider world view, her church was fun in that junior high sense of the word. We'd been invited to the rally through the church by David, the nearly twenty-year-old youth counselor. David was friendly, drove a car, gave credence to the thoughts and concerns of teenagers, and enjoyed photography. Within a month of our hanging out, I would realize he was secretly and seriously dating my thirteen-year-old friend. Standing in the fading light of that rally, surrounded by bloodied fetal posters, and an unrelenting "God loves you—and therefore you must hate" preach spewing all around me, it became clear that these people of Christ, these lovers of the church, loved the unborn so much that they felt completely justified in hating their fellow living, breathing humans. Irreconcilable. Raised with understanding and forgiveness, taught to love and feel loved by an all-knowing God, I could not in good faith advocate or conform to this level of condemnation. Soon, my heart walked me away from that church, David, and my friend. That event exposed me to hypocrisy, seeing first-hand how complicit we all are in judging, shaming and blaming others, despite being taught to judge not. It revealed how savagely superior and dehumanizing we can feel in our belief and zealotry, how selectively we forget the free will described in the good book.

Other valuable books found me, steeping a rich brew of series and stories into my soul. Pouring myself into another sacred space, the local library, I still keep a certificate for the forty-four books I completed one summer. Hearth and home were tightly woven into Laura Ingalls Wilder's pioneer family adventures. *Grimm's Fairy Tales*, which were dark then, seem much darker now. Beverly Cleary's Ramona and Astrid Lindgren's Pippi helped me see the spunk in myself. Nancy Drew shone a light on my curiosity, and the undertakings of the Hardy Boys and the Boxcar Children held fascination for me. Judy Blume, Edgar Allan Poe, Roald Dahl, Marguerite Henry, Louisa May Alcott, Frances Hodgson Burnett, Jack London and Lucy Maud Montgomery, among others, captured my imagination, enhanced my spelling and hinted at the magnitude of history and place.

Christmas mornings found our small family room stuffed with us in pajamas, robed and slippered in front of a small stack of gifts, with gratitude in our hearts. Mom's packages were tagged with Dad's endearments, and Santa always remembered a few key gifts for each of us kids. We felt fortunate to have all that we did, and we played with our new games and action figures throughout the winter breaks. Snow days had us all horsing around in the yard, cheeks shiny with Vaseline, beaming. Running inside for cocoa, the chafe of our legs burned red beneath long johns soaked under our jeans. We peeled down the wet layers, fighting for space over the metal heating vents, warming ourselves and drying last year's boots faster. Warmer days provided us with grill-outs, gardening and memorable rides on the back of Dad's motorcycle. Long evenings wrapped our arms around him, strong and in control, the wind, sun and smiles on our faces.

Remembering occasions with cards, Dad also sent gifts and thoughtfully mailed postcards home from his work and road trips, signed, *See you soon, Love Dad*. I love postcards, those in particular, and looking back on his handwriting I sense timelessness in the word *soon*.

Divorce and visitation are difficult on both parents and children, even in the best of circumstances. After parent visits, John, Heather and I each came home obliviously happy, holding Barbies or Kiss albums in hand, the plastic treasures traded for time. Favor waved in Mom and Dad's faces, unwitting tension trailing behind divorced children and parents into the home. Though frequency or consistency were rarely found, Heather and I saw our father, Jack, even less than Little John saw his mother, Lorraine. Not long after Mom and Dad's marriage, visits Heather and I shared with our father dwindled to none, while further distance stretched between Little John, his mother and other two sisters.

Over the first handful of years together we occasionally saw Big John's oldest daughters when they'd visit our house. As a young girl I couldn't possibly understand just how tough all around it must have been on Lorri and Tina, seeing their Dad with a new family, with two little girls no less, but they weren't anything but kind to us. Before long they started their own families. Children and marriage happened young for both of them, and being prepubescent myself, I couldn't help but feel light years removed from their realities. One Christmas, Lorri and Tina thoughtfully brought Heather and me prettily boxed birthstone sets. I still have the emerald necklace in a memento box somewhere.

Still, in the children of blended families, complications of loyalty often arise.

4

dad [dad] *noun* Informal
1. one's father
    verb
1. to act as a father toward; act paternally toward

T HE BEST DISTINCTION I'VE FOUND for a "dad" versus a "father" was in *The Daily Republic*, in Solano County, California, where Kathy Mitchell and Marcy Sugar write, "A father is someone who believes that by donating his sperm for your creation, he has done his duty in life. A dad is someone who gets up every day and does whatever he can to put a roof over your head, clothes on your back and food on your table." Maybe, like me, you've had both.

Jack Brians was part of the earliest chapter of my life. Called "Daddy" by Heather and me for early slivers of our time, Jack had a previous wife and first-born daughter, Jennifer, our half-sister, who is nine years older than me. She and her mom, Jackie, are dear to us. They endured the same indiscriminate moony mess from a man who simply knew no better than to find a bit of fun when the going got rough.

Jack, my father, hadn't grown up any better or easier than John, my dad, had. Neither were able to fondly relive childhood memories, as Mom so easily could. Neither were given the daily or steady example of how to be a father or husband, but between the two of them, it was Jack who couldn't force himself into either of those traditional roles.

Working a variety of jobs, Jack, more like a child himself, followed whims and fancies in the evenings while his young working wife stayed home. As a newborn, I learned to cry out my loneliness since Heather, a toddler struggling with asthma, needed more of Mom's time. With emergency trips to the hospital for breathing treatments the first eight years of my sister's life, my first lesson was to comfort myself. For far too long my thumb became an indispensable way to do so. Heather's health and temperament often claimed Mom's energy until late at night. When my sister would finally sleep, I'd cry out, sensing a window for some one-on-one attention. From the start I learned how to wait with myself, to bide my time, before demanding the care I needed.

Jack held his babies and posed in photos as a family. He wasn't unkind or completely invisible as a father, at first. He tried out that disappearing trick as a husband instead, ducking out to bars after work, meeting up with other women. Mom would shoo us up the stairs when he came home intoxicated. Some nights he was angry enough to throw something around the room—not someone, just something. Jack had decided young that he would never hit a woman. Heather and I made ourselves small to peek through the banister rails in the darkened hall above, leaning in, listening to his drunken tirades, wondering if we would be able to come back downstairs and finish our Valentine's cards or desserts. Mom believed me too young to remember these times. When I asked as a teenager, Mom and Heather had to confirm my earliest memories.

Jack was handsome, with silvery hair and impressive sideburns framing his face. He had enough affability in him to dance and sing, drink and party with the best of them. Lighthearted, lithe and good-looking, he didn't take things too seriously and didn't spend time evaluating his behavior when he was misbehaving. Jack did care for others but was simply incapable of taking care of them.

Discovering her first husband's character flaws, Mom still "hung in there tough," as she likes to say. And much like his first wife, Jackie, Pat put in her time with enough nights spent waiting and wondering when or in what state he'd come home, before she realized there'd be no change big enough to satisfy. The couple had separated once by the time I was born; I am the bonus from that rekindled marriage effort. But some things can only be borne so long, and inevitably, Pat learned to expect better for herself and for us, her daughters. Right after I turned four, Mom, hurt but not hateful, took Jack out for lunch after their divorce proceeding and wished him well.

Crying from the front porch for my Daddy, I can still see him driving away from our house on Shaffer Avenue with a borrowed truck full of his things. Youth understands the basics, and basically, I was left with a profound wish to have him back. Contact with Jack waned after the divorce was finalized, and significantly more so when Mom began seriously dating Big John six months later.

Jack also made a new life, with Rosie, a new girlfriend, and her grown children in Colerain at new apartment across town. For a while he still picked us up for the occasional overnight at their apartment, showering us with Barbie townhouses and storebought Easter baskets, attempting to make up for his longer and longer periods of not being around. Daddy drove us in circles around the empty mall parking lots at night, with his hands in the air and only his knee steering the wheel. He seemed impossibly cool. Calling me his Princess carried him further with me than it ever did with Heather who, older, knew not to be fooled by his boundless charm. Never one to squirrel money away, Jack soon fell behind on child support. At age seven I understood that money was an issue for him. Curled into the cord of a bedroom phone, I whispered a promise that I would grow up and take care of all that my father needed, hoping I might be enough to keep him close. Fewer Princess calls came when I turned eight. That summer Mom and John married, and then he stopped calling at all.

Naive and young, I could not comprehend that Jack dropping out of our lives was predicated on *his* behavior—not on anything Heather or I could have done. I incorrectly correlated the timing of Mom marrying John as the reason my father couldn't be with me. It doesn't make sense, but when we view the actions of children through the expectations or experiences of adults, it is often the children who lose. Besides, children don't allow a little thing like reality to narrow possibilities in their world. We divorced children often and already blame ourselves for parents splitting, and any shitty games adults play after that fact are just more fuel for therapy. Unable to accept being unwanted, I manufactured reasons outside of myself that Jack had left. Built up in my mind to such exaggerated proportions, the level of cool to which none could achieve, he seemed like a silvered Elvis. An active imagination regularly returned Jack to me in dreams throughout my childhood, and I built a relationship out of thin air with a magician who had disappeared. Today, I can't imagine voluntarily leaving my child, though, now, I also understand what circumstances might lead to a separation like that.

Barely eight years old then, I could not reconcile that Jack bailed on me for good. I still held him in my mind as *Daddy*, which was confusing, because my other dad, Big John, was also my Daddy, as I scribbled on homemade cards for him and my Mommy.

As with all starts in life, we are shaped by those we know, love and lose. It may sound strange, but the relationship I had with my father is an important part of understanding this story about my dad.

Big John and I loved each other. We got along really well and still, somewhere along the way as I grew, we got messed up. Though I'd embraced Big John's place in our lives, was happy to have a home with my new family, after contact with Jack stopped, I became resentful. Mom and the man of the house were left to bear the brunt of my belligerence as inside I withdrew in small ways. I wasn't outwardly rude, because most children simply weren't then, and yet I denied Big John the chance to remain "Daddy" for me.

In seventh grade at Delhi Junior High school, a group of us divorced kids met once a week during lunch. Seated in a large circle in the choral room with the school counselor at least let us know we weren't alone. We, the "split down the middle" children, were fast becoming the nation's majority. Maybe you have walked the same obstacle course of mixed feelings for more than two parents.

Growing into a teenager, that unrequited loyalty to Jack prevented me from forgiving small infractions with Big John. Looking back now, through the lens of three decades, I am able to see that for better and worse I loved both of these men, one very real and one very imaginary father figure. For a reason I've yet to define, it left me feeling inexpressibly torn. What my father of birth was, and mostly, what he was not to me over the years, deeply affected my relationship with Dad.

Jack's mother, Clara, my Grams, wore coral lipstick that smacked of wit and whimsy. Eyebrows arched over her cat-rimmed glasses, her sky-blue eyes spared no nonsense and stored a squint of mirth. Playfully Gram's pipsqueak of a laugh would snap the air when our antics were no match for her. Possessing the dogged strength of a woman who's seen her share of battle, she stood scarred, but smiling. Coincidentally, Clara lived in Over-the-Rhine when she gave birth to Jack. His 1938 birth certificate lists an address across the street from my home today.

Jack's father, Harry, ran off during Clara's five-year stint in a sanatorium, a typical regimen for tuberculosis in the 1940s. Her two boys—Jack, age five, and his older brother, Larry—were then sent to stay at Oakley Children's Home, an adoptive and foster facility, for those years. By the time Clara returned to reclaim the boys, Jack was ten years old, and she had met and married Rich. As I've said, blending families is hard. Jack grew believing his mother deserved a better man, one who wouldn't raise his hand to her, and when he couldn't stomach Rich's abuse, he and Rich had squared off. I've heard that it was a nasty business. Jack's point was clearly made at the end of a gun pointed at Rich's head, delivered with a promise to act if Rich ever beat his mother again. Ongoing strife in the house led to Jack leaving home. Lying about his age, he joined the military at age sixteen.

Long after, when Jack married my mom (his second marriage), Rich and Jack played nice for the ladies at get-togethers, but rarely spoke.

Rich sported a gray crew cut, smelled of pipe smoke and was the other Grandpa Heather and I knew. Other than his polite smiles, Planters Dry Roasted Peanuts jars and an ashtray at his elbow, I have little recall of the man. He sat in a chair on the porch or in a chair in the living room, in front of the television, so Grams spent time with us or with Neil Diamond crooning in her sewing room.

Mom would drop us girls at Grandma Clara's house for sleepovers now and then, when John was on visits with his mother. We loved helping Grams sew or make her delicious chocolate fudge with the magical Marshmallow Fluff folded in. Coca-Colas from her Frigidaire slipped into our systems. Grams was the more outlandishly fun grandparent. Rule and order were not the language she spoke to children. She crafted ridiculous outfits, plaid suits and bunny onesies we were forced to wear by our mother. Oh, she was funny. Playing hide-and-seek or kick-the-can with other children in her neighborhood, we would then run back to her cozy corner house tucked above the sidewalk. At bedtime she'd give Heather and me a can of beer we were told to share to get us to sleep. After all that sugar, it's no wonder.

On those overnight visits to Clara's house, I would sneak through her sewing room looking for traces of my father. Nosiness or intuition paid off when I found a single photograph, a Polaroid of Jack, older than I had ever seen him, secreted under her sewing basket. Dated on the back in Clara's hand was a very current 1983 and the word, "Mass." On the front, a middle-aged blonde sat hand in hand on a rock wall by Jack's side. Heather at fifteen had long ago given up the ghost of her silver-haired father, but for me, at nearly thirteen, I had not only discovered Jack's alternative life; I realized that adults who love you, will lie.

My relationship with Grams changed then. Incredulous that she purposely kept my father's whereabouts secret, I withdrew from her. Looking back, it seems clear that Jack deserved my scorn, who in five years had not once reached out to me. My sisters were able to see that. Again, reality isn't always the plane we walk upon. No, that Elvis-like persona became all the more mystifying when I discovered Grams' deception. Clara was protecting her son, and no matter my pleas, would not share his contact information. I hadn't learned by then to wield anger against anyone other than myself, so I turned the betrayal inward, questioning my value, sparking a deeper want for my father and setting a boundary around my love for her. As a pre-teenager, desperate for identity, I felt an intrinsic part of myself had knowingly been hidden from me.

Out of loyalty, she hid a son who requested not to be found, because he couldn't meet his financial responsibilities to the family he'd abandoned. If my own child asked me to keep this kind of secret, knowing the imbalance on this left-behind side of the equation, it is safe to say I would not.

In the early 1980s, I would regularly slip downstairs into our blue-paneled basement and rotary-dial the operator for assistance. Thick phone books with Bible-thin paper printed zip codes into the front pages, and I worked my way through. After I found that photo of Jack, I called Massachusetts and New England states' operators repeatedly. By the mid-'80s, telecommunications progress had me pressing 4-1-1 onto a raised-button phone. No comfort was found in the voice on the other end of the line, with few Jack Brians in each state. My age couldn't understand that the phone bill simply was not in his name. My impatience with adults grew: Even the operators were keeping him from me.

I was not sorely misunderstood or mistreated at home. I had no good reason to seek a father outside the one I had in John Powell. My father withheld tempted me, like the possibility promised by a lottery ticket, the kind Jack spent his life buying.

IN THE PARALLEL LIVES of two paternal figures, considerable similarities stand between John and Jack. They shared great instability in their childhoods; both their fathers had abandoned them. Growing up without much, both were robbed of their own mothers for significant periods of time in their childhoods, due to illness. Both worked with their hands, married and fathered children fairly young. Both had enjoyed motorcycles and drinks with friends. Both had loved my mom. Both suffered the pain of divorce, both struggled to build a bridge to their own children who had grown distant from them.

The contrasts are more stark. My dad, John, was reliable, a man who worked hard and played hard, but placed responsibility over a chance to party. Caring for his mother and sister had made John less capable of selfishness; self-respect made him loyal and level-headed. It would take years before I could recognize and appreciate these qualities—years before I would admit that it was John who had chosen to be there for us despite his own demons of loss, mistrust and longing, day in and out, good times and bad. Becoming a father figure as inescapable as Elvis remained aloof, John not only showed up; he stayed. As Mom had wished, John was my dad. He earned it.

Strong-willed at seventeen, a year after my dad had been killed, I dramatically, as teenagers can do, used guilt to coerce Grams Clara into telling me where Jack was. At long last, breaking from that sense of duty to her son, she told me he was living with that woman in the photo and her children in Massachusetts. They had feared that Pat might have gone after him for unpaid child support. All those years, a dollar sign had kept us apart.

Jack ran from reality, dodged trouble. Though in his own way, he loved his first wife and first-born daughter, and then loved Heather, me and our mom, Jack couldn't stick. His upbringing could not have taught him how. Not surprisingly, he didn't trust Mom well enough to know she would not attempt to squeeze blood from a turnip. Mom would not prioritize pursuit of money over a father in the lives of her children. Pat Powell is too forgiving to hunt someone down for past failures.

Instead, ever supportive and understanding, Mom booked my flight, my first long-distance plane ride, that very next weekend to visit Jack. Rather than ask me how in the world I could be so delighted to finally hear from a man who'd left me behind for no good reason, she simply smiled and said she was happy for me. In her magnanimity she paid for an expensive flight, an uncommon extravagance, while feeling concerned about handing me over to meet a man who'd left her holding the bag. She knew Jack had no parenting skills, and now lived with God-knew-who, and that her daughter was only seventeen. Wonder if I could be so gracious?

Getting what you want doesn't always turn out to be the best thing. Reconnecting felt so important that what other issues may arise simply never crossed my mind.

After this visit, Jack showed interest here and there when it occurred to him. He attended my sister's wedding when I was a few days shy of twenty. Mom had earned the right to walk Heather down the aisle and Jack, seemingly uninjured, sat smiling in a pew. We were glad if not surprised that he was there to celebrate Heather's lovely day. In photos, he looks handsome in his grey suit, next to the beautiful bride, despite the heat in the church. But Jack left as soon as the booze-free reception began in the church basement. He continued to phone me several times a year, ever his Princess on each of those calls, but I had outgrown our kingdom of make-believe, and the relationship slipped sadly into an unannounced biannual phone conversation.

Tragedy breeds itself. That much is clear. Naive and emotionally ill-equipped as a late teen, I could not predict or prevent more pain at that time. I would also realize just how unprepared Jack was to properly parent or live up to my expectations. Decades later I would learn how foolhardy those expectations were. When humans hurt, we latch onto anything we think might alleviate the hurt, seeking anyone who may divert us from the loss of another. Jack was a dream, dashed. Harsh realities are lessons in survival.

Maybe I didn't know how to be a daughter anymore, telling myself I simply wasn't lucky or worthy enough to have deserved a real father. To avoid confusion in my mind and with new friends, I decided that I would refer to Jack only as "my father" or "my birth father," since I already had a dad. This helped me own a reality I had denied myself, one I shared with Big John, even if he too felt like a dream stolen.

Bartending for cash, but not pouring the best version of myself into my education and psychology classes, I lingered in a failing relationship before leaving Bowling Green State University halfway through my third year. Worth became an argument I frequently had with myself. Returning to the safety of Mom and my dog at home, I attempted to figure out my own path, one that couldn't be certified on university paper. That winter I did odd jobs, and in late February 1993, I started bartending in Cincinnati. Though I had made clear choices, I still had much to learn about what and who I brought into my life, and how it affected me. Distance proved healthy, and that spring, when I broke up with that longtime boyfriend—even though I had caused hurt too—I said, "You don't deserve me," and found myself believing it. We'd both done things the other couldn't forgive, and the official ending was overdue. At twenty-two, pushing boundaries, realizing responsibilities, proving my strength with boys becoming men, I didn't have the mindset to take care of others at that time.

By April Mom helped me move into a two-family walk-up in Clifton, where I played house and played the field. My old friend Karena, studying at the University of Cincinnati, had been looking for a roommate, and we reacquainted ourselves as young women. Gordon, a regular at the bar and an often-traveling businessman, asked if I wanted to be his personal assistant—help him set up a new apartment and home office, organize his files, make appoint-ments, that sort of thing. The salary was too good to refuse, and though I enjoyed tending to customers, I longed for something more intriguing that might expand my horizons. Gordon certainly wanted more than a secretary. With about sixty years on him, he wanted to feel something new, spend time with a younger woman to enjoy his nice meals and keep good company. Though physically respectful, he was verbally suggestive and inappropriate, as so many men could be. I regularly provided reminders of the boundaries of our business arrangement. Gradually, Gordon settled his efforts and came to enjoy the organization I brought to his life, along with our nice lunch conversations.

A few months into that job, the summer of '93 found me on a long-awaited road trip southwest across the country to Arizona and New Mexico, initially plotted with my friend Holly. When her plans changed at the last minute, I turned the excursion into a solo trip. Being alone was no bother to me, and I had taken the time off work. Gordon knew my mom was a wreck at the prospect of me driving alone. With his help, and his mileage and car rental points, I booked a plane ticket into Phoenix, looking forward to a personal journey. Keys to adventure and a red convertible Cavalier waited to drive me to Tucson for a few days. At a gas station on the way down, I called Mom from the payphone booth. Watching the sun bake the dessert at 102 degrees, I told her that I was definitely moving to Arizona, that it was just a matter of when.

In Tucson by the pool, I tested and enjoyed my solitude. Books accompanied me to dinner at corner tables. Dating myself, I became fascinated by the new object of my affection. Alone, I was not lonely. Chatting with nice strangers at the hotel or on local hiking tours, while I enjoyed being friendly, it occurred to me that I didn't need a person outside of myself to feel whole.

The white sands of New Mexico led me to Alamogordo, where I stayed with Jack's firstborn, my half-sister Jen, and her then-boyfriend Jim, a.k.a. Jimbo (now happily my brother-in-law). Jen, nine years my senior, was a nurse in the Air Force. Over the years she'd sent colorful bags from Turkey and hand-painted sake sets from Japan to her teenage sisters stuck in Ohio, who had yet to try rice wine. Jen had seen a lot of the world on her tour and thankfully thought to share glimpses of it with me through postcards. At this time, my oldest sister's life was settling into a house of her own, where she welcomed twenty-two-year-old me on one of my first adventures, in a world largely unexplored.

Jimbo and Jen took me to local sites. We saw where Billy the Kid left his mark, joined cookouts with their friends, and visited the Mescalero Apache Reservation. We ate a fancy brunch with champagne at the Inn of The Mountain Gods. We cracked jokes and got to know each other as grown-ups. We drank beers in the evenings, a buzz slowly pushing me to bed in the guest room I shared with their pet tarantula named Bitch. We listened to Bruce Springsteen and ate omelets with low-fat cheese. We visited the officers' club on base; I quickly owed a round of drinks that Jim helped me cover.

Not lost in a world without her biological father, Jen talked with me about the blood we shared. We were happy Jack wasn't the only tie that bound us. Equally we appreciated her mother's dry humor, and quoting it liberally, we laughed and laughed.

Experiencing distinctly different parts of the country, I considered myself in places I hadn't before. Feeling closer to my half-sister, and grateful for my stay, I left New Mexico and drove back into Arizona along the wide streets and stucco walls of Scottsdale, to stay with Karmen, a BGSU college friend who had left her small town to wait tables in the sun. Dust devils blew dry and wild across the desert, and I felt just as carefree.

Life makes its own plans, I have found. The southwestern stars then threw Damon Ragusa, bright like a meteor, across my sky. The concept of a soulmate was no longer fantastical. An immediate and undeniable connection formed with this intelligent, confident, relaxed being, and we began a long-distance relationship flecked with a few golden visits filled with chemistry and honesty. With the steadiness of a mountain, he stood by me as I stumbled up and down for my place on that hill. For seven months he waded through my morosely optimistic, enthusiastically fatalistic, confusing and typically bifold, Gemini view of the world. Damon did not question my dichotomies; he did not shun the vibrancy of my nightmares or mind the insomnia which actually worked well with the time zones between us.

As providence would have it, we discovered that his father, Don, had been my Quantitative Statistics professor at Bowling Green. Damon had likely graded my papers. Don's greying beard, elbow patches, mock turtlenecks, conspicuous intellect and bonus questions about wine on exams had me intrigued enough for a front-row seat and office hours. Unbeknownst to me, Don had been a glimpse of my future.

Our long-distance phone bills had grown out of control, totaling more than our combined rent, when Damon and I decided to take a risk on shared expenses and space. In February '94 Mom followed behind me in her minivan with my dog Matti, as my cat, Miller and I steered through rare snowstorms over Texas and Oklahoma, crossing the country so that I could find my home with

Damon.

Shortly after this journey, I found out from Grandma Clara that Jack had moved to Florida.

❖

LIVING TOGETHER BROUGHT the lessons of love and lenien-
cy. Galley kitchens will hear laughter or bitching, depending on
the two cooks wedged in, and Damon's mother, an artist, created
a pie-baking task to help us learn which sounded best. Damon
and I made new friends and got to know our respective families.
Every few months we'd attend showers, gatherings, weddings or
graduation ceremonies. Happy as I was for our friends and loved
ones, the parental pride posing in photos or walking down aisles,
sweeping daughters into fathered dances, pained me. Tears sprung
up simultaneously for both beauty and loss, as I questioned who or
what I was mourning. Had I betrayed Dad, or was I betraying Jack?
Guilt and confusion overwhelmed me at times. Unlike most of my
friends, visions of my own future wedding were few and did not
include traditional symbolic moments. In dreams I always walked
the aisle in winter, alone.

When Damon and I did decide to marry, a spontaneous elope-
ment to northern Arizona fit us both perfectly. With a judge from
Flagstaff overseeing our bond in the beauty of an outdoor cathe-
dral, there was no parent to miss, no aisle to navigate—just us and
a beginning. Confiding our plan to Mom by phone, only her joy
accompanied us that day, without logistical or emotional hassles.
We cherish that day; it endures as a beautiful reminder of how we
forged our own path to love. After the ceremony we called both of
Damon's parents and mailed a wedding announcement to Jack.

Newly married, working, and trying to start a family, the steadiness I sought wasn't found in calls from Jack. We remained lightly
in touch twice a year even when Damon's job took our family from
Arizona to Georgia and then back again to Arizona.

Before our firstborn was two, in 1999, Grandpa Rich and

Grandma Clara passed, within months of each other. With each of their deaths, I did not hear from Jack; it was Mom who called to tell me. Immediately I regretted any anger I'd levied at Grams. Filled with remorse, I understood the chance I had missed to make things right between us. Jack called a month later to tell me that since his parents had died, he now had Gram's old clunker of a car and the little money she left him. That was the last I spoke to Jack for a very long while. Birthday cards bounced back, stamped "RE-TURN TO SENDER."

A year and a half later, pregnant with our second child, we planned a move back to Ohio. With four years' worth of holiday cards returned, and no answer from Jack, I slipped into numbness. Back in Cincinnati, Damon and I built a life, and I happily got to see more of Mom, Heather, John and their families. We gathered for holidays, birthdays and play dates. My children finally had family close by and often played with their cousins. We visited my sister Jen as she moved across the country with her growing family. Too young to understand, my children weren't bothered to know about Jack. How could I introduce a grandfather who had ducked out, or explain his complicated, chosen absence from our lives? Raised with the constant affection of their paternal Grandpa Don, whom they were blessed to know, they also knew Grandpa John, the face in a frame they'd never get to meet.

Maybe Jack had his place and time. With no trace to follow, for all I knew, he might have already died. At peace, finally, in my skin and my mind, happily married, parenting two incredible children, I no longer needed *Daddy*. Grateful, I watched each day as my husband was every bit the father Jack could not be. Parenting is the battle faced in the mirror of your children's eyes. What I saw wasn't a glowing reflection of my efforts. I kept trying, often too hard. Clarity on Jack's parenting choices came from recognizing not everyone is cut out for that particular war; indeed, it was hard some days even to ride out to meet my own expectations. I came to understand that the parent lacking in Jack was exactly that: just something lacking, not maliciously withheld.

That nagging question of his mortality hibernated in my mind for over six years, festering until the spring of 2006, when finally the ache to know if he was alive or dead overpowered indifference. Reaching out across that glorious World Wide Web, still novel in its scope then, I looked to find and reconcile with Jack. Whether successful or not, I was ready to accept that my father, Jack, gave me life; he was a contributor to who I was, as much by his absence as his presence, and I liked who I was. Jack and his flaws didn't mean to harm anyone, especially not his daughters. After considering all this, I knew I could live without a response, but I could not live without making the effort. With good intentions over expectations, I paid a small fee to a private investigator service online to get an address for him. Shortly, my $39.99 made his whereabouts known. In a stamped letter, I set ground rules for reconnecting with the simple request for honesty and a sincere wish to be a part of each other's lives in some meaningful way. My father called days later, the minute he received and read my letter.

Not girlishly glad, but sincerely happy to connect, I took healthy steps to cautiously open my heart and mind again for this man that I had built up as a child and torn down as an adult. To face our own histories and choose to move through life, loss and disappointment without anger is truly empowering. Forgiveness is freeing. Jack was willing to answer me honestly; he didn't dwell in darkness. Living a smaller life in Clearwater, where habit became routine, and routine became safe, his simple pleasures included his good friends, a good game on TV and a McDonald's sandwich in the morning.

The next day, at one of our favorite family restaurants, Damon and I sat in a booth facing our eight- and five-year old, explaining over black beans and quesadillas that they had another grandfather. There were questions, as I shared that Jack had been in and out of my life and was back in. Explaining what I could about his absence, I then apologized to the kids for not telling them sooner. We ask so much of children. Youth's beauty lies in resilience. Possessing less cynicism and hope in heaps, both of ours lovingly accepted the concept of Jack as a new addition to our family.

We began with a phone courtship about twice a month to catch up. Seeing Jack as this nearly seventy-year old man, wholly, for who he was, for what he could give, I extended my hand and he took it. It was enough that we had chosen to care. "Bullet," as he was now known to friends for his early head of silver hair, had aged in other ways, his dancing feet slowed to a shuffle. His favorite activity was "bull-crapping," as he described it, over beers or coffee on the patio with the few friends he kept close to him. Clearwater locals were his family. He was often called Uncle Bullet.

Damon and I started paying his phone bill to ensure consistent access to him, and if I'm being honest, just in case he decided to go missing again. The phone became a safety feature as he aged, and helped him meet tight monthly ends. I was providing for him, just as I'd promised long ago. I got the strange sense that things tie themselves together in the end. Not once did Jack complain or ask me for anything, but he graciously accepted care packages and letters sent to his doorstep that I hoped might cheer or comfort him. At ten and seven, our children were able to meet their new grandfather when we flew him up to see us in Cincinnati. Giving the choice to these wee people of what to call Jack, they settled on calling him their Jack. Though hoping for a grandpa title, he quietly understood. Jack's admiration and respect for my husband filled my heart. Seeing his wish to do right by his grandkids was gratifying. We hosted a cookout in our backyard on a lovely May evening, inviting Mom, Heather and her teenage children, who were also excited to meet their grandfather by birth. Being with us all together meant a great deal to Jack. That my children had the chance, albeit small, to know one of my fathers, is priceless to me.

Visiting Jack in Florida I discovered what a Social Security income will and won't afford. For Thanksgiving weekend 2013 we flew him back to Cincinnati, where Jack was well met and seated with the extended family he'd married into so long ago. Warming his hands around hot cocoa at our favorite Christmas tree farm, a beloved annual pilgrimage, Jack's strength couldn't walk him into the field with us to cut down the tree.

Health issues arose and mounted, and with his lungs in decline, travel was no longer advised. Jack's doctor visits began to fill his weeks, and the results of blood clots, COPD and emphysema spilled through the phone to me. Cigarettes smoked since he was sixteen were collecting their toll. His pace of life swiftly lost steam. Each time I saw him, it was he who grew thinner, his breathing more labored. Eventually lung cancer settled in with him, and his best friend became an oxygen tank.

These fragments we pieced together into a beautiful end. I flew to Florida to be with him as he passed away in August 2016. Brave in the face of a terminal diagnosis, he chose to die in the comfort of his home without much more than he started life with, and few misgivings. In the end he understood life very differently from how he saw it start. A dreamer, without any foundation to be a father, was mine. Those last ten years Jack Brians was consistent, and without doubt I felt his love and pride for me, for my sisters. We created a meaningful decade and closed a circle. I treasure that last chapter with Jack.

Sometimes I wonder what a second chance would have looked like with Big John—if I could have taken better advantage of my time with him. With Jack I have no remorse, owing to the full weight of regret I carried for my dad.

5

upend [uhp-end] *verb*
 1. to affect drastically or radically, as tastes, opinions,
     reputations, or systems

E XIT 13 ON I-75 NORTH staged and witnessed Dad's accident
that afternoon of July 8, 1986. John Powell's badly damaged,
un-helmeted head and unresponsive body were life-flighted to
University Hospital, leaving the wreckage of his motorcycle scat-
tered on the roadway.

He had been riding to the General Electric plant, just north
of Cincinnati in Lockland, where he worked as a union plumber
and welder. One more turn off the long exit, and he would've made
his shift. *Old Farmer's Almanac* recalls the high temperature around
93 degrees that afternoon, the kind of heat that discourages helmet
use. On that scorching, hazy summer day, the strong silent force of
John Powell, intimidating and unflappable in my childish eyes, was
disrupted. He was in critical condition.

The hospital called the house, asking for Mrs. Patricia Powell.
Mom wasn't home, so I gave them her work number, as was done
in the 1980s: Telephone handsets, mounted on a wall or seated on
a desk, would ring loudly, and the person nearest by would pick up
the receiver and politely answer. A twisted phone cord could stretch
across a room in order to jot down a name and number on a piece
of paper. I didn't think to ask why, when the caller insisted they
needed to speak to my mother; I simply gave them the number.

Catastrophe plays cruel tricks on a vulnerable mind. When

Mom received that call notifying her of the critical condition of her husband, she was overwrought. Leaving work, it's impossible to say what fear-filled visions must have passed behind her eyes as she attempted to focus on the road. In her state of agitation, she ended up driving to the wrong hospital. Obviously distressed, when no one could find a record of her husband being in the emergency room at Good Samaritan Hospital, it occurred to them to call around to other emergency rooms. Carefully Mom was redirected to drive over to University Hospital.

Our grandparents also lived in Delhi Township, less than a mile from our home, in a sweet little mid-century tri-level on Chantilly Lane. Soon Al and Kay's Buick was in our driveway. Corralling us kids, all they knew was that Dad had been in a motorcycle accident and we needed to meet Mom at the hospital. Heather, seventeen, Little John, fourteen, and myself, fifteen, quickly got in the car, uncertain of ourselves and the situation—as is the case with most teenagers in even the best of circumstances.

Joining Mom with tight hugs, tears and worried faces, we were immediately ushered away from the crowded emergency room lobby and into a private family waiting area, where squared chairs cornered the bland carpet of a windowless room. Here, we learned, is where they put families in the most serious cases. A wooden door stood guard between the average emergency and our family.

Airlifted directly into extensive surgery, Dad was fighting for his life. Mom, beside herself with worry, waited with us in our tiny room. There was nothing else to be done, with no mobile phones existing then to divert or educate. Hospital staff held no answers, aside from cafeteria whereabouts. Worrying ourselves and each other, we passed several hours before a surgeon updated us on Dad's still-critical condition. Using layman's terms, the surgeon gently spoke of severe head trauma, a collapsed lung, broken bones. Dad had also suffered deep flesh wounds, burns of hot blacktop embedded into his arms. He had been given a necessary tracheotomy for placement of a breathing tube. Indicated already by the privacy afforded us, it was made abundantly clear that Dad was hanging between life and death. Detailed medical descriptions, given to a family unable to grasp their full meaning, were poorly received. In that boxed space, with nothing to compare or relate this predicament to, no search engine at our fingers, there was no way to comprehend just how bad things were—until, post-op, a nurse walked the four of us through doors we never wanted to go through.

Up to that point, little in life had prepared me for how precarious our human existence truly is. Thrust into that sterile room, beeps and hums of life-saving machines covered choked-back tears as we stood witness to what only hours ago was the whole, upright and undeterred person we each knew as Dad or husband. Inescapable, life's terrible turns. Our responses to his state were overwhelming. Intensive Care Unit nurses stood grouped against white walls and metal beds. My mother and her three children stopped in shock at the sight of their critically wounded family member, attempting to take in the irrevocable, unbelievable sight before us, sobbing at the severity of his injuries. Heather nearly passed out, and nurses swooped in to seat her safely, put her head between her knees and fortify her with orange juice.

Seared in my own mind, from that ICU visit, is the abnormally large swell of Dad's shaved head, staple-sewn, where a train track of trauma now steered across his skull. Scorched with road rash, his once-capable arms burned in our brains as they lay across white sheets. Skilled as he was on a motorcycle after more than twenty years' riding experience, Dad had not been wearing his helmet that day, when someone swerved to miss a semi-truck and hit a family man's motorcycle instead. That 1979 Yamaha we'd all ridden time and again, always with helmets on our own heads, had skidded, thrown him into a pole and across the searing roadway.

I cannot speak for my family or say exactly how they felt, though I know we each were experiencing something completely unsettling and devastating. I can barely communicate any one particular emotion tied to that moment. Shock. That word is defined as a sudden upsetting experience, a complete surprise, a blow. Yes, a piece of me was blown away in that Intensive Care Unit, like summer unexpectedly pushing a storm into a previously calm day.

Intense energy, once stirred, needs the entire sky to simultaneously contain the tempest and allow it to escape. Blown out of myself, a part of my mind swept away from that time and space, leaving numbness to observe the first sight of Dad's wreckage. Certainly, more than one measly physical plane was necessary to absorb what I was seeing. When I blew back into myself with a physical jolt, the tears came.

It sucked at my gut to see Dad so incapacitated, so close to death. My body ached for him. Nerves of empathy ran down my legs, leaving me unsteady. I had little reference for mortality, only having attended one open-casket funeral for a nice lady in our church community. Staring down at Dad's badly misshapen head and damaged body, I acutely sensed how close we each stood to death. The sick pit in my stomach told me that any moment could end his life, or any of ours.

His raw skin cut at me, to his bone, to my core. My heart felt exposed, beating outside myself. The connection to my mind was stripped so bare that my thoughts jumbled, incoherently, and no words were able to form the depth of feeling untapped in my fifteen years. Heartbroken for him, for my mom, for us all, misery was all I could feel. Later in life I came to realize I was already mourning, grieving the loss of who and how we knew Dad to be. Time colors past pains with the glow and grief of possibility.

Openly weeping, we told Dad how much we loved him, feeling it might be the last time we could. Comforting ourselves and each other as best we could, we took in the full weight of his condition. Mom was seeing the man she loved, broken. Though her heart must have been exploding in pain, an assured future severed from her dreams, here she was, tears pouring forth, hugging us, making sure the three of us children were okay.

Nurses, kind and responsive, were forced to limit our time in the shared space. Other critical patients lay in their own beds around the ICU, and other families waited. We were told we'd be allowed more visits throughout the evening.

I cannot imagine the strength it takes for nurses and doctors to handle the visual scars cut into a mind upon seeing all those broken bodies, experiencing such physically disturbing sights at work each day. Healthcare staff stand witness to all manner of pain, bringing comfort to both patients and their families with wounds obviously and invisibly ripped open. I stand in awe of the armor and strength they wield in their chosen profession.

❖

LATER THAT FIRST EVENING, with strength renewed, Heather, as the eldest child, made the mandatory calls to extended family from the hospital lobby payphone. Numbers were found listed in the dangling phone book; coins dropped repeatedly into the slot connected her to those who needed to know our situation. Alerting our pastor, aunts and uncles, and a few dear friends, she carried that load for Mom, explaining to concerned voices on the other line the seriousness of Dad's injuries. Little John and I paced every inch of that tiny room. Stepping into the hall, stretching our legs and continuing, anxiously, to wait for news, we were terrified of what news might come.

Recovering in intensive care after his long and complicated surgery, Dad was comatose. Part of his brain had been surgically removed. He was alive, for now, though doctors were not hopeful. New as we were to all of this, we could not know what to hope for or to think. I can still hear Madonna begging "Papa Don't Preach" low over that ICU radio speaker.

Peculiar how strong a memory can stand: 1986, a summer we never could have imagined and can never forget. Vague recollections remain of being driven in and out of cold concrete parking garages that hot July. Grandparents, aunts and uncles all pulled double-duty to help, knowing Mom was still putting in forty hours a week trying to maintain her job and our family, with no more sick days. Survival mode kept the house running. We each did our chores, folded laundry, vacuumed, emptied the dishwasher—pulling our weight without question. Family and friends got us through with labeled dinners and meals dropped at the door with loving instructions. Thankfully, we didn't have to worry about losing both our house and our loved one as the bills mounted. Saving us from complete ruin was the medical insurance that GE provided to its employees.

My fifteenth year, though, was profoundly sad. Any amusement felt was quickly dismissed as inappropriate or ill-placed. Guilt surfaced for seeking or experiencing an ounce of joy, as each day slowly dragged our family behind it. Mom somehow held herself and us together. If only our deepest strengths could be measured, she would win weightlifting contests. Her warmth and faith did not fail her.

Friends and family visited often, sitting with us, especially in the beginning, expecting what seemed imminent. In its vegetative state, the doctors determined, Dad's brain patterns did not show promise—and so, together, several days after surgery, we made the difficult decision to take him off the breathing machine.

Still strong and silent, he began breathing on his own.

MOVED TO A ROOM upstairs at University Hospital once his vitals had stabilized, we could not imagine what Dad felt or heard while in his coma. Considerably less was medically known then. Along-side family and friends, we spent days watching over Dad, talking to him, searching for the slightest hint of hope.

Becoming familiar with the ins and outs of a major hospital, we shared a new, distinctly different landscape, drawn in concrete and glass. Stacked wide with levels, tile hallways ran uninterrupted through the thresholds of secured doorways. Perched at every junc-ture, a nurses' station granted access to countless infirm rooms, each a fractal of another. The recurring family tale of woe fully imagined next door and the next.

Each floor had an identity, a purpose, a personality. Nurses roosted at each end as doctors and visitors flocked. No smiles or balloons welcomed us as they did on the Maternity ward, no pink and blue crepe paper announced a reason for joy.

This was the serious and critical care ward, where prospects and bank accounts withered. Every tired, tear-stained face in the elevator was a mirror image to our own. The debilitated, in varying ages and states of ill health, occupied gurneys and worried minds. Nurses shared tasks among numerous IV units and patient charts, lending skill and fluctuating degrees of warmth to their patients and their visiting loved ones. Aides ran through with food trays, bedpans and clean sheets, turning patients to prevent bedsores. When Dad's changes were made, we would step out of the room to leave him his dignity. Separating one tragic life from another, thin flowered curtains hung from the ceiling, sparing no privacy, each whisper and diagnosis shared with intimate strangers.

Summer days were spent indoors in stages of hurt and healing. We ate cafeteria Jell-O wishing we were at the pool with our friends, though we didn't dare admit it. We prayed for a miracle as Dad lingered in a purgatory unknown, his mind hidden within the protective shield of his body.

Forearms, once so strong, now lay still and scabbed-over with plum contusions, glossy beneath ointments. In the weeks that followed, as yellowed bruising began to fade, so too did our hope of any animation or awakening from his coma. Convinced that doing nothing was not an option, Mom bought a pair of white high-top sneakers at Payless, insisting the care staff keep them on Dad's feet to prevent his toes from falling further forward, as they'd begun to do with inactivity. With the professionals focused on life-saving techniques, routines and procedures, there had been no thought given to his muscles beginning to atrophy. Would he ever need them again? The doctors at University Hospital were not optimistic. Speaking honestly about their findings with us, they never raised the possibility that Dad would live to recover.

It was obvious to this teenager that we were in the way of these physicians. University is a teaching hospital, so ever-shifting squads of residents, trainees, instructors, practitioners and observers often filled our small space, their fascinated demeanors carrying something less than a bedside manner. Yet as Dad stayed alive, we all remained vigilant for the smallest signs of progress. Hope pinned itself into that all-too-familiar hospital wall without anchor for every twitch or shift in Dad's body. My mind still sees the strange bump of high-top sneakers sticking up at the end of his bedsheets. Such stillness in a body is unnatural, unnerving. We talked to Dad, read to him, moved and rubbed his hands and fingers. I faced my own fears of inadequacy and discomfort at his bedside. Averting my anxiousness, I started just doing: tidying, talking, reading, running out for things. Any task felt better than the crushing sense of powerlessness.

A mind digs into moments like these, moments when life is being thrown at you. A type of robotic trance kept me in motion for the sake of moving. Involuntary reflexes stepped up to prevent a barrage of feeling. All the emotion in the world was inside me with nowhere to go; it was either going to propel me forward or weigh me down. Without action I was in danger of stopping, and I couldn't stop. None of us could. Among our family we each experienced these pushes and pulls. Life has a strong arm and keeps throwing. If we didn't move out of the way, we could easily get knocked down.

GLENN WHITAKER WAS AN attorney in the Graydon Head law firm in Cincinnati in the 1980s and '90s. Aunt Lori, Mom's youngest sister and a paralegal in the practice, had referred him to her sister Pat.

Glenn has since retired. When we spoke in April of 2017, it was obvious how clearly he still remembers first meeting my mother, Patricia Powell, in the summer of 1986.

"The first time she walked into my office," Glenn said, "I remember thinking what a nice, kind lady she was." He then said, "On a personal side note, at that time in my life I was heavily considering buying and learning to ride a motorcycle. Well, when Patricia showed up with the traffic report, where someone had crossed over two to three lanes of traffic, and told me of the severe head trauma John had endured—her story scared the hell out of me!"

Turns out that Glenn decided to buy a convertible instead.

That first meeting they talked about John's condition and a potential lawsuit in the traffic accident. Investigators were still determining who had swerved and why, and were going about getting identities of drivers and police reports together. No clear case stood out as of yet, and so Glenn and my mom parted ways, but he asked her to keep in touch.

In 1986, I was an upcoming sophomore with a strong interest in boys, friends, books, music and makeup, mostly in that order. There were many things I'd rather have been doing that summer more closely related to hair, clothing or tape deck choices. "Boy crazy" might not have been exactly the right descriptor for me, but wasn't far off: Not uncommonly for a teen, my decisions were influenced by the new crush of the moment. Those symptoms of puberty are terribly important, as frivolous as they seem outside of that time and place. Prince and Cindy Lauper understood, and I seemed perfectly rational to my friends. Whatever strangeness that lives inside a teenage mind seems logical there. Still, I could not escape feeling wrong, thinking about cute crushes and eyeliner while our family was going through this.

My struggle with the superficial began then. Deciding often, at times begrudgingly, to lay aside want over need, freedom over obligation, I waffled daily between what seemed to matter to my peers and what actually mattered with my family. This upheaval that touched my family so deeply, revealed for me the difference between truth and trivia. It was to be a defining moment for who I would become.

6

hindsight [hahynd-sahyt] *noun*
1. recognition of the realities, possibilities, or requirements of a situation, event, decision etc., after its occurrence

W HEN I SAW MY DAD that midday in July, just before the accident, there in the kitchen between us was the tension often present with an angst-filled teen—and boy, could I fill a room.

I see him. Still. Readying his lunch at the counter, standing mere feet from me in a tank top and jeans, placing a soft cap on his head, closing his Little Mate cooler in hand. "See you later" was all that walked out the door with him as it shut behind. Standing inside our enclosed porch just before he left, he sorted himself out, keys in hand, putting on his sunglasses. No questions delayed him, no thought for his well-being, no hug or message of love left with him. My ears still register his bike roaring to life and fading as he drives away.

I was the last in the family to see and speak to Dad before the accident. Hours later and still today that is unreal to me.

You see, I rue the years wasted childishly wishing for Jack, the man who was unable to be present, whatever his reasons, when John Powell was standing in front of me. Teens often have troubled times with their parents. Divorce doesn't help.

I have to assume Dad knew that I was waiting for Jack to show up. Only later was I aware how painful that must have been. Neither Dad nor I would scream or rant when we were upset. Our tendency was to flee the scene on a bike, mine taking me as far as the power of my anger and legs could go. I would read or journal to escape; he'd tinker. When my anger boiled, letters were sent, mostly addressed to Mom. She kept a few doozies I aimed at my sister.

Happy to pretend or dive into a book, I prized being alone. And since I wasn't into sports, I figured Dad and I had few points of commonality, even when I might have sought his company. I wasn't always a peach to be around, coming across standoffish or sensitive at times. If I found myself the least bit uncomfortable— hot, cold, itchy with poison ivy—everyone would hear my fussing. I couldn't stand it when the elastic on my pants or the smocking on a shirt rubbed wrong, or the music volume was too low or too loud. My family grew annoyed at the injustice of my claims. If I were a child today, I would likely be diagnosed with sensory integration disorder and anxiety, and given tools to understand and better manage those conditions. But this was the 1980s.

True, my stepdad didn't do well with conflict, having his own particular quirks. No one is without fault. I can't imagine the doubt on his end, raising two young girls when it hadn't gone easily for him the first time he tried. Even as a junior high student, I felt guilty sharing a home with my dad, knowing I wasn't giving him a real chance, pitting Mom against him and insisting she choose me.

As a boy, Dad had learned not to trust a renegade parent. Knowing what he must have endured, waiting for his own father to return, he may have found my aloofness, as I daydreamed for mine, foolish. Perhaps he worried (with reason) that my dreams would be dashed. Perhaps he understood me better than I knew, having felt his own heartache over a missing parent, one you've built up repeatedly only to have to tear the idol down again in your heart and mind. Not a big communicator, John Powell couldn't say any of that to me, and I wouldn't have been ready to understand if he had. Instead of using words to connect, he'd make a beautiful belt buckle with my name engraved on it or offer to take me on an evening motorcycle ride. In return I'd clean the house or dust his dresser and fold his handkerchiefs nicely. My annually crafted cards for Father's Day were lovingly received. Innocence cuts through sadness to create happiness.

Glimmers of opportunity appeared in kind notes, in silly jokes and across dinner tables, providing doors for both of us to walk through or slam. As I grew, reaching out or apologizing became more difficult, after a disagreement—good intentions and construction paper could no longer easily glue us back together.

One spring, when I was eleven or twelve, our family slept on wheels for a week in a pop-up camper borrowed from my Aunt Lori and Uncle Jeff. Trailing behind Dad's van, the hand-cranked house rose into being and just as quickly collapsed down to hit the road again. Heather and I were made to share a tucked-away bunk. Campsites around Williamsburg, Virginia, crowded families into the same economical spring break trip. One evening, Mom and Dad settled into lawn chairs near the fire ring, drinks in hand as evening fell. Heather, the oldest, ran around camp, but Little John and I were kept closer. Feeling slap-happy and goofy inside the camper, my brother and I were probably acting out more than we should, getting loud, chucking things back and forth at each other—a typical sibling battle, born out of boredom.

At one point I threw Little John's sock at him. When it landed in the little camper sink, getting wet, he was indignant. Laughing at my small victory, as any middle sibling would, my smile faded fast when Dad's cheerless face opened the camper door. Our shouting had likely disturbed other campers, maybe even embarrassed him. For all I knew, we'd been on Dad's nerves all day.

When Little John pointed to the sink, saying I'd thrown his sock, Dad was quick to respond. Before I could say a word in my own defense, Dad grabbed my arm, pulled me out of the camper, spun me around, and spanked me hard on my bottom several times. Having only felt Mom's light hand in the past, I was a stranger to real spankings. My body wasn't prepared for the force of the blows, and my bladder released from impact. Pee, in warm rivulets, ran down my legs, pooling into my shoes. Anger and shame welled in my eyes. I could handle the sting of the spanking, but was mortified by the attention drawn to me, the resulting damp pants, and even more painfully, the injustice of Dad's rush to punishment.

Parents occasionally lose control. If pushed too far or lied to,

Dad would intimidate, spank, and maybe hit. This was the way of our childhood. Back then, no fault was found with parents rearing their children however they saw fit. Times are different, though bastions still support this type of physical discipline. No manual is provided when children become yours. I wasn't abused; I was spanked, and not often. Depending what lines you draw, other parents gave it far worse. Still, if a spanking can stay with me this long after the point of impact, how hard must the force of regular beatings or a constant string of verbal assault hit the heart of a child? I'm fortunate that wasn't my fate. Looking back, I've determined that Dad lost it sometimes in part because he never really learned how to communicate with words. Repression is an incubator for anger.

My pride was deeply wounded that evening, and bitterness sat with me for a long time after. Little John, not realizing what ratting me out would lead to, felt terrible the rest of that night—and I let him. Mom didn't have a say in her husband's quick reaction, but to my mind, she had allowed it to happen. Not knowing I'd peed myself, she didn't rush to help as I ran to the camp bathhouse. For days my family received daggers thrown from my eyes.

Eventually I got over myself. Most of us usually do.

Attempting to connect later, in seventh grade, I asked Dad if he would take me on a motorcycle camping trip. Feeling the need to incentivize this proposal, I promised all "A"s on my report card if he would consider it. Dad's noncommittal response saddened me, pushing me harder at school to prove myself. Despite my efforts, when the time came, one "B" spoiled my row of "A" letter grades. Standing with me in the kitchen, after I'd faced up to my failure, he said, "Well that's that." No other mention was made of our agreement.

Maybe he didn't comprehend how important this hope of a father-daughter camping trip had been to me, or how hurt I was by his dismissal. If he knew what it meant, he couldn't have so easily shrugged it off. For my part, not once did I plead my case or fight for that campout. Dejected and prideful, I walked away to console myself. Why hadn't I just asked him to take me, without tying a string to it? What did I need to prove?

It really stung when Dad took Little John camping the following weekend. Withdrawing further inside myself, I preferred the world of make-believe, easily found through books and my own imagination, to the real world of John Powell.

Later that year Dad accidentally walked in on me in the bathroom, and, as a preteen, I was humiliated. Surely just as mortified, he quickly closed the door, but I didn't respond with grace, and stayed bent out of shape for weeks. Pubescent girls are a tricky business, I know, but why couldn't I just forgive him, for something that seems so small now?

After events like this, I wouldn't talk to Dad for several days. Fear and insecurity kept me from yelling, but internally I found my ways to punish or rebel. I might steal twenty dollars off his dresser, saying later I found it on the floor at a store. I might pretend to get sick in the morning so I could stay home and watch *Spider-Man* and eat snacks all day, because I didn't want to face school. I would hide out in my room. The small means by which a child can wield power. Days would pass, and I'd feel like I'd somehow evened the score—and then Dad would surprise me with how gentle he could be with a baby animal, or how thoughtful or playful he could be with Mom. He was an enigma to me. Returning from trips with trinkets or souvenirs to show that he'd thought of me, mailing postcards addressed to me. Sharing smiles and jokes at dinner. Then he'd ignore something I found incredibly important or forget a plan we had together. One time he went out of his way to dismiss my ethics and trick me into eating the deer he had hunted, killed and cooked into chili for dinner. He pushed, and I pushed back. It was our way. We could still joke when we were in the clear of each other, and we could hang out and watch a program or enjoy a meal together. It wasn't that our life was horrible; it was the complexities of life and our personalities coexisting with us. Still, when Dad and I were off, we were really off. Whatever excuses I made or attempts he denied, were the chances we both missed.

By the time I reached adolescence, I couldn't be told a thing, "I knooooow-wah!!" was heard from me regularly, accompanied by the obligatory eye-roll. Independent, resentful of needing anyone, I was sure that I could handle just about anything without assistance. Aimee Mann and *Voices Carry* understood the bravado I sought. The make-believe power teenagers wield. Mom regularly became a necessary fallback position; at no time did I feel weak in her eyes.

Heather and I didn't see eye-to-eye; as she was far more shy, I would prank her just to annoy. That modesty in Heather was easily set off by my bluntness, even when I wasn't trying to embarrass her. Mom had to read her fair share of persuasive essays chronicling my sister's faults and the discrepancies of her parenting between the two of us. Not easily flustered myself, I understood some of life's lessons sooner, and usually Heather benefited from my experience. Then, and still today, even Mom would joke that I'm the real older sister.

Discontented teens will manipulate winds to blow in their favor. I blew hard. While Mom was busy with work and caring for all of us, I took advantage, playing on my mother's emotions to obtain permissions or promise of benefit. Dad saw through me and didn't have time for my shenanigans, not wanting to give an attitude undue attention. Little John smartly kept out of the fray. Screaming matches did not ensue—Dad and I were not prone to yell—still, small dramas lived on in my mind, and boiled over there regularly. I believe I am accurately describing that I was every inch a teenager.

Our everydays were absent drama, and ordinary rigors of family life woke us early, placed us in carpool rides to junior high, or maybe a friend's ride to and from high school. Conversation happened at dinner before we squared off to our own spaces after dinner. Weekends would put us back in each other's spaces for breakfasts, maybe with Dad's pancakes and plans for projects around the house, or an outing. Family gatherings piled us into the car and unloaded us into other homes, where cousins peeled us away from our parents.

Looking back, my friends also had either very boring or strained relationships with their own parents. Dinners were eaten in silence across many of the tables I shared. Being disgruntled here and there with our folks wasn't something that seemed awful or out of the ordinary, though the underlying tension always chewed at me. I can almost hear its gnawing cut through a room. With Mom, I could recover the situation; with Dad, I was outmatched. Every time we played psychological chicken, he would win. Resolution never came with hugs and apologies. Eventually I lost my resolve and moved on, and then so would he.

After Dad's accident, I became consumed with guilt for ever causing him pain. Internalizing everything, I vacillated between hiding out or acting out, seeking any way to avoid dealing with what became a heavy emotional burden.

11-1-86

Dad,
I came to visit you today, it's been a long time. You are doing a lot better since then. You have to get better and come home to us. You moved your right leg and arm and were awake on and off. Happy belated Halloween.
I'll see you later
I'm Sorry,
Love,
Holly
[Silly face doodle]
Smile God Loves You

IN THE HOSPITAL I found a way to make things right. Remorse faded with each visit, and so I increased their frequency. Accompanying Mom on those evenings after work, meeting the aides and fellow visitors, decorating Dad's room and talking to him, I rebuilt our relationship in whatever place he was ready to receive it. All pretense and power positions dropped. Having almost lost him made me more aware of what had been there. Days at his bedside presented an opportunity, a second chance for more than I had allowed between us.

While being on a chronic care ward isn't for everyone, with the smells of fear, feces and fading life flooding my nose even now, I worked through it for redemption, to claim what I hadn't fully before. John Powell was my Dad. He'd been by our side, at our dinner table, on the couch and in my heart all along. I just hadn't recognized it until I was once again threatened with abandonment. Recently I was talking to my brother about that very thing and finally was able to explain to him why I had so often been at Dad's hospital bedside, and what it meant to me and, I think, I hope, to Dad.

I wasn't alone in this parent-child incongruity: Heather had to deal with her own issues of abandonment. She's walked her own road with that, and it has made her love her children fiercely. Around 2011, my brother John's mother, Lorraine, and his two older sisters, Lorri and Tina, rediscovered each other after a long separation. They were finding a way forward, as I had with Jack. Strained and distant family relationships can't help but present challenges with so much history, time, and miscommunication embedded, but it's important that Little John had some reconnected years with his mother before she passed away. I think he feels better for it, much as I did with Jack. It has been really good to have someone like my brother John to talk to with such similar stories in and outside of our immediate family.

Siblings don't always get along and aren't always born to the same parents. These are the facts. John, Heather and I found our individual ways to function within the blended marriage, and within the nightmare we experienced through Dad's murder. Each of us went our own way after high school or college, studying, working, keeping and meeting friends, making our own families. Even when we struggled to find the right words we kept in touch, we sent stamped letters and then sent emails and now we send texts, evolving with technology as we catch up on each other's lives. Anniversaries weren't remembered alone. Love is strong, and over time an even stronger bond has expanded communication and reliance between us. Family is good work if you can get it, and I dearly love mine.

Back then, though, more than forty years ago, merging into one household—boys infiltrating girls' spaces, different styles of parenting threatening to undermine and overthrow—there were fights and disagreements. I was not born the middle child; I became one. Developing my inner diplomat, I grew to be the go-between. I carefully drew and color-filled signs to hang on walls of the house, with taped corners, encouraging us to count to ten when angry, reminding us to smile and be nice to each other. Not claiming to have followed that advice any better than I offered it, these peacemaking projects were something to do when feeling powerless, other than writing in my diaries. Have I mentioned that journaling saved me? Repeatedly. Opening a confidant inside myself built faith and confidence in my identity, and to this day I trust my intentions implicitly—though being human means they are riddled with bad execution.

Through it all, there was Mom, bridging divides, conquering every crisis and mishap with her best foot forward, always looking at the sunnier side of life. I am certain that Big John must have loved this about his wife. As irritating as overt kindness and positivity can be when you are tired, grumpy or already done in by rowdy kids, after a full day's work, it's probably hard to be too upset with a ray of sunshine preparing your supper. To see the industrious woman you chose, still in her coat, purse dangling over her shoulder, smiling steadily at you—she must have been his eye in any storm. Mom had a habit of moving her body as she stirred at the stovetop, as if the action in her hand couldn't be separated from the rest of her body. Dad would walk up behind her as she swirled her stew or soup, holding onto her hips, grinning as her movement became his. This remembrance, and the giggles Mom and Dad's affection brought to us all... I just love about them.

11-10-86

John,
You slept most of my visit but you looked at the picture I brought and I felt
you knew I was here. Hang in there, Hon! That's what I'm doing.
Love,
Pat

JOY STACKED TO TEETERING on plates most weekend mornings, all for Dad's fluffy, pink-and-green food-colored flapjacks. Food coloring is inexpensive fun, and Dad loved making each expertly flipped cake squared-off at one corner, from the handled hot griddle pan he liked to use. His son and daughters create the same puffed-up colored love for their children. Hard-earned Friday night paydays took us away from the kitchen to national or local food chains, Red Lobster, T.J. Peppercorns and Frisch's Big Boy, for our favorite dinners twice a month. I preferred the places with free refills on Shirley Temples (with extra cherries). Fun family campouts and road trips took us winding through one-lane country roads, eating fried dough in tiny towns or walking tamed pathways at the Cincinnati Zoo. We explored close to home and didn't feel we were missing out on a wider world. Car-ride vacations took us to Metamora, Indiana; Williamsburg, Virginia; Madison, Wisconsin; and Gatlinburg, Tennessee. One splurge trip drove us all the way to Disney World and the beach at St. Augustine.

We embarked on an at-home family adventure two years in a row when we rescued four and then five baby raccoons born in the flue of our old, unused basement fireplace. The third year Dad's careful covering of the chimney worked to deter the mother. Dad showed us how to bottle-feed the babies, and we raised these little black-handed bandits together, walking them on harnesses and leashes, bathing them, using mini-marshmallows to get them to come to us. As they grew older, as much as we loved the racoons, we turned them out to Fran and Joe's wooded hilltop, where their descendants must still roam today.

Mom and Dad both loved animals, and while on a 4th of July motorcycle ride in Indiana, they rescued our first family pet. A tiny white fluff popped her head out of the tall field of grass just in time to be seen as their bike approached. What turned out to be a defenseless puppy ducked back into the greenery as they slowed to a stop to see what the downy speck had been. When they found her, it was obvious she had been cast off too young. With no means of protection, she'd been bitten on her back by some larger critter, the wound deep and nastily covered in maggots. The poor thing was terrified and in a state of complete malnutrition and infection. Dad scooped her up, wrapped her, and they carried her on the bike all the way home against Mom's chest inside her shirt. Finding an open emergency vet close to home, they saved the pup's life. We all fell in love with her and considered naming her Freedom for the holiday on which she was found, but Muffin, with a bite out of her, won out. Our first dog (not the last), she lived and was loved for seventeen years.

Difficulty washes over most familial spaces, securing the knots we lash to each other. Home propagates contentment or resentment, while also holding our routines and making allowances for authenticity. While celebrations become preferred parts of our history, tradition is often built on simpler footing. Less remembered are days of tightly packed schedules, songs sung in cars, rained-out practices and chores done before supper. Unremarkable moments pass into the months and years we overlook or reflect back on. Dinnertime advice wasn't lightly received. "Almost" didn't carry much weight with Dad, who would wisecrack, " 'Close' only counts in horseshoes hand grenades." Accidents were signs of weakness or thoughtlessness to him. He was a precise person, and if ever I dropped a fork during dinner, much to my chagrin, I heard, "Two hands for beginners." In those moments, it was easy to feel small in his considerable presence.

With that tough exterior, Dad saw things clearly through the lens of his principles. Accompanying a firm stance on cleaning our plates were the lessons in how to handle bullies. He didn't coddle and used common sense, encouraging us three kids to stand up to the one bully in the neighborhood because numbers were in our favor. He offered perspective in learning our limits and not taking too much guff from someone. "You don't need to throw the first punch," he said, but I'll be damned if he didn't show us how to properly tuck our thumbs down right there at the table. We ended up taking his advice and found he was right. Our boundaries and confidence grew the day we banded together to defeat the bully. We even ended up friends with him, still in touch today.

Leadership came naturally to Dad, who was also a Scoutmaster for Little John's Troop 483, which met at St. Dominic's church. From meetings to campouts, he put a great deal of energy into that time with his son and that group of young men. At this same time, Dad had also joined a new motorcycle club with Joe. Having both served in the same elected roles in The Pleasure Seekers from 1968 until around 1984, John left the club after a disappointment by what seemed to him a coup from the younger members. River City Motorcycle Club offered more than a hundred strong bikers, with quite a few police and firefighter members expanding his circle of friends.

Skilled as he was, Dad tirelessly worked on our Delhi township home, creating function and form in every weekend effort. His son John cares for that same home now. I can't help but think how wonderful it would have been for the two to have shared in their carpentry or construction projects over these years.

Dad's keen focus supported his interest in things like hunting and photography. There he is, in my mind, bent with a camera, focusing on flowers along the Blue Ridge Parkway. After he died, his 35mm Minolta was passed to me.

His ability to concentrate, though, also meant that he thoroughly digested every word on a historical placard before moving on to the next, often leaving impatient kids to invent their own fun while waiting. In October of 1982, the Cincinnati Art Museum held a special exhibit in town from the Tower of London, which we all truly found fascinating. Still, the overriding memory is that it took forever for Dad to get through the galleries, and we were bored stiff. He possessed patience, alongside true curiosity, and was always left hungry to know more. Retaining all new information that came his way, he preferred television that led to discovery, such as *Mutual of Omaha's Wild Kingdom*, or any history show. I'd deliver his evening ice cream as he reclined on the soft blue fabric in the family room, watching his programs. Funny, it's now me who likes those kinds of informative shows and won't easily pass by any interpretive placard.

Weekends might find our young family attending regional car shows, roaming between all that parked history and mechanical magnificence. Loving forward motion, Dad relished engines built to take us places, caged in creative metal packages. Once a year, we would head up to the Dayton Air Show and watch those winged devils dare to scrape the earth and defy gravity. Paying a small fortune, as a special treat one year, he sent us kids up with a pilot in a small twin prop, providing my first bird's-eye view. I couldn't have been more than eleven or twelve.

When I was nineteen, I dated a guy who acquired a motorcycle he found in Youngstown, Ohio, and we drove up together to bring it back on a rented trailer. A Yamaha FZ750 crotch rocket, white with royal and red detailing, was now in his possession, along with a need to learn to ride it. That summer we both signed up for a motorcycle driver class through the State of Ohio—me on a dirt bike borrowed from my friend Nick, though, as it was not considered roadworthy, it was not an option to test on legally. The FZ750 was far too much bike for me to attempt a road test on, so I walked out an unlicensed yet more attentive driver. Dad's accident had already made me very aware and protective of motorcyclists on the road.

Must have driven my mom to madness with worry when I rode around on that motorcycle, even though I always wore a helmet, no exceptions. Knowing myself, I had to get back on a motorcycle, replace dread with education, and face that fear head-on. Hands-on experience made me less anxious and a better person behind the wheel of any vehicle. Each of us had really enjoyed riding with Dad, and did so regularly. Mostly, I just wanted to remember what he loved about it, and I needed to relive a joyful part of his life. Feeling the temperature drop in the dip of a wooded valley, sensing the warming sunset alongside me on the roadway. There is little else as freeing as wind-whipped hair, the sway of a body in tune with the lean of a bike, and the sun in your squint. To feel deeply what mattered so much or so little on the seat of a bike, to know what amount of risk was worth your body, to free your mind. Possessing better knowledge, I can see what a freedom it was for him.

WHEN I FIRST MOVED IN with and then married Damon, he was traveling a lot. Given my history of important men leaving my life, I struggled then with his absence. Feeling an acute sense of loss when he'd leave, relief of having him safely home didn't always alleviate a distanced welcome upon his return. My behavior suggested he needed to be forgiven for leaving me. Fear is a bad bedfellow. That first decade of business trips, I wouldn't wash the bedsheets when he traveled, just to keep his scent on the pillow in case he died. We all grow into or out of fear, and our sheets are regularly washed now despite his travel.

Over our early relationship, I regularly played the game of "What if?" with Damon. For some reason it helped calm me, mentally preparing for scenarios beyond my control. I've always wondered what the other side of situations might look like. For years my mind had played this game alone, with terrible outcomes, horrific scenarios, creating countless ways to hide or get away from a killer, to free myself from attack or a trapped situation. Knowing the need for answers stemmed from my personal history, lovingly my husband would pour us a drink, turn off the TV, and entertain my endless stream of questions with as much stamina and patience as he could muster. He acknowledged my worry, my monsters. Have I mentioned how much I love my life partner? With Damon I had someone waiting at the end of those dark corridors for me.

Benign or injurious, many of my questions landed like bombs he could help me diffuse. What if we bought a house or got another dog? What if we decided not to have children? What if we did?

What if we weren't good parents? What if just one of us could go to Mars, would you go? What if the house caught fire, or someone broke in? What if we lost everything? What is everything? How big is the universe? What if we are nothing or our lives mean little? Would he still love me if I were maimed? What if either of us ended up in a coma? How long might he let me live on life support? Would he pull the plug or wait for a sign? What if we ran out of things to say, lost common interests or worse, fell out of love? What if we were too tired to talk things through? What if one of us were seriously injured? What if the world ended? How would my life go on if he died?

I had some fears to contend with. My husband lives far better in the here and now, and with humor he would often remind me that death wasn't a maybe; we all would eventually die.

I play this same "What if?" game sometimes on my own to better remember my dad. There was much to the man that I didn't place significance on when he was alive. What else had I missed?

What if he had been able to wheel himself home from the hospital? What if he had been able to walk again someday? Would he, if he could, have ridden a motorcycle again? What if he'd been here to accompany us down our wedding aisles? What if he had been able to meet all his grandchildren? What if Mom still had her husband to see her through life? What would he say if he were here right now?

What if we were more alike than I knew?

What if I had tried harder?

What if I had been a better daughter?

What if I had kept Dad in our kitchen for a few minutes longer that day in July?

7

Caregiver [kair-giv-er] *noun*
1. a person who cares for someone who is sick or
   disabled

A LMOST EIGHT WEEKS AFTER Dad was set down on the he-
lipad atop University Hospital, doctors there ascertained they
could do no more to further his progress, and it was suggested we
seek other options. Mom began looking. Most of us were surprised
Dad had survived at all. Stable, but without showing signs of improvement, he needed a place geared for chronic cases. This is when
we moved Dad to a continuing-care facility where he could get the
attention, exercise, and treatment he needed if he had any hope of
recovering.

Drake Memorial Hospital of Cincinnati was the only option
near town that made sense for his particular injuries and possible
rehabilitation. In early September, we followed Dad's ambulance
there.

BEFORE WE CONTINUE on that road, a short detour into local history. As Dr. Maya Angelou said, "I have great respect for the past.
If you don't know where you've come from, you don't know where
you're going."

For more than 15,000 years, the Shawnee, Ojibwa or Chip-

pewa, the Seneca, Lenape, Erie, Chickasaw, Iroquois, Wyandot
and Delaware tribes, as well as people of the Adena and Hopewell
cultures, lived and moved around this Ohio River Valley region,
named for a Seneca (Iroquois League) word meaning "beautiful
river": "*ohi:yo.*" In the 1660s, France was the first European nation
to claim the "Ohio Country," as a part of New France, and by the
mid-1700s, white settlers had moved into this region, beginning
trade with Indigenous peoples and marking land for themselves—
which of course led to conflicting claims and decades of bloody
battles, with ruinous consequences for the Native inhabitants. All
over the Americas, colonial expeditions at this time were intended
to thwart Indigenous populations and cultivate the land for gain.
Here, from the massacre and forced removal of Native clans to the
uprooting of sacred burial mounds for downtown development,
this thieving of land and culture seeped into our city's foundation.

Cincinnati came into being when, in 1788, three white men—
Matthias Denman, Israel Ludlow and Robert Patterson—bought
800 acres from an earlier settler, John Cleves Symmes. The land
ran along the Ohio River up to the mouth of the Licking River,
good for farming and a magnet for commerce. They then plotted and divided the land for future settlers, and named the town
Losantiville. The name later changed to Cincinnati, for the ancient
Roman citizen-soldier hero Lucius Quinctius Cincinnatus, and the
Society of the Cincinnati, an association for former Revolutionary
War officers, of which Arthur St. Clair (the Northwest Territory's
governor at the time) was a member. Fort Washington had been
completed in December of 1789, and with protection afforded to
non-Native people, the town began to grow. The surrounding land
was fertile, and the soil brought bumper crops of corn that settlers
distilled into whiskey for the soldiers and militiamen at the fort,
which kept the first Sheriff, John Brown, busy. The Ohio, meanwhile, brought trade and immigrants to the new and booming hub,
Cincinnati, the Queen of the West.

Hamilton County, named for Treasury Secretary Alexander
Hamilton, was formed in 1790 as the second county of the Northwest Territory. Today it lies in the furthest southwest corner of

the State of Ohio, abutting Indiana to the west, and Kentucky, a stone's throw across the Ohio River, to the south. Among other local services, the county ran what was once known as the "Hamilton County Home," a nursing home and infirmary for the poor, since 1924, on Hartwell knoll near Longview Hospital. Originally it was the City Hospital, built on that same knoll, and established in 1851. The Cincinnati City Cemetery was also once on property, final resting place for generations of inmates. Unlike a pauper's grave or potter's field, the death certificates claimed "City Infirmary Cemetery, Hartwell." There is no information showing that bodies have ever been moved from that piece of land.

In 1952, the county infirmary was rebuilt into a five-story, 340-bed hospital renamed the Daniel Drake Memorial Hospital, after Daniel Drake, who had received the first medical degree earned west of the Appalachians. He also established the Medical College of Ohio, and though there is some controversy regarding his ties to the medical community then, he is certainly regarded for the focus he brought to medicine, establishing asylums and institutes, and the well-trained medical professionals he coaxed to our region.

By the 1960s and '70s, Drake Memorial Hospital turned its focus to rehabilitation and long-term or chronic care, and local property taxpayers approved the funds to support this work for more than fifty years.

SHIFTING OUR ROUTE AND ROUTINE, Galbraith Road brought us safely to Drake Memorial Hospital, where we got Dad settled onto Ward C-300. Anticipating uncertainty and discovery each day, I learned the new halls of both that hospital and the Oak Hills High School building, where I started as a sophomore and prepared for my coming lessons.

Visiting often, our trek through campus from the parking lot and each turn of the boring corridors became sadly familiar. We met nurses, orderlies and cafeteria staff we wished we didn't have to know, yet were grateful we did. Each of us endured personal levels of discomfort within those wearisome hospital walls of Drake— none so much as Dad, who still lay comatose.

Mom, employed full-time, was grateful for the visitors, friends and family covering time with John while she worked and also drove her children around town. I saw she was exhausted, yet she kept going. Everyone offered help, and our dear friends Joe and Fran Suesz could always be counted on. They often took turns spending lunch hours at Drake visiting Dad. Longtime family friends are invaluable. "It takes a village" is an understatement. We relied heavily on ours.

New hospital faces were polite as we learned their names and tasks in regards to Dad. Less anxiety hung on these walls, though a somber crowd filled the cafeteria, and patience ran the length of this slower-paced hospital and its hallways. Not understanding then that chronic-care facilities are for patients with uncertain futures at best, most being far on the downward side of life's curve, we discovered that dignity and comfort were the main treatments offered.

Worry woke us each morning, and uncertainty welcomed us each afternoon as we confronted our deepest hopes and fears at Dad's bedside. Routinely we felt sickened—the putrescence of life obstinately clinging to flesh penetrated our nostrils, and was enough to keep Little John and Heather from wanting to be there too often. Uneasy in our shared experience, weary with the seemingly benign task of waiting, we stood vigil, forced to linger, waiting on doctors, nurses, bed changes, and shift changes. Powerless and surrounded by bodies betrayed by age and illness, we kids struggled to show politeness and cheer in the face of such a sad place—but not Mom. The nurses warmed to her immediately.

All medical charts and condition updates then lived on paper, clipped to boards passed in and out of skilled hands. Daisy Key was the experienced head nurse on Drake's Ward C. She, along with nurses Sandra Huber and Judith Sander, and the orderlies, Donald Harvey and James Hale (or "Big Daddy" as he was fondly called), among others, were kind, welcoming, as we settled into this unfamiliar environment and Dad's new routine. We took comfort in the care, treatment and humor they provided.

Thoughtfully, Fran prepared two visitors' logs to keep at Dad's bedside. Covering spiral notepads in soft fabrics, she hung green fuzzy yarn tied to a pen held at the ready. When one filled, the next journal began. Mom could catch up with the day every evening when she arrived and feel the support of those who had stopped by, those pages a window into the times she couldn't be at her husband's side. These two notebooks spilled over with handwritten well wishes from loved ones, and more importantly, served as our own chronicle of Dad's progress during this difficult time.

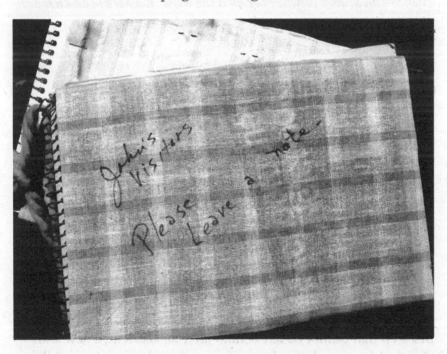

Visitor logs created by Fran for John Powell's bedside at Drake Hospital

Between the frequent sign-ins of family members and close companions, were longtime but distant friends who had only recently heard about John's accident, and rallied to his side. Notes and phone numbers were left, calls returned, prayers gratefully received. The uniquely familiar, unaltered and angular loop of Mom's left hand left her messages. While documenting her love, she also logged Dad's efforts on that long journey, encouraging others to do the same. Details of Dad's every movement indicated hopeful changes and, just maybe, some progress.

10/21/86

John,
I was here for a meeting with the staff
They are all so good to you — caring is the word. You were in an awake time and you looked comfortable in your chair.
Your right leg moved.
Love
Pat

Never one to leave a page unmarked, I signed the book regularly as well. Strikingly odd now, at middle age, seeing my teenage penmanship. Strange for the aging and for the change in my handwriting. Schools today aren't actively teaching the carefully curled cursive drilled into me as a child and left so jauntily angled upon those journal pages—entirely dissimilar to my handwriting today. Unlike my mother's, my hand over the years followed each state of my altered mind, so broken with convention that now it spreads my thoughts in a fractured and impatient combination of cursive and print. So changed am I, that I can no longer recreate that same carefree cursive. This change I would equate to a noticeable hitch in a step that cannot be left behind after an accident, a new and distinguishing mark that becomes an outward expression to others of what you've endured. Despite decades of attempts, it proves difficult to evoke that younger self, the naive state of mind which produced that handwriting.

Mom and I eventually came to better know the staff, easily recognizing the smiles that met us each day. Dedicated nurses greeted us by name, asking about our day and freely providing updates about Dad, in very thoughtful ways. Knowing Mom's schedule, they also regularly phoned her with news. Nurses M. Hinterlong, A. House, S. Huber, K. Marshem, A. Metz, A. Mueller and J. Sander, were always on shifts at Dad's side. Aides such as Big Daddy and Don Harvey were assigned to help the nurses, clean the patient, change the bedclothes and make Dad comfortable. Alternating shifts, we got to know the aides and nurses who were working toward the common goal of getting Dad home. Cracking a joke or anticipating tears with a box of tissues, they made things more bearable. Big Daddy was a favorite: tall and strong, he won us over with his humor and confidence.

Donald Harvey, by contrast, was a petite man, not much taller than myself, with dark, leveling eyes set in a face framed by black, curly hair. Though I remember seeing and interacting with him in Dad's room many times, one of the last days I clearly recall speaking with Donald Harvey was in mid-January, a week or so past Dad's forty-fourth birthday. Returning from the cafeteria, we ran into him near the lobby elevators. My family and I had noticed he hadn't been on the ward lately; we said hello, got caught up and asked where he'd been.

He then told us he sometimes was asked to work different positions and shifts within the hospital, and that he "actually really preferred Pathology." At fifteen, and as a reader, the word stuck with me; I remember the joy it seemed to bring to his eyes as he discussed his move to the lower levels within the hospital. We stood and made small talk. He was both serious and a bit silly. He had a polite manner bordering on demure, pulling his lips over a smile he seemed worried about expressing fully; he wasn't gregarious. His eyes, though, could lock on to a person, and they did so then as we spoke. He listened intently as I shared some updates on Dad's progress. Without recalling specific words, after thirty years, I do remember telling him that Dad clearly was on the road to recovery. I remember Don Harvey's slight smile as he responded, his best hopes for Dad delivered in that distinctly soft, Appalachian drawl.

We thanked him, and wished him well.

8

record [verb ri-**kawrd** noun, adjective **rek**-erd]

1. to set down in writing or the like, as for the purpose of pre-
    serving evidence

History is a love of mine. I adore digging for it, discovering the lives, truth and lies hidden within it. Inestimable wisdom rests in understanding how we've gotten where we are. Winners have written what we currently know, which means as of yet there is not a full account of history, and that excites me, knowing there is far more to learn. I believe wholeheartedly in continuing to educate myself. I see the value in learning something new each day, opening doors to new people and places, peering into worlds beyond books, belief and my own imagination. Arrogance and certainty rely on slim sets of facts, yet time has taught us that we cannot ignore wider truths. Personally, I like a broad understanding of my world, and don't dabble in selective ignorance or propaganda. I do not mind being challenged or becoming uncomfortable with a topic. Discomfort is an internal signal that I have something more to learn. Khalil Gibran wrote, "Perplexity is the beginning of knowledge." Curiosity is born from lack of understanding. I find delight in proving myself incorrect or finding new paths to long-held certainties.

While I do not condone language and actions that harm or oppress my fellow citizens, I can listen to opposing views. Annoyed as I might be at times, I still enjoy learning how a person arrived at their view. Sympathizing in another's perspectives, considering their upbringing and experience, I can even comprehend how folks might come to label, blame or hate someone else, including myself.

I look forward to a time when all stories are told and can be reconciled.

Research led me on some rather fruitful tangents, furthering my understanding of this case and all the arms that reached into it. The overarching themes of county responsibility, federal protections, freedom of speech and of the press, journalistic and criminal investigative integrity, public safety, trust in the justice system and media in general, as well psychological and forensic applications, all apply.

Irrefutable, the full effect this story had not only on myself, other victims and their families, but also on this city. Throughout this process I've become a better-versed Cincinnatian and can claim "above amateur" status in my understanding of criminal legal processes, media representation, and healthcare administration, as well as the city's political and corporate structure.

Particular to Dad's case, a record has been set, a chronology exists. Credit newsmakers of the day for establishing an enduring account; journalism is the first rough draft of history (a quote often attributed to Phillip. L. Graham of *The Washington Post*). The value of early reporting cannot be overlooked as a necessary step in seeking accuracy, and concrete facts.

First, a few words on the onus of a free press. The Bill of Rights, comprising the first ten amendments to the United States Constitution, was adopted in 1791. As the First Amendment was being debated in Congress in 1789, James Madison put it this way: "The people shall not be deprived or abridged of their right to speak, to write, or to publish their sentiments; and the freedom of the press, as one of the great bulwarks of liberty, shall be inviolable."

I'm afraid the bulwark Madison envisioned has, in our digital age, become a flimsy cheesecloth of agenda-driven sound bites, misinformation and distraction. Readers today seem less interested in news that leads to discourse and a deeper understanding. Despite Madison's conviction of its indispensable service to democ-

racy, the press itself has become oppressed, politicized, and ostra-
cized. Forward-thinking editors and truth-seeking journalists are
now unwanted, especially if they disagree with us. Our personally
curated news feeds give us only what we want to hear.

With our own channels of preference and bias, streaming
24/7 at our fingertips, we disparage others rather than seek to
understand. Our reliance on social media is undeniable, yet people
remain ignorant to the use of data-powered algorithms driving
our information sources. Targets all, we will read and share what
supports our leanings—and for the marketers, who know our
weaknesses all too well, every moment of our attention is money in
the bank. In this media echo chamber, absolutes drown out nuance.
Vitriol shuts down healthy debate. We allow belief to be claimed as
truth, at the expense of fact, and if one side is "right," the other side
must be damned. This is all bad news for our democracy.

I believe wholeheartedly in a free press, and have great respect
for the intrepid reporters who dive deep into stories, willing to
drown in the details in order to bring truth to the surface. Supporting details, responsibly sourced accounts, irrefutable fact—these
are the components of the best news stories. Of course, journalists
are humans too, and being human, sometimes they make mistakes;
sometimes these mistakes make it into print, or get repeated on the
air. Though you'll hear frustration from me here, when misinformation or plain bad reporting plays a part in my own story, you'll also
note my reliance on both archival news sources and current media
outlets to help me set the record straight.

To question the media does not necessitate hating the media.
Rather, it is incumbent upon us all to hold ourselves, and each
other, to higher standards of inquiry and accountability. Facts that
disprove our own thinking must not be shunned in order to make
our preferred fictions more believable.

The notion of a free press was built into our nation's founding
for a reason. Though we citizens must assess the worth or credibility of any agent of the media, to paint the press with one brush as
"the enemy of the people" is a dangerous step toward a propaganda
state. To only want freedom for your own speech, on your own

T-shirt, but not for others and not for the press, is nationalistic, not patriotic; it is not freedom for all. Whatever "bulwark of liberty" we have left, it's our shared responsibility to protect it, by supporting real journalism in our communities and understanding the media's role in our democracy.

IN 1987, AT THE TIME of Dad's murder, Hamilton County's local stories were most commonly published—alongside national news, sports, arts and lifestyle coverage, opinion, and more—in *The Cincinnati Enquirer* (the daily morning paper) and *The Cincinnati Post* (its afternoon counterpart, more popular on the West Side and over the river in Kentucky), among smaller suburban weeklies. Most folks woke to their news delivered by the sound of bicycle spokes whirring by and a paper boy's best toss in the direction of their driveway. With paid subscriptions and a strong advertising base funding quality reporting and editing, daily metropolitan newspapers across the country allowed readers access to the most timely and relevant news in and around their towns, and Cincinnati was far from unique in having more than one. We also had morning and/or evening TV news broadcasts, on four networks (five if you count CNN, just seven years old then), and radio news playing on the hour in our cars—but for a vast majority of Cincinnatians, the daily paper was a common denominator.

Fascinating, now, to sift through the stories of these newspapers themselves. First iterations and intentions, family lines of succession, prominent purchasers, corporate buyouts, employee investment, local or national achievements and editorial leadership were all offered up in my discovery. Invoking all the intrigue of a Netflix docudrama, the history of our city's flagship paper, *The Cincinnati Enquirer*, is worth relating here.

The *Enquirer*'s origins date back to its first predecessor, *The Phoenix*, founded in 1828 and edited by Moses Dawson, who was an activist, teacher, politician, writer and immigrant from Belfast,

Ireland. Of English descent and well educated, Dawson was swept up in the political currents of Ireland under British rule in the early 1810s, in his native Belfast, working toward an independent Ireland. Escaping political persecution in Glasgow, Scotland, he came to Philadelphia in 1821 and began a career as an associate editor. After losing all his books and papers in a fire, by 1823 he relocated permanently to Cincinnati, becoming editor and sole proprietor of what was no longer the Phoenix, but now, *The Advertiser* and later, *The Commercial Advertiser.* In 1838 it was then renamed *The Cincinnati Advertiser and Journal.* Dawson was by then a prominent Cincinnati public figure and author, framing opinions of the day.

What began as a daily afternoon newspaper, excepting Sunday, *The Cincinnati Advertiser and Journal* offered a morning edition started in 1841 by John and Charles Brough as a "newspaper of record." Dawson's death in 1844 revealed interest by one James J. Faran, a graduate of Miami University of Oxford, Ohio, and attorney admitted to the bar in 1833.

James Faran took over running the paper. In 1848, under his proprietorship, *The Cincinnati Enquirer* became only the fifth paper in the country to offer a Sunday edition. Faran went on to become a member of the U.S. House of Representatives from Ohio's first District; he was named Commissioner for the State Capital of Ohio and elected Mayor of Cincinnati from 1855-1857. U.S. President Pat Buchanan also named him Postmaster of Cincinnati in 1855 until 1859, and he served as a delegate in Baltimore at the 1860 Democratic National Convention. He ran the paper until 1881 and worked the newspaper up until his death, in 1892, and is interred at Spring Grove Cemetery (where generations of prominent Cincinnatians have wrapped up their résumés).

Given his positions of note at the time, in 1848, Faran sold some interest in the paper to Washington McLean and his brother S. B. Wiley McLean. By the 1860s Washington McLean had bought out Faran's interest entirely, and sold it to his son, John Roll McLean. John McLean owned and ran the paper solely until his own death in 1916. Rather than leave the paper to his only child, Edward Beale or "Ned" McLean, John McLean uniquely placed the *Enquirer* and his other paper, *The Washington Post*, in trust with the American Security and Trust Company, headquartered in Washington, D.C.

Before long, McLean's son Ned had broken the trust for *The Washington Post*; however, the *Enquirer* remained in the trust until 1952, when *The Cincinnati Times-Star* offered to buy the *Enquirer*. In a last-ditch effort to keep the paper independent, 845 *Enquirer* newspaper employees rallied and lumped together their assets to compete with their own $7.6 million bid, and actually won the sale. Unfortunately, the *Enquirer* employees failed as business managers, and the paper was sold in 1956 to the E.W. Scripps Company (which already owned the *Post*).

Interesting side story: John Brough and his brother founded the *Enquirer* in 1841. He then became governor of Ohio in 1864, during the Civil War, though the *Enquirer*, his own former paper, did not endorse his candidacy. The then-owners, Faran and McLean, were anti-war Copperheads who opposed abolition and President Lincoln. The government attempted to silence dissent from the *Enquirer*. In April of 1865, the Enquirer did close for one day, so the newspaper employees could celebrate the end of the Civil War. President Abraham Lincoln was shot and killed on that very day. The *Enquirer* was caught behind in delivering the story.

The *Enquirer* endures as the main local paper in this region, with Cincinnati.com as the dominant online news source. In today's world of instant "free" news, though, the printed paper sadly resonates less and employs fewer, year by year—as in most other American cities with once-proud newspaper legacies. (*The Cincinnati Post* folded in 2007; *The Cincinnati Herald*, voice of the Black community, still publishes weekly out of Avondale, while the remaining suburban *Community Press* newspapers have gone on-line-only.) Lost advertisers, shrinking subscriber rolls, and consolidated ownership have meant less local news, fewer free opinions, and a loss of public accountability, in too many places.

❖

BUT IN 1987, IT WAS a different story. As I said, most Cincinnatians either began or ended each day with newsprint smudges on our fingers. My siblings and I were instructed to clip grocery coupons from the Sunday flyer, a chore rewarded by time in turn with Garfield, The Peanuts, Dennis the Menace and The Far Side comic strips. Pressing Silly Putty onto the inky paper stretched cartoons and our child-smiles wider, while grownups got serious with the articles. Newspapers familiarized citizens with local officials, elected or appointed, who spent our tax dollars, enforced our laws, and oversaw public services—county services such as the rehabilitation provided at Drake Hospital, ongoing investigations and the prosecution of crimes.

Some names of top Hamilton County officials at that time, many of whom played important roles in the Donald Harvey case, might still be familiar to Cincinnati readers. Art Ney served as Hamilton County prosecutor from 1983 to 1992. Joe Deters (Ney's successor, and the current prosecutor) and Terry Gaines both were assistant prosecutors on the Harvey murder case. Frank Cleveland was the Hamilton County coroner at the time. The sheriff was Simon L. Leis, Jr., and the Cincinnati Police Department chief was Lawrence Whalen (no relation to Harvey's attorney Bill Whalen). The Hamilton County Commission was presided over by Joseph M. DeCourcy; Peg Goldberg, Norman A. Murdoch, and Robert H. Taft II were commissioners. Jean Corbett was president of the Drake Hospital Board of Trustees, with Robert A. Pierce as vice president.

Politics and the press have always gone hand-in-hand: Many early American newspaper publishers were also active politicians, as was the case here with the *Enquirer*, and while non-partisanship has become the professional standard, at least for mainstream journalists, even today's most "objective" reporters still have to play politics sometimes, to keep their sources talking. Media outlets, too, have always had to weigh the risks of litigation and other costs when deciding how tough to be on the powers that be. But in

1987, in the midst of the Donald Harvey case, the *Enquirer* did the right thing.

"Drake Hospital, Medicare cutoff illustrates another failure in government," ran a banner headline on December 15 of that year, alongside an impressive statement signed by the paper's entire executive-level staff: Chairman William Keating, President and Publisher John P. Zanotti, Editor George R. Blake, Vice President Thomas S. Gephardt, Associate Editor Craig A. Moon, Vice President for Advertising Francis M. Price, Vice President for Production William R. Johnston, and Vice President for Circulation James A. Schwartz.

"The men and women who have looked to Drake Hospital for medical care deserve better than they have been getting. So do their families and the taxpayers of Hamilton County," the "A" section article goes on to say. "The public is entitled to assume that every public institution is being conscientiously administered, that standards are being met and that the services in which tax dollars are invested are being provided. That, unhappily, appears not to be the case with Drake."

MY GRANDPA MYERS WARNED me to be wary of the media, ideology aside. He was part of a generation who looked around at their community as they read and listened to their news, before the broadcast world exploded onto every available flat surface. Relying on the likes of Douglas Edwards and Walter Cronkite, they trusted a news stream that, at bedtime, turned to static, insisting you close the door on the wider world to focus on your own. A man of his word, Al Myers saw through the cowardice of insult and fabrication. Grandpa saw which way the wind was blowing toward truncated TV punditry by the late 1990s.

As a young teen interested in our world, I questioned being asked to cower beneath a desk for nuclear drills in junior high. I watched an assassination attempt on President Reagan from a

19-inch TV on a wheeled cart in my 5th grade classroom. I wrote letters to Presidents and enjoyed debates and mock elections at school. I remember being stunned when Walter Mondale chose U.S. Representative Geraldine Ferraro, a woman, for his running mate on the 1984 Democratic ticket. I would espouse my political ignorance at family dinners; it was my Uncle Robert who always asked me for my sources. He sparked an awareness in me about claims made, ideologies promoted, anything put out by others that I might repeat without examination. My uncle and grandfather didn't agree politically, and yet both of these men showed respect for each other, sought multiple news sources, and knew propaganda media when they saw it. Their early examples and advice have rendered me vigilant, so that I'm as choosy and comprehensive with my media diet as I am about the food I eat.

Having experienced it myself close-up, I can say, finally, that good reporting matters. It has the potential to inform our most important decisions, to protect us from harms of all kinds, and even to save our lives. Today's journalists have to work harder than ever in pursuit of accuracy; editorial backbone is critical. Any newspaper or network today has to struggle to maintain their heading and bearing, in the current media storm, and too many local papers are getting lost. Thankfully, there are shining examples to the contrary—as recently as 2018, here in Cincinnati, with the Pulitzer Prize given for local reporting to the *Enquirer*, for a multimedia series on the human toll of the heroin epidemic.

Freedom of the press cannot be free of cost to the public. We have to be willing to pay for professional, ethical journalism in our communities—or be prepared to pay for its absence, as I fear we are already doing. Those of us who have experienced tragedy first-hand know how important it is that these stories be told, and be told truthfully.

9

recover [ri-**kuhv**-er]
    verb (used with object)
    1. to get back or regain (something lost or taken away)
    2. to make up for or make good (loss, damage, etc., to oneself)
    3. to regain the strength, composure, balance, or the like, of
        (oneself)
    verb (used without object)
    1. to regain health after being sick, wounded, or the like
    2. to regain a former and better state or condition

11-18-86

John,
Heather, Holly, John & I had to come see you again because you've been
making so much progress. You communicate with nodding. Your right leg is
moving a lot more. We love you.
Love,
Pat

I feel compelled to tell the part of the story most often lost in this
entire tragedy:

My dad was recovering.

Painted inaccurately in countless news stories, attorney sidebars
and defender's books, John Powell was described as a non-respon-
sive invalid and nearly always labeled a comatose patient in the

news at the time of his death.

Make no mistake: That was not the case. Though his first days, weeks and months after the crash were uncertain, the patient's resolve was not.

First, while in his new room at Drake, Dad remained in a coma. But small signs indicated that he would not stay under for long. Comatose from his crash on July 8 to mid-October, awakening was slow but noticeable to those of us who had been witness to mere muscle spasms and twitches before.

Noon 10–20–86

John
Saw you 1st time in a week. R. leg moves left arm moves. I swear you're trying to communicate—
Love ya
Fran

We watched, amazed, as small movements became more pronounced and intentional. Dad's eyes began to open, and though at first we didn't know what he perceived, as he searched our faces, his relief was apparent when he recognized his wife. Aside from early confusion with new faces in the room when he first awoke, his eyes soon lit in recognition for us all. Physical therapists began to work with these new improvements to strengthen his muscles and gauge his responses.

We started small. With his tracheotomy, there could not be words right away. After three months under, and with such extensive physical damage, Dad had to relearn the simplest things. It was obvious early on that he'd only come out of his accident with meaningful use of one side of his body. He'd rub our hands with his thumb as a way to connect and show his affection or even his frustration. His hands, formerly those of a laborer, so long unused, had grown incredibly soft, his fingernails elongated with a seashell sheen that the harsh soaps and chemicals of his working days would not have allowed. The once weathered skin on his face, expressionless for months, was so smooth it appeared as though years of his life had been stripped away.

Dad was returning to us. A deliberate stroke from his thumb told me he knew I held his hand. A leg moving or a foot bending made us unbelievably happy. When his eyes opened, the man we knew was behind them. Indeed, Dad was strong, mentally capable, and recovering. He was responding in a way that seemed astounding to so many at Drake, the nurses and orderlies started calling him "The Miracle Patient."

11-15-86

Dad,
I came in today and you were wide awake. You look a lot better. Mom and I brushed your hair. You looked straight at us. It snowed yesterday and it's really cold out. Thanksgiving is coming up. Sorry you can't spend it with us in Illinois, but how 'bout coming home for Christmas, huh?
Well I'll be back.
Get Better.
Love,
Holly

Friends and family noted in bedside logs about Dad's waking times, tired days, smiles, and stirrings. They made comments about his heading out or back from therapy sessions. Without this record, I doubt one would believe what significant changes were seen as John Powell threw off this supposedly unyielding coma, revealing the tenacity and strength of the man who lay beneath.

12-11-86
Pat,
Fred Bosken stopped to see Johnny — He is making great progress

Dad learned a way to communicate by blinking his eyes in response to questions: two blinks for "yes," one for "no." One example I can easily recall was when I asked if he knew what day December 7 was. Dad blinked "yes," and when I tried to tease him into another option, he blinked "no." When I asked if it was Pearl Harbor day, he again firmly blinked twice: "yes."

12-13-86

Dad,
You were up a little bit but you were real tired. We stayed until you were too tired to listen, so we went to do more Christmas shopping. I still don't know what I should get you. I'll think of something. It's really cold outside, but it's sunny for now. Winter is really here. We have to decorate your little space for Christmas. We have a lot to be thankful for. This should be the best Christmas since you are finally coming back to us. Keep it up!
Love,
Holly

That December, as we decorated the shared hospital room with a small tree hung with tinsel, candy canes and paper made ornaments cut from old Christmas cards, we were all hopeful for a speedy recovery. Dad was moving his limbs more regularly, his head nodded in response to our questions, and soon he was getting out of bed, with help, and sitting for part of the day in the reclining chair in his room.

Speech and physical therapy were his daily workouts, and he was working hard. Wheelchair rides, rather than gurneys, took him out of his room to appointments throughout the hospital, and he became known to the entire staff as a remarkable success story. Young and strong as Dad was, everyone at Drake believed that he could recover well enough to be released to go home in coming months. We were all praying for that outcome.

12-30-86

John,
Looks like you're making great progress.
Know you're going to make it.
Best of luck to you
Happy New Year!
Bob Sahand
PS — Looking forward to having a few beers together this summer on Grossepointe

As Dad progressed in strength and mobility, he helped get himself to therapies, independently wheeling his chair there. As he worked his one good arm and leg to nudge the chair down the hallway, a smile of effort and pride also moved across his face.

Evenings after work found Mom at Dad's side, often with me in tow. Extended family visited as they were able, leaving notes, checking in with Pat, their sister or daughter. Weekends, all three of us kids were at Drake with Mom. Fran and Joe continued their every-other-day visits at lunch, alternating time with their dear friend. The hospital staff knew them well.

Over these weeks and months, Mom checked in periodically with her attorney, Glenn Whitaker, to update him on John's progress. Knowing Glenn was a part of this story from its beginning, I reached out to him early in the process of writing and was grateful when he responded to my request for an interview. I phoned him on a spring afternoon in 2017. With fingers poised on my laptop, I listened through the phone as he shared how he'd retired and moved to Colorado—but before anything else was said, Glenn added that he would never forget Dad's death, 'a once-in-a-lifetime case."

We mused over the decades that had passed since he'd last spoken to Mom, and I assured him that she was healthy and doing well. He asked about the family, hoping there had been better days for us since then. His voice was kind, his words direct, and he was adamant about helping with my project in any way he could.

I asked Glenn what he remembered of this particular time, in the fall of 1986 and into winter of 1987, when Dad was recovering.

"We had one in-person meeting during the time John was at Drake, and I remember that though things were still tough for John, there was good news—he was starting to recover," Glenn said, adding that he remembers feeling very hopeful for our family. I told him how strong a memory that remained for me as well.

Hearing his account solidified what I knew. There was nothing new in his remarks about Dad's progress, though to hear the clear memory of an outside observer so involved in our story, yet distanced for more than three decades, moved me. That part of the story felt significant, as I long believed it was: the undeniable truth that Dad had been recovering.

As Dad's condition improved, his doctors and nurses were excited along with us. It was a time of possibility. We dared to hope. Everyone could see how hard Dad was working toward coming home. Wheelchair access was being considered for our house, a confirmation that we'd have him home with us, that we would be able to care for him, however many months away that may be.

1-2-87

Dad

We (Mom & I) came again today. You were up in your wheelchair. You looked really good. Your work is paying off. We rode you around to the lobby before your therapy. I accidentally bumped your leg in the door I think you were mad. Sorry

We'll see ya later.

I'm going to Dyan's this weekend so I won't see you.

Bye

Love,

Holly

P.S. your occupational therapist said you had a good day.
We were real pleased with your progress today
Love,
Pat

Dad celebrated his forty-fourth Birthday in January 1987, with a small celebration for him at Drake and slices of cake for us all in the cafeteria. At the height of his recovery, this celebration was about far more than completing another turn around the sun; it promised future turns that Dad would live to make. A clear path of work and continued progress lay in front of him.

Therapists were excited to recount his successes to us after each session—his occupational therapist most of all. In regular updates and daily conversations with the Drake staff, we heard and saw how incredibly impressed they were with his recovery. Months ago they hadn't expected him to live, let alone wake or communicate, and nurses and staff shared their surprise with us. Cheers and smiles met Dad every time he wheeled around the corridors with us. One doctor discussed with Mom the hope of soon removing his trach, so that eating and speech therapy could move forward. Reward was easily seen on the faces of Dad's team of support at Drake, chronic care professionals unused to seeing such happy results. Filled with the promise of better days, we were all so proud of Dad, marveling at how far this patient, under such diligent care, had come. His next stop, surely, would be home.

1/18/87

Dad,
Mom & I came tonight but you barely even opened your eyes. You must be working hard in Therapy. You were so tired. So we're going to leave.
Keep up the good work,
Love, Holly
And Love, Pat

10

descent [dih-sent] *noun*

1. the act, process, or fact of moving from a higher to a lower
    position
2. a downward inclination or slope
3. a passage or stairway leading down
4. derivation from an ancestor; lineage; extraction
5. any passing from higher to lower in degree or state; decline
6. a sudden raid or hostile attack

Our bright, hopeful start to the new year in 1987 fizzled out
toward the end of January. Confusing to see Dad doing so
well, then have several sudden and unexplained declines—what was
going on? Pressed concern replaced staff smiles, heads tilted toward
us with pity and empathy. Several concerning episodes of breathing
and bleeding rushed Dad in ambulances back to University Hospital for emergency treatment. Staff at Drake struggled to understand
Dad's symptoms of excessive sleepiness, very low blood pressure,
abdominal bleeding, and eventual seizures, though the nurses knew
he was a chronic care patient; sometimes patients just got sick. The
entire ward worried as their Miracle Patient foundered, without
clear reason.

At University Hospital, Dad would stabilize, recover, regain
strength, and days later be settled back at Drake, only to suffer

another setback over the next week or two. Fearful that pneumonia might be setting in, the doctors ran tests that did not provide conclusive results. As our family's worries grew, hope ebbed but didn't fade; after all, Dad was on a hero's journey, and this was just another hurdle, something we and he could manage. Little did we know how much was out of our control at this time.

By mid-February, he'd already been back and forth to University for emergency care twice. Returning to Drake, in his uncertain state of health, Dad's therapies were halted. There was no more joy-riding in his wheelchair. Confined to bed, all his energy could be concentrated on his healing.

One evening in particular, Dad's agitation was evident the moment Mom and I arrived to visit. At that point, due to his weakened condition, his eyes and head were his only means of communication, and he began moving both in an attempt to tell us something. He rolled his head to the right repeatedly, and when his neck tired, his eyes took over the job. What was he pointing to? How could we possibly imagine what might be wrong? We tried in every way we knew to comfort him, rubbing his hands and feet, brushing his hair. He shrugged us off. Mom and I were so frustrated for him, bothered we couldn't guess what he was trying to say. Closing his eyes a long time, as if in thought, he'd then open them, blink and look meaningfully to the side. Dad had behaved this way one other night in the hospital, motioning his eyes to the side of the room where another patient, whose family we had gotten to know, lay. We could not decipher what he was trying to say. Shortly thereafter, that man passed away.

Without speech, Dad often couldn't get his message across. We'd usually talk, ask, or guess until we eventually figured it out, but no luck was had that night. Again, we tried to soothe him. Exhausted, eventually his eyes remained closed. It was late, it was a Friday night, and we had stayed a while past visiting hours. The nurse came in and assured us that physically, Dad was all right—not in his best condition, but not in pain. Still, Mom and I felt terrible for not helping him find peace. I remember us talking together on the way out, wondering what we'd missed.

❖

FOR YEARS I HAVE REGRETTED not putting it together sooner.
Mom and I both knew something significant was being commu-
nicated; we just weren't receiving the signal. Dad was very unlike
himself those two nights. He knew something bad, that much was
clear. In fact, his life was at stake, and I missed a chance to save it.

What's more disturbing is that Dad likely didn't feel safe
over those final weeks. Given what we now know, for more than
a month he must have guessed his coming fate and had to resign
himself to it, without our understanding his fear and without any
means of protection.

Ultimately, we failed him. Each nurse who had also come to
love this patient also failed him, by not screaming their concerns
to anyone within earshot, by not revealing to John Powell's family
what they secretly suspected. I can forgive my fifteen-year-old self,
now, for not understanding what Dad was trying to tell us. Who
could have guessed that one hospital patient, lying silent in his
bed, had witnessed the unnatural death of another, at a caregiver's
hands? Police officers with years of horrific experience could speculate that I, as a teenager, might have taken my own father's life—
yet even with my wild imagination, I could not have known someone else was killing him, and it was within my power to stop it.

1/21/87
John —
Sorry you're not real up today
Be back soon.
Love
Fran

1/24/87
John,
Joe & I stopped to see you

I could not keep you awake.
I am hoping you start to feel better.
Teddy

1–27

John –
You tolerated my visit pretty well considering you had a rough weekend.
Pat is recovering from her cold.
We'll check on you in a day or 2.
love
Fran

FRAN, WHO OFTEN VISITED Dad during her lunch hour, frequently saw the nurse's aide, Donald Harvey, on duty. Fran believed they were in partnership for John's care and they'd often talk. In February, she began to express concerns to Don, about all the discomfort John had recently endured.

As he was moved from room to room between critical care units at University, and then returning to different rooms and beds at Drake, Dad's personal items were all packed up—and so our visitor log tapers off at the end of January, as did his health. But we were all there, praying for any sign of improvement, waiting for some reason to renew our hopes. At times our patience was rewarded. We'd allow ourselves a moment of excitement, over some positive indication, only to fall back into despair. On February 12, Dad was sent to University Hospital for the last time, staying nearly two weeks to regain his strength. When he returned to Drake, his loyal friends Fran and Joe feared for his condition, improved as it seemed, feeling uneasy because they had to be out of town that first week of March and wouldn't be around to watch over him.

They were right to worry.

John Powell's medical report - March 5, 1987

2:00 P.M.
Temperature 102.7. Wife contacted by Charge Nurse, A.
Metz , RN.
Respiration less labored at 40 per minute, radial pulse 164
per minute, easily palpated. Blood pressure 82 over 60. A.
Metz, RN.

3:00 P.M.
Temperature 101.8 degrees Fahrenheit. Wife at bedside.
Laying on back, head of bed elevated, feet cool to touch
with right foot cooler than left foot. Hands slightly cool to
touch. At this time resting quietly with eyes closed without response to verbal stimuli. Cool wet compress to lips
elicited sucking response. A. Metz, RN.

5:00 P.M.
Family members at bedside
<end report>

MOM AND I VISITED DAD on the evening of Friday, March 6.
Dad's doctors were still worried. Stabilized, Dad remained unresponsive in bed with his head elevated slightly for the night; no
light shone above him. Late winter darkness covered him and the
other patients in the room, all sleeping. Though Dad had been unable to respond during our visit, we were comforted that at least he
looked somewhat peaceful. It had been a rough few days of seizures
and coughing, and we were relieved he was resting quietly. Two
days earlier, the clinical term "heroic measures" had been explained
to Mom: these were extreme treatments performed in emergency
situations to prevent death, not necessarily to improve life. Doctors
asked if these actions should be taken in Dad's case. After fully
understanding and following their advice, Mom agreed that heroic

measures were not to be taken. He'd endured so much and was so very ill. We only wanted Dad to be well, but sometimes the best outcomes aren't of our choosing.

Talking in low voices to him and each other, we rubbed his arms and hands, telling him he'd get better again and come home soon. Our concerned looks to nurses had them assuring us they were doing their best to make him comfortable and would call with any news. Not knowing it was the last time, we kissed him good-night, gave him our love, and walked out of the room to let him rest.

LONG GONE WERE THE DAYS when we'd find a soft bite of home in a stack of Dad's fluffy pancakes, alongside Saturday morning cartoons. Eight months had passed since Dad's accident, and his teenagers had grown into young adults fully aware of the danger of living. Eight months ago I might have been sleeping in on a week-end, in typical teen fashion. I might have been on a sleepover, or dressed for a day at the park or the mall with a friend. I may have been ignoring my family by choice, rather than being forced to live without some of them. Childhood ends when you realize that unlike Wile E. Coyote, we won't rebound from a fall.

Dad had transformed our house over the years. Kitchen, yard, every inch of the property felt his hand. Three teens each had our own rooms after Dad renovated a bathroom in the daylight base-ment and fashioned a bedroom in what used to be our playroom for Little John. With skill and vision, he created another haven for Mom. He beautifully bricked-in the enclosed front porch as a three-season room for her plants, giving a facelift to the front of the ranch-style house. Mornings, Mom often took her coffee there. Evenings, we sat among colorful cushions on a wicker sofa with our dogs or any injured or lost animals, the birds or strays Mom regularly rescued. Our cozy home was small enough that from any room, we could hear and talk with one another—less annoyance than circumstance of living.

We cut each other a lot of slack those days, but still got done what was needed to be done. Since I often went to the hospital with Mom, I missed some of my chores. My laundry was put through a few more of its paces before washing. Saturday and Sunday afforded time to play catch-up, at home and in my half-assed efforts with schoolwork.

Mom's career at Hi-Lo Powered Scaffolding occupied forty hours of every week, and her only time off was the weekend—if you don't count motherhood, that other full-time job. Between paying and managing the bills, keeping up with us kids, doing the grocery shopping, and visiting Dad, she hardly had a minute to herself. We children took care of dishes, laundry and cleaning the bathrooms. Warming weekends allowed Mom a few hours for working in her yard, only now, most of that time was spent in the hospital. Sundays, we had church. Saturday was the one morning Mom didn't have to rush, and could get a later start.

Before Dad's accident last July, on a typical Saturday morning, our TV might be filling the family room with the trusty voices of the news or the tumult of cartoons. Local Q102 radio personalities or 80s pop tunes might be forced through small speakers on my combination clock and radio cassette-tape player, as my bedside alarm blared. Slumping sleepily to the kitchen, I may have poured myself some juice or milk, then floated a few flakes in the fish tank before plopping onto the sofa to start the day. I would hardly break fifty steps in the tight circle of our home.

Fewer sounds woke me now; fewer smells tempted me out of bed. Since Dad left our kitchen for work eight months ago, rather than waking up to one of his big breakfasts, only a scavenged piece of toast or a bowl of cereal fed me there. I heard none of the normal Saturday-morning racket of Dad working in the garage or rumbling his motorcycle on the driveway, or of Mom mowing her lawn; what had become normal now on Saturdays was a visit to the hospital, and without doubt today, we would be heading back to see Dad, as soon as we were all up and got ourselves dressed.

This Saturday, March 7, 1987, as the sun sifted into my room, a telephone call broke the silence, just past 8 a.m. My bedroom was closest to the kitchen. Half-awake, I knew Mom was alone with her coffee when I heard her soft "hello" pick up on the second ring.

Without knowing who called, I immediately knew why.

Hearing Mom's voice catch, she said "It must be God's will."

I sat up in bed.

Before that moment, my small room held an unimpressive desk and chair; a narrow chest of drawers; a rarely touched, second-hand piano keyboard; a twin-sized bed; and a daughter with a dad. After that moment, that same room was a fortress, built with my fellow soldier, denial, keeping out the realization that my dad had died. Frozen half-upright above my comforter, I scarcely breathed as Mom spoke another minute on the phone, saying she needed to be at home with her three children. As a mother myself now, I can't imagine having to face your children to tell them their other parent has died.

Heather must have also heard the call. Edging into my room and onto my bed, her face spoke the volumes we didn't want to hear. Mom then appeared in my doorway, tears sliding down her cheeks. Taking a deep breath in, she said again, to the two of us, that it must have been Dad's time and God's will.

Moving into the room, she gathered with us on my bed. Comforted by the weight of holding onto each other, Mom and Heather cried openly, my own eyes moistening with the heaves of their sobs. Sadness pours differently into people, sifting through our layers before reaching the sieve of our senses. My tears weren't ready. Denial wouldn't leave me, even when Mom broke away from our huddle, feeling the pull to her other child, who still slept unaware.

Down the stairs Mom went toward the other John, the one left alive in our world. No more "Little" stood in front of his name, as she stood just inside the door at the foot of his bed. He clearly remembers the exact words she said: "The good Lord took your father today." He says he can still hear her say it.

Out of my element, uneasy, in a fog, I was hugged by the few friends and family who stopped by to sit with us in our grief that morning. Detached: the word I have since understood to be the feeling I embodied most that morning. Emotions don't run because they should or can; they come when we can each accept the incremental weights of them, and that morning, unlike my iron-willed mother, I couldn't carry any more weight.

When the funeral director came to the house around noon to discuss the details of a memorial, I became restless and couldn't cope. Just past noon, two newer friends at school, not knowing what had just happened, called to see if we could all hang out on what was becoming an unseasonably warm and sunny Saturday in early March. One was able to borrow their dad's convertible and thought it would be fun to drive around with the top down. Quietly, I shared over the phone that this morning my dad had died. A silence fell before they responded with condolences. Rather than hang up, they offered to still come get me out of the house, if it would take my mind off things.

I didn't even consider a shower. When Mom said I could go, I just grabbed my closest pair of jean shorts, pulled on a royal blue sleeveless top, and tied my hair back. Dad's death wasn't real yet. Just last night I saw him. Just last night I was holding his hand, talking beside him. I just needed to get outside and forget all that had happened since his accident last July, and not be the girl whose Dad had died. Denial drove with me that day, taking me away from home for those few hours to escape dealing with Dad's death and the sadness of my family. Apparently, this kind of response to a loved one's death is fairly normal—whatever that means.

Needing to be out of the house, I sat in the back of that sporty white Corvette, letting the wind whip my ponytail hard against my face, beating a rhythm away from my life. Jen sat up front in the passenger seat, tuning the radio, as Sherry drove her very-much-alive father's car. Jen cranked up the volume to Bon Jovi's "Livin' on a Prayer" and I sang along. Sherry laughed, and I laughed. When Whitney Houston asked, "How Will I Know," we screamed back, above the wind, "If he really loves me?" When my friends talked about how fun the car was to drive, I smiled and nodded. It could have been any other day. We made the rounds of Cincinnati's West Side, winding roads and hairpin turns, the day as warm as summer without a bud yet on the trees. We stopped at Delhi Park, where pasty, shirtless boys played basketball as girls stood watch over their boyfriends and perfected their lip gloss. Bared arms and legs, long hidden in a grey Cincinnati winter, were soaking up daylight.

Sherry dropped me home, and I cannot remember the rest of that night. Some memories we must store up, to get through leaner times, and this was one of them. That sun-shiny day helped me ease into a process nobody wants to prepare for. I will always be grateful to those friends for those few glorious hours in the sun, delaying the darkness of death, allowing my last unadulterated teenage afternoon, beneath cloudless blue skies above, to blow a clean wind in my face.

Reality still hadn't settled in my head by that Monday evening, as we prepared for Dad's viewing at the funeral home. Passenger in the car, I could just as easily be on our way to the hospital, except we weren't. My heart hadn't relinquished the hope that had lived there for the past eight months. Assessing how to dress appropriately for a funeral, while brushing my hair, I was confronted by the absurdity of making the effort. Angrily pulling my hair into a low ponytail, I hastily threw on a dark-patterned sweater over a long red skirt, stomped into a pair of black pumps, folded myself into a coat, and got in the car.

WHEN I MET WITH FRAN and Joe in April of 2017 to ask about their memories, there were a few surprises. As I've mentioned, Fran is sharp; she doesn't miss a beat. No wallflower, either, she knows our extended family well from years of gatherings, from John and Pat's wedding and countless holiday parties. Our friends all knew each other. Birds of a feather, flock.

On top of Joe agreeing with everything she said, Fran keeps proof. Printed copies of both her and Joe's depositions from the police waited on her table for me, along with a copy of the traffic report from the motorcycle crash, photos taken at the crash site shortly after Dad's accident, and vintage photos of their group of friends, including some I had never seen.

Fran told me what she saw at Dad's viewing the evening of March 9, 1987. It could have been last night, she remembered it so plainly. She remembers everyone who was at the funeral home, and could name them all—everyone except the one stranger in the back of the room, a man in a long, dark coat. To him, she hadn't spoken. But she was aware enough of his uninvited presence that evening to follow his movements as he left for his car, which was parked up the hill on Pedretti Road.

Later we learned it was a Cincinnati Police detective.

THAT HOPE I'D HELD onto for so long at the hospital didn't die with Dad. It had survived his accident, his brain surgery, his coma, his therapy, his emergencies, recoveries and declines. It had survived the last two days despite knowing, logically, he was dead. To kill that hope would also kill off my chance to rebuild a relationship with him and to have him once more in my life. Arriving early before visitors that Monday night at the funeral home, I slowly walked up to my dad's suited and still body, resting in a satin-lined casket. Staring down at his forever-closed eyes, I saw no sheen of life lingering on his skin, I felt no radiating warmth. No longer could a hospital gown dress his condition; there would be no recovery. Holding his unnaturally cold hand, I laid a white carnation on his chest, and in that gesture allowed my hope to fall away. Realization of his death hit me full-on. Floods of tears from the last fifty-six hours, from the last eight months, from the last eleven years, burst forth, and I broke down openly, heaving with sobs before his open casket.

How long I cried, I don't remember. I was inconsolable, even when multiple hands helped me up from my crouched position on the floor. Though expressive, generally speaking, I maintain my composure. Call it calm or controlling, call it what you want—I've always had that kind of presence, and only death could elicit this truly unrestrained response.

Finally, my tears ran out and emotional exhaustion set in, and for one of the few times in my life, I was void of perception, unaware of my surroundings. Other guests must have filtered into the room and spoke their kindnesses. Extended family would have hugged my drained shoulders and kissed my tear-stained face.

If I spoke to you that night, I have no memory of it.

Especially when we are young, without the words, tools or experience to guide, the path leading us to go on is filled with shadow and uncertainty. There were times I experienced hopelessness. Today's children and parents have an internet full of resources at their fingertips, a thousand ways to know they are not alone in their grief. I did not. Time, books and proper support helped me though. Someone I cannot remember to thank thankfully gave me a copy of Eleanor Craig's *P.S. You're Not Listening*. Reading to know my pain was shared and understood by others, and learning to speak the words of grief myself, made the most difference for me— whether silently on paper, as I prefer, or openly with peers. Misery loves company, and eventually I found human connections to help me better cope.

Some grief comes all at once, some in slow leaks. Some grief battens down the hatches and holds it all together on top of the storm. For some, it feels like a tsunami: a deep earth shift, forcefully pulling back from the griever, opening up an eerie silence; a moment of portentous stillness before the body is overtaken, engulfed, overwhelmed, wrung out until it can stand no more, until the mind is wiped clean and we collapse into sleep.

That night at the funeral home was my tsunami.

Mom told me that after I was calmer and safely seated away from the casket, she went to address the line of visitors. They began to flow through the doors, bringing the same misty, chilled, late-winter wind I'd walked in with. Around the room, sympathy-givers snaked, Mom said, and the condolences and hugs went on and on. Hundreds of people moved through the viewing room, leaving Mom on her feet for hours with no break, not even a glass of water to drink. She faced them all, honored them all, and as exhausted as she was, she appreciated each person's grief for her husband. No one brought her a chair, or any relief. She still remembers the utter expenditure of the evening. Everyone has always relied on Mom's strength.

Grief is worthy of space and time in any form, and it's important to recognize and reconcile it. There is no right or wrong way to grieve; much of it, anyway, is involuntary, so we couldn't do it properly even if we tried. I've experienced a wide range of responses to loss in my life, but at fifteen, I'd had none of that—I had no reference point or healthy perspective as to what I was feeling, or not feeling, in the wake of my dad's passing. What I've learned since then is, there is no greater or lesser grief. Death, that undeniable part of life, no matter our age, becomes life-altering.

❖

MOTHER NATURE'S PALETTE had been on full display during the week, offering chilled blue skies and clotted cream clouds to preside over Dad's funeral service at St. Dominic's. Immediate and extended family, and scores of friends, paid their respects to a man lost too soon. The pews and parking lot were packed. Dad's best buddies were his pallbearers. Friends from both Mom's Presbyterian church and Dad's Catholic parish flooded the aisles and held us together in prayer. Boy Scout troop leaders, motorcycle club members and officers, neighbors and classmates were all there. Father Jim Meade presided.

Heather had a few good friends and a boyfriend present, supporting her. Two of my newer high school friends, Michelle and Carrie, attended for me. My brother, overwhelmed by loss and the crowd, sat in his coat and tie in the back of the church, alone on a couch, keeping as far away as he could from Dad lying so unnaturally still in his casket. After the church cleared, and before we left for the cemetery, we three siblings stood alone at the back of the narthex. John remembers me taking him up to see Dad one last time. I was worried because he hadn't yet cried.

Dan Vanderpool, a friend and officer, professionally routed the large funeral procession with his motorcycle over to the Bridgetown Cemetery, where our Dad, John Powell, was laid to rest under stone and pine. My two friends who attended the service were a helpful distraction. Fearing another breakdown, like I'd had in front of Dad Monday night, I took comfort in not being too comfortable yet with these friends, their newness encouraged control over my emotions.

My grandparents hosted a small reception at their condo on Montana Avenue. John's ex-wife Lorraine and daughter Lorri joined us there after the burial, and Fran and Mom talked with them for a while before they left.

John remembers feeling numb; Heather, too shy to draw attention, remained quiet, and Mom was unselfish in her attentions, even when weepy. Nothing could have prepared me for the emotional reaction I would have to the loss of my dad. It was a strange and desperate first few days. I went back to school the next day, looking to find some normalcy in routine, and ended up crying in a hallway and leaving early, unable to be "normal."

Normal. I abhor the word. The only useful application of "normal," I'm convinced, is as a setting on the clothes dryer—never as a descriptor of human behavior. What a strange set of benchmarks we have set for ourselves to fail to meet. Who decided on this normal? When did boring become best? Children will continually miss their own potential trying to fit such narrow definitions. I know I did.

I do not understand what is so good about being "normal" anyway. By definition, it means common, standard, conforming, usual, sane, rational. While I'm not advocating for insanity, I am rearing against the definition of sane. When grieving, when growing, when adapting, often our human reactions and responses do not conform any norm. I did not conform. Many of us cannot conform and actually hope to stay sane.

Prince, for example—revolutionary musician, poet and producer, a formative genius of my teen years—challenged norms. He succeeded in bucking convention, in every aspect of his life and career, and uplifted countless others to do the same. The music of Prince might not seem wildly out-there today, but in 1983, '84? Utterly mind-blowing. It is our uniqueness, our boldness that makes us strong. "Normal" boxes us in. There's no shame in trying to conform; often it's shame that makes so many of us want to fly under the radar. I simply want those who don't meet society's arbitrary standards, whether by choice or circumstance, to be treated equally. And I take pride in those of us who refuse to settle for the norm of "normal."

When I went home crying from school that first day back, unable to pretend to be alright, I knew at that moment I was forever separated from everyone else in my school. The Holly they had known before, didn't exist anymore. Experiencing loss removed me from mundane, pushed past petty, and sling-shotted me into what felt like a parallel universe. When I finally did return to school, I had learned to play the part that made things easier for others, old and new friends alike, thereby making life smoother for me. Acting my way through my days, I went about the things I did before and pretended everything was fine.

Until, as I'll explain, it wasn't.

11

suspect [verb suh-**spekt**; noun **suhs**-pekt; adjective **suhs**-pekt, suh-**spekt**]
verb (used with object)
1. to believe to be guilty, false, counterfeit, undesirable, defective, bad, etc., with little or no proof: to suspect a person of murder
2. to doubt or mistrust: I suspect his motives.
3. to believe to be the case or to be likely or probable; surmise
verb (used without object)
1. to believe something, especially something evil or wrong, to be the case; have suspicion
noun
1. a person who is suspected, especially one suspected of a crime, offense, or the like

12-12-86

John,
Your hair is getting blacker instead of greyer. I guess when this is all over I'll have more grey hair than you. I massaged your arm and you didn't want me to stop. You went to sleep. We'll be back soon.
Love,
Pat

MY ENTIRE YOUNG LIFE, Mom was the adept and well-liked administrative office assistant at the Hi-Lo Powered Scaffolding company. Though the business managed scaffold work all over the country, it was family-owned. President Wayne Mauldin, the

VP Dave Robards, and all the employees were good friends, looking out for each other.

Visiting the place where Mom went about her business felt special to us as children. She wasn't in charge, but she kept the office humming with smiles and proficiency. Her work family knew us well and were kind to kiddos interested in forklifts and the choreography of large trucks. Mom was happy there; valued.

Easily I conjure her to mind, sitting behind that desk, wearing a pretty blouse or sweater, a short silk scarf tied about her neck, with waves of soft, hot-rolled curls framing her face and shoulders. A vision, she could still be sitting at that L-shaped desk, hands on her typewriter, against those wood-paneled walls. We adored the Hi-Lo branded ballpoint pens and notepads she allowed us to take home. Posted mail carrying office invoices, receipts and letters from all over landed on her desk. Thoughtfully Mom would rip the corners of cleared stamps from envelopes and bring them home to me, to add to the collection of yet-to-be-traveled places a young girl keeps in a glass jar.

A Chicago firm bought Hi-Lo Powered Scaffolding from the Mauldins around this time. Coming in, the new boss had assured a dozen longtime employees that all their jobs were safe. Ten days after Dad died, he sat at the end of Mom's desk. Dolores had just been let go that very day, and Millie, last week. This hard, horrible man sat in front of Pat Powell for an uncomfortably long time as she finished calls, filed papers and completed each task until the very last minute of her shift. At exactly 5 p.m., after watching her put in a full day of work, with his unnerving stare, he told Mom, "I am letting you go. This is your last day. You can pack up and leave."

Mom, whose life was literally coming loose at the seams, remembers saying to a man she describes as a tyrant, "Well, I had a far greater loss two weeks ago, and if I can handle that, then I can certainly handle this." Pat Powell placed her years of dedication into a box and carried it out with her.

❖

A FEW DAYS LATER our doorbell rang, unraveling the final strands, leaving little to hold us together.

Perhaps that inner strength I mentioned earlier is what got Mom through losing her job so shortly after Dad's death. No question it carried her a few days later, when, without any support around her, she learned how the man she loved had actually died.

We'd all been walking around like zombies in our grief, adjusting to Mom's new schedule at home. She'd worked our entire young lives. Latchkey kids—that is what we three children were termed then, getting ourselves on the bus to and from school, coming home to an empty house and then starting on homework and chores. Now, Mom was at the door greeting us after school. Another change to navigate.

Two-and-a-half weeks after Dad died, mere days after Mom was let go from her job, a pair of detectives appeared on our enclosed porch doorstep. Hands full preparing dinner when the bell rang, Mom waved a dish towel, asking me to get the door.

Two suits with ties and walkie-talkies said, "Hello." One suit announced, "We are looking to speak with a Mrs. Powell." I quickly went inside to get her.

Wiping her hands on the towel, she walked out to meet them, Heather and I watching from the kitchen window. We saw Mom nod to them, then turn back to come inside. The men stayed and waited. Back in the house, Mom laid aside the towel, quickly grabbed her coat and told us to turn off the stove. She said that these men had asked her to come with them to answer some medical questions and discuss Dad's death. Heather and I were confused, and, so it seemed, was Mom, but she took a deep breath and said she'd be home soon.

Watching her walk out the door, alongside people openly wearing guns holstered at their hips, we felt helpless. From our window lookouts, we followed the men as they crossed to the other side of the street, where a dark sedan was parked, and opened the back door for Mom to get in. Something felt off. Unsure what to do, if anything, Heather thought to take down the model and license plate number of the car before they drove away.

The importance of this visit was something we could not antic-ipate. We did not question how quickly our mother threw on her coat and drove away with the badges; we just wondered what had prompted them to take her, and at dinnertime. We were teenagers, uncertain kids really, with no way to reach our mom. In 1987, there was no thought of capturing the moment on camera, and far fewer frames of reference to understand what might actually be happen-ing.

Finally, Heather thought to call Grandpa. Explaining what had gone down, I heard her give him what information we had. He told her that he'd make some calls. Dinner was cold when the phone rang, and I ran to answer it. Mom's friend Mary Jane was just calling to check in on Mom, what with all that had gone on over the past few weeks. I had to let her know there were new de-velopments, that Mom had just driven off with two police officers coming to ask her questions about Dad. Nervous for Mom, Mary Jane pressed for details, but we didn't have any to give.

Hours passed, and we waited. It was getting late when Aunt Lori called to ask us specifically what we saw and what Mom said when she left. Apparently, Grandpa was driving around downtown hoping to find her and calling home for updates. Recounting what little we knew, we all began to worry that something was seriously wrong. Why take a mother away from three teenagers without a number to reach her, and no real explanation? Mom had not called to let us know she was okay, or would be returning late.

The late-night news was airing when the phone rang again. This time, thankfully, it was Mom, saying she'd be coming home, but didn't know exactly when. She told us not to worry. We told her Grandpa was looking, and she said that, yes, she had already talked to him. Very short and unlike her, giving us no other details, she hung up. What else could we do now but get ourselves to bed? Mom had said she was all right, and after all, we did have school in the morning. Still, only after I heard her come in the door later that night was I actually able to fall asleep.

The next morning, Mom drove me to school—the only perk

from being fired was time with her children—and I probed and prodded for what had happened the night before. She wouldn't say a word. Always tenacious, I figured I would try again after school. Once home, I put my things away and proceeded to follow Mom around the house, pestering, until finally she acquiesced. Sitting down on the floral comforter under which she now slept alone, Mom raised her shoulders then sagged into a heavy sigh. At length she spilled everything, starting with how those two men politely opened the back seat door of their car for her, talked nicely and chatted all the way downtown to the old Alms & Doepke building on Central Parkway. Mom hadn't known it then, but that was where the Homicide Division of the Cincinnati Police was housed. (Today, the late-Victorian landmark across from the Courthouse is home to Hamilton County Job & Family Services, among other public departments.)

The detectives again mentioned they needed Mom to answer some questions about Dad's medical record. Always a people-pleaser, not one for making waves, Mom went along, participating in the detectives' incessant small talk, ready to comply with anything they needed. Once they arrived at 222 East Central, and as they walked Mom through the building, the officers kept the conversation going until they reached a back room with a long table. Sitting across from her, they casually began reading her Miranda rights, saying it was routine to do that with anyone they talked to. Distracted and confused, Mom assented, assuming they were just doing their jobs. The detectives were overly polite, even kind in their tone, Mom remembers—and yet they did not offer or allow her a phone call or provide anything to eat or drink during the long hours of interrogation that followed. She hadn't eaten the dinner she'd been making, being pulled away and thinking naturally she would be returning home to her children soon.

One of the men began to explain how they needed to investigate and rule out any role Mom may have had in the death, since her husband, John, had been poisoned.

Pat Powell, caught completely off-guard, could not believe what she had just heard. Did they just say "poisoned"? In her shock, she exclaimed, *"What?!"*

Until that moment she had no idea that her husband had died by anything other than God's hand, and she certainly hadn't considered anything nefarious when she'd been taken from her home to answer questions. Her disbelief made her nauseous. The detectives then explained how John had been poisoned with cyanide—"enough cyanide," they said, "to kill an army." Her husband, John Powell, had been murdered, and if that was not enough to digest in the moment, Mom was beginning to understand that *she* was the main suspect.

Detectives employ all kinds of mind games to get a confession. Asking first for details about Dad's medical condition in those final weeks, intimating how miserable he must have been, "I wish someone would do the same for me if I was ever in that situation," "It's a loving thing to do, rather than watch someone you love suffer..." Sitting with me on the bed, Mom recounted all the ways the officers had baited her.

When Mom didn't break or confess to anything she hadn't done, the detectives moved on, asking directly if it was possible, somehow, that her daughter Holly, a high school sophomore, might have acquired a quantity of cyanide and killed her dad with it. "After all, she was with you the night before he died," one of the investigators said, as if laying common sense at Mom's feet. "You two were the last visitors to see John Powell alive."

Supposing they really did have to rule everything out, Mom assured the officers that she and I were together the entire visit with Dad, that we hadn't left each other's side, and there was no way that her daughter could have done such a thing.

Six long hours of questioning later, the detectives seemed to realize that Patricia Powell could not possibly have been the perpetrator. They finally permitted Mom to call her father to come pick her up, and to call home to tell us children not to worry. Grandpa rushed downtown to the building where Mom was being held, and into the waiting room. He was made to sit without access to his daughter while she had consented to being given a polygraph test. Having had her rights read under false pretense, nearly seven hours prior, her emotionally exhausted, uncorrupt mind did not think of enacting her right to an attorney before the lie detector test, nor did the detectives remind or again offer one to Mom.

SOME TIME HAD PASSED since Glenn Whitaker and Patricia last spoke, and so when she again came to see him at the law firm the day after her interrogation, he greeted her warmly and asked, "How's John?"

Mom answered flatly, "He's dead."

Glenn told me he was beyond shocked at these words. "I felt like a jerk for asking, but couldn't have known otherwise, because last I remembered, John was getting stronger and showed promise of coming home."

Then, he recalled, "She sat down, and proceeded to tell me the most horrific tale.

"Pat explained that she had been picked up at her home by two police detectives who then deceivingly took her in for nearly six hours of interrogation at the homicide station, with no food or drink, and no phone call." Glenn clearly remembered seeing Mom in tears in his office, as she recounted to him the harsh means by which she learned that her husband John had, in fact, been poisoned.

"After all that questioning," he said, "she told me that by the time they had finished with her, she actually felt bad because she *hadn't* killed John! It was an awful ordeal for her."

Listening to Glenn share this version, hearing through the phone his deep and lasting memory of this event, I began to realize how truly horrible the experience must have been for my mom. Though I'd known about Mom's ordeal through her own words and understood it to be difficult, my empathy swelled to hear someone else with a lifetime in the legal profession describe how utterly traumatizing it was for her.

At the beginning of her account, Glenn remembered feeling affronted that Mom hadn't called him in as her lawyer right away—until she told him how the officers had downplayed their reading of the Miranda rights, and that they had never suggested or offered Mom the chance to actually call an attorney. After hearing this and more from Mom, Glenn was enraged.

"I did criminal work, and the idea of the officers treating Pat in that way, who was such a nice woman and under such emotional stress, really upset me," he said. Immediately he became involved in the case on Mom's behalf, though to what end they couldn't then know.

"Something not easily forgotten," is how Glenn summed up those early meetings. Decades later, his thoughts and feelings still rang clear—and now our conversations were clarifying things for me. I'm grateful to Glenn for all the help he gave Mom over those years, and for his assistance and well wishes for our family.

THE POLYGRAPH TEST—which, as expected, Mom passed—still revealed her heart rate racing so high that the detectives suggested she see a doctor immediately after leaving the station. They then swore her to secrecy, as they were fully investigating everyone involved, including any and all family and friends who had visited John at Drake. They also wanted to see the lovingly filled visitor logs to determine other possible suspects. It didn't occur to Mom for a second that hospital staff might also fall under suspicion.

Al Myers, having waited all that time, finally drove his troubled daughter home. Upset as she was, Pat couldn't help but fill him in on the awful truth of her situation. Other than her parents that night, and we three children the next day, no one could know what had happened to John, or we might lose the chance to find the real killer.

Later we learned that for insurance purposes, an autopsy is commonly performed to confirm whether a patient has indeed died from their injuries due to a traffic accident. In a state of new grief that morning of March 7, Mom had not understood how important a decision she was making, when asked if she preferred the Hamilton County or Drake Hospital to oversee the autopsy. She confirmed the county. Ultimately Mom created an opening for the truth to come to light in what would become this investigation. Patricia Powell's choice set Harvey's secretive and murderous plans on a path for discovery.

My Dad's full autopsy report has been made a public document, available online by request. I've read it. It is downloaded on my computer. How else could I know that when my dad's heart stopped, it weighed 425 grams? My own heart raced as I scanned such personal physical details while sitting on my sofa, our dog chewing a bone at my feet.

After we learned that Dad had been murdered, suspicion wrapped itself around family and friends in my own mind. Mistrust laced new conversations and shadowed past kindnesses. Conceptually, thoughts turn to crazy when weighing who amongst us might be a secret murderer. This was no game. If even I could be considered by the police, then everyone was a suspect.

After hearing about Mom's interrogation, I was incredulous. Left with too many of my questions that she could not answer, days later, on March 31, Mom returned to the Homicide department, with me in tow. Detective Jim Lawson had agreed to talk with me and fill me in on what was going on. The officers were deferential and kind in this instance, answering my questions, informing me that since this was a murder case it was important to operate with secrecy. They strongly encouraged me to keep my comments private, only talking to my mom about it. As Mom and I were about to leave, the detectives were warned that photojournalists and reporters had crowded out in front of the building. Whether by a leaked source or an intrepid reporter requesting public reports, the press were already sniffing around the coroner's report, waiting for the news of a fresh killer.

In a gentlemanly gesture, Lawson moved Mom and me quickly to the back of the building, into a freight elevator that emptied us into a back alley. From there, we made our way back to the car and home. Though we were relieved not to be bombarded, that courtesy of avoiding the press also served the detectives' interests.

A WEEK OR SO passed, all of us under tremendous stress while going about our lives. Without work to occupy her mind, Mom worried each day through. Everything in my world felt off-kilter: my family was a mess, I wasn't sleeping, school demanded as it does. During French class one day I was overtaken by a flood of emotion. Vividly I remember staying in my seat as long as I could manage, as panic set in, my first real encounter. Feverish flames licked at my face, the heat of feeling everyone watching you burn. Panic rarely turns back; it must drill through to the other side. My mind, that unsteadying house of cards, was collapsing inward. Hot tears splotched the papers before me on the desk. At first, I thought to become embarrassed—a highly unusual response for me. Bent over, hiding my face, my body shook as I became increasingly tense, a coil tightening. The embarrassment passed quickly. Any energy spent thinking about onlookers slipped away, seeming far away from what I could handle. My focus narrowed to only me, to the small place I occupied and to my mind dying to get out. I felt like an animal trapped with no concern for dignity in escape. The surrounding walls, desks, and people faded.

I was scared. That classroom held no power over me. There were much bigger things happening than that classroom could know or teach me. Unable to control myself any longer, I bolted loudly from my chair and ran out into the wide hallway. Heart beating, cold sickening sweat eating at me, I turned toward the girls' bathroom for refuge, but the sound of giggling inside repelled me back into the hallway. Looking for safety, unsure where to go, where I could be, as I was… I noticed the overhead fluorescents were off, saw daylight beckoning from a nearby window, and I focused on that. Madame must have taken pity; shortly after I fled, she motioned to one of my friends to go check on me. When Karena hurriedly came out of class looking for me, she asked what on earth was going on.

Being under strict orders not to tell anyone about the investigation was a heavy burden to bear at any age, but especially at fifteen. Without the coping skills of an adult, going to school day in and day out so soon after your dad has died, pretending your grief is the only thing upsetting to you, is no easy feat.

Quickly words tumbled out to Karena, without details: "There is more going on than just losing Dad." Alone in my thoughts and fears, I felt forced to share the secret to lighten my load. Conveying the seriousness of what I was about to say, I grasped her forearms and begged, "You can't tell anyone. I mean it."

When she nodded, I blurted out that Dad had actually been killed, without saying how, and that we were all under a gag order to be silent about it while the police pursued every lead. Karena had not visited the hospital, wasn't under any suspicion, and I felt sure it wouldn't hurt the case if she knew—but again I reminded her that she couldn't tell a soul.

Attempting to comfort, she said, "Holly, I'm sure it will all be okay."

"No, it won't," I said. "There is an investigation going on to uncover the murderer who killed Dad." I thought it would make me feel better to say it out loud, but I felt no relief, and found little comfort, as dubious as Karena appeared. Years later she told me that, at the time, she wasn't sure if she believed me. How could I blame her, when what I had divulged seemed like such an inconceivable story—even to myself?

Days later we would all have to face the truth, whether we wanted to or not: The police were narrowing in on a lead suspect.

11-20-86

John,
I visited at lunch time.
You smiled when Don* said "This is the person you took for better or worse?"

You're doing great. You're determined and very strong. You'll make it!
Love,
Pat

*A reference to nurse's aide Donald Harvey

FRAN REMEMBERS MOM stopping in at Joe's retirement party in
1987, around the first of April. Very unlike herself, Pat was with-
drawn and quiet; her friends chalked it up to grief. It had been just
three weeks since her husband John had died. Fran remembers Pat,
as she walked out to leave, strangely stopping to say, "I never knew
people could be so cruel."

Mom also remembers herself saying exactly that. Questions
and suspicion ran through her mind. Under orders to keep the secret, unable at that time to say anything to Fran and Joe about the
murder of her husband and their friend, she was sharing in her own
indirect way the horror she was enduring.

Mom, at home, out of a job, was isolated. Dear church friends
concerned for well-being thought it would be good for her to get
out. Nearly a month after Dad died, in early April, they offered to
drive her up to Dayton on a Saturday evening to see Sandi Patti,
the popular Christian singer, in concert at University of Dayton
Arena. Somehow keeping her spirits aloft, Mom was pleased to
have anything to look forward to. My siblings and I were glad she
was going; she deserved a treat to take her mind off of our situation. Leaving the restaurant name and number with Heather, Mom
left with her friends. Difficult to imagine today, it was ordinary
then to leave an itinerary and landline phone number for people
to actually get in touch in case of emergency. On this night, the
precaution was well-taken.

An hour after Mom left, Heather received a call from police
detectives. I was at a sleepover at my friend Dyan's house, next door
to my Aunt Karen and Uncle Stan. Heather had just turned eighteen, and after confirming that fact, the homicide detectives left her
with the directive to tell our mother that they had just arrested an

orderly at Drake Hospital: Donald Harvey had confessed to Dad's murder.

Standing in a Chi-Chi's Mexican restaurant in Dayton, Mom took the call from Heather on a curly-corded telephone line at the hostess stand, surrounded by her friends. Hardly able to fathom the incredulous news Heather conveyed, Pat felt her shoulders lighten. For the first time in weeks, she let go of silence and arcane suspicion of those around her. Fear gave way to mixed emotions of personally knowing her husband's killer, and of suspecting others. The horror and relief of Heather's call brought a much-needed release of tears, as mom began to weave a tale her friends could hardly believe. Everything she'd been holding in for a month burst out, ending with the bombshell that a man we knew, someone assigned to care for her husband, had now confessed to his murder.

12

arrest [uh-rest] *noun*
1. the taking of a person into legal custody, as by officers of the law
2. any seizure or taking by force
3. an act of stopping or the state of being stopped

12-27-86   7:15

John,
Joe & I visited & brought you a flower.
We did texture exercises — you handled coins & small nuts & bolts
You seemed glad to see us.
We love you.
Fran

1-10-87

John,
You were resting comfortably and you smiled a lot.
Joyce & I had a nice visit with you.
Keep hanging in there,
Love,
Pat
P.S. I told you that you were looking good and you smiled with pride.

ON SATURDAY, APRIL 4, Donald Harvey came in for a poly-graph test with Cincinnati Police Homicide division, after having canceled one previously scheduled on April 1. Declining the lie detector, Harvey was interviewed instead for four hours, con-fessing to Detective Jim Lawson what he called "ending John Pow-ell's suffering." Charged with aggravated murder, he claimed mercy motivated him. Lying came as naturally as poisoning to Harvey.

Two days later, the Findlay Market Opening Day Parade flooded the streets of downtown Cincinnati, in hopes of a Reds baseball victory against the Montreal Expos (the home team won, 11-5). That Monday morning the media market began peddling their wares: Local news sources were reporting that a nurse's aide had poisoned a man in Cincinnati, at a prominent, county-funded hospital.

The Cincinnati Post headline on April 6, 1987, rests under a banner celebrating Opening Day 1987, announcing in bold, black letters, "Orderly charged with slaying patient." In the accompa-nying photo, an unshaven Harvey casts his eyes away from the camera. As explained in the *Post* staff report article, the Hamilton County Coroner's office performs an autopsy whenever a traffic accident is involved in a patient's death. This routine autopsy "re-vealed an unusual amount of cyanide" in Powell's system, Detective William Fletcher is quoted as saying.

On Friday, April 10, *The Cincinnati Enquirer* reports that Har-vey had a history that hadn't been known to Drake when they'd hired him. "Poison case suspect had prior scrape," the headline reads. Below that, it says, "Drake didn't know about problems at VA Hospital."

David Wells of the *Enquirer* then continues his report with an interview with Donald Ziegenhorn, the local Veterans Affairs Hospital administrator in 1987, who said Harvey had been allowed to resign from the Cincinnati VA and let off with a federal citation when, after explicitly acting against the rules, he brought a firearm to work.

The Federal Privacy Act of 1974 would have prevented that

kind of information from reaching prospective employers, unless the subject signed a waiver. Michael Hawkins, the attorney for Drake Hospital, said there was no policy at the time for running police checks on job applicants, and that such a procedure still would not have revealed the past incident with Harvey at Veterans Hospital. Harvey had worked there since 1975, first in the morgue as assistant, then as a cardiac catheter unit technician. The VA Hospital citation left him with no criminal record and only a $50 fine. Ziegenhorn said Harvey was allowed to resign because the hospital wanted to avoid the trouble of a dismissal and more severe criminal prosecution: "This lets us close the book on this case and end the matter."

The Privacy Act, intended to protect individuals, has ended up covering a lot of corporate asses.

ARTICLES WENT TO A LOT of trouble to discuss Harvey's state of being: who he was, who he had been, where he had lived and worked. Neighbors and trailer park managers were interviewed and quoted, saying what a good tenant he was.

John Powell, the deceased, did not receive the same consideration. Most news reports merely stated (wrongly) that Powell had been comatose since July.

Harvey's possible motives, meanwhile, were much speculated on in the media. Was this, as the accused had suggested to the authorities, a "mercy killing"? Despite public evidence to the contrary, some reports described Harvey's past as untainted; a neighbor and teacher recalled "Donnie's" sweet nature. Harvey's birth date, classmate memories and character assessments, the idea that he was known for being really well liked… everything that was printed or broadcast about this killer seemed to tug at the heart strings.

John Powell, the victim, had, at most, one line per article—and that, inaccurate. Where was the focus on the victim? What about statements from his neighbors or classmates? Where was any interest in his nature? What about his motive, to recover and make it home to his family?

In the limelight live the killers and the corrupt. They're the ones people want to read about. Perhaps we will signal a turning point for humanity when victims are given prominence over their assailants, when stories of survival serve as guideposts, when the truths of human suffering amount to more than entertainment. When reporters must shovel more sensation than substance into the minds of the public, journalism fails. Vultures will circle smut and feast on feculence. So long as filth and outrage deliver more "hits" than dignity and altruism, that's the news we're going to keep getting.

If any of those headlines in April of 1987 had read, "Father and husband, 44 years old, poisoned and murdered as he recovered," or possibly, "Drake Hospital 'miracle patient,' age 44, dies by hand of one of their own," would that have made a difference to anyone? Maybe not. But it would have mattered to us. Truth *matters*, especially when our story is all that remains.

13

investigate [in·ves·ti·geyt] *verb* (used with object), in·ves·ti·gat·ed, in·ves·ti·gat·ing
    1. to examine, study, or inquire into systematically; search or examine into the particulars of; examine in detail
    2. to search out and examine the particulars of in an attempt to learn the facts about something hidden, unique, or complex, especially in an attempt to find a motive, cause, or culprit

AGONIZING, WHEN I LET my head dive into the physical struggle and mental torture Dad endured in that hospital bed. Doubtless we've all been laid up sick in bed for a day or two—a more common occurrence among us, two and a half years into the COVID pandemic. The body aches at inactivity. Stuck in one position, my hips and legs literally throb from being unmoved, my coccyx screams for repositioning and a stretch after five hours on my laptop propped against my headboard or hunched in a chair. There is no comparison to anyone with a long-term mobility impairment, yet it is in these moments when I can feel an ounce of the pain and discomfort Dad was subject to. Eight months of my body inactive, completely dependent on others: What would that do to my mind?

Surprising all of us with his tenacity, his sheer will to move past the accident, Dad traversed the long road of his recovery. Hard-to-reach waystations of his journey stretched before him: opening his eyes, wiggling a finger, bending a leg, each milestone exacting its toll. The apparatuses of his arm, hand, leg and foot all were retooled with industrious effort. With deliberate steering he coaxed his machine into the steep climbs and tight turns of repair. Gaining control and mobility, wheels furthered his path, as they often had, navigating the halls and grounds of his new landscape. Yearning to arrive safely at his destination: home. To have set out with such ambitious aim, to have scraped for each inch of that road, to have transported himself so far, for so long, only to have met his end at the hands of a killer... Even now, I cannot fathom it.

Unfortunately, for all his returns to the University Hospital ER, no one thought to run labs on Dad for possible poisoning. Even if they had, cyanide does not stay in the bloodstream for long.

An autopsy on March 18 confirmed Dad's death by cyanide poisoning. Cincinnati Homicide squad was contacted the next morning, and the investigation was begun. The team on the case was comprised of seasoned investigators: Sergeants Morgan, Jay and Guy, Police Specialists Camden and Lawson, as well as Detectives Fletcher and Arnold, along with other members of CPD and Homicide.

Hospital staff, including aide Donald Harvey, were questioned on March 22. Among other things, Harvey cast doubt, telling investigators that he thought John Powell didn't respond well to his wife, Patricia. Homicide notes on this day recall Harvey as "very helpful."

These forensic professionals filed nearly 150 pages of detailed reports. Dad's visitor logs were sought, secured and reviewed; John Powell's family and friends were contacted. Cyanide was extensively researched. Requests to the coroner's office for further autopsies were logged, though after eighteen such procedures were administered, no new cyanide cases were discovered. Assessing motive and opportunity, the specialists conducted exhaustive interviews with hospital staff, drew conclusions from numerous polygraph examinations, assessed truth-telling, ran down leads, deduced and narrowed a list of suspicion. Presenting as coroner's investigators, they visited Drake Hospital on numerous occasions and learned everything from shift change protocols to feeding tube procedures. They had done a thorough job of breaking down the case, including suspecting Mom. They questioned a life insurance policy, a GE employee benefit that paid out to Patricia when Dad died and explored dark motives for her wanting a letter from Dr. Varmer or Dr. Sarkar about John's disabilities, and a healthcare Power of Attorney for her ailing husband prior to his death. Leaving no stone unturned, investigators went so far as to bait Patricia Powell, suggesting her own daughter may have committed the crime.

All possible leads were followed.

Nurse Judith Sander told investigators, on March 27, that she remembered hearing Donald Harvey repeatedly discuss being tangled up in questioning about other unexplained deaths in other work environments. Though no formal accusation was made, word got out that Donald Harvey seemed to be around an awful lot when patients died.

Harvey backed out of his April 1 polygraph.

On April 2, 1987, Cincinnati Homicide discovered through Homer Brown and Renee Peel, two of Drake Hospital's security detail, that a detective, Maurice Loeb, had been assigned to work undercover at the Veteran's Affairs Hospital specifically to gain covert information on Donald Harvey when he worked there and doubts and concern arose about his performance. Loeb detailed his findings around Harvey's satanic worship, vindictiveness, destructive behaviors, and keeping a loaded .38 revolver in his work locker, plus thievery of books, samples, tissue and body parts. After a bust Loeb supervised on July 18, 1985, Harvey was allowed to resign..

This key piece of information finally pulled the other clues together and focused the squad on Harvey. His confession to Dad's poisoning was received April 4.

Jan Taylor, Drake administrator, informed detectives of a list of suspicious deaths that had been slipped to management around or just after John Powell's death, and Taylor then confessed to worrying about other deaths at the hospital.

Another note, in talking with JAN TAYLOR last night and TAYLOR was
quite concerned about the possibility of other deaths being involved here,
and our suggestion to him was - and this is the stand that we pretty well
feel we need to take - is that the Coroner's Office is not going to be able
to identify any other bodies as being cyanide poisoned and in lieu of not
being able to prove that they were poisoned and the fact that DONALD HARVEY
is not telling us that he did anymore, then we'll just have to stand on the
conclusion that that's the only one that we have and can prove at this time
and stand firm on that issue.

COMPLAINANT:	JOHN POWELL	OFFENSE:	DEATH	
INVESTIGATOR:	SGT. JAY & CAMDEN	DATE: 4/5/87	PAGE	6

ON APRIL 28, ATTORNEY Bill Whalen entered a plea of Not
Guilty by Reason of Insanity on behalf of his state-appointed client, Donald Harvey.

From April to June 1987, I somehow finished my sophomore
year at Oak Hills High School, having missed quite a few days.
Even when in attendance physically, I wasn't exactly what I would
call "present." The only bright spot I can recall in the building then
was Mrs. Gibbons. She taught 10th grade English, now more commonly known as Language Arts. I had Dee Gibbons after lunch,
and usually arrived early, loitering outside her room until she might
motion me in to sit until class started. She was the only teacher
who actually seemed to give a damn about what was happening
with me. Basically, I was a mess, and though we rarely talked in
depth, she watched the news. She understood why. Looking back
through a dark veil, I remember her assigned sophomore curricu-
lum book, *Cry the Beloved Country*, sharing my tears. Alan Paton's
South African social protest novel addressed the complexity of a

murder leveled there, becoming a direct point of reference outside of my own life, connecting me to killing in ways my classmates had yet to guess.

I can remember distracting myself with crushes, messing around with boys but committing to books—otherwise, the specifics of that time have dissolved. Decisions weren't thought-out. I wasn't amassing a résumé for higher education; I wasn't even writing. Future was simply a word, not a concept. Notebooks filled in previous and following years, remained largely empty that spring and summer. For the first time in my life, I had been hit by something that was just too much to put on paper.

Home was a refuge—an extension of both our parents, who'd left their marks throughout. Mom, with an eye for artful arrangement, had attended University of Cincinnati's DAAP program for interior design in 1960, as a college freshman. Her color palette lived on the walls and sat beneath us on furniture. Knickknacks lounged on sills next to pots of greenery. She persevered as a gardener, pouring soil and seed over her sadness, filling pots to overflowing. Her efforts provided a sanctuary where Heather and I could sun ourselves, glazed in Johnson's Baby Oil those hot afternoons, while John either slept in, or had regular visits with his videogame therapist named Atari on the basement couch.

Dad's hand was unmistakable on a large shed he had built in the backyard: a house in miniature, adorned with window boxes hung under paned glass for Mom's garden tools and lawn mower to look through.

"Handy" didn't begin to describe Dad; his ingenuity and care were everywhere around our home. The largest project he tackled was the outdated kitchen. When we moved in, reasonably priced microwave ovens hadn't yet made it to our neighborhood Sears store. Old metallic appliances and battered turquoise cabinets hemmed in the small square of a space. A two-paned window centered over the sink, at shoulder height, allowed a tiptoed view into the backyard. A small table tightly packed us under the window opposite, which looked across the driveway onto the street. The garage door took up valuable space on the main kitchen wall, squeezing the refrigerator up against the cabinetry. When Dad built out that enclosed porch, he strategically moved the ill-placed garage door out of the kitchen and onto the porch, creatively enlarging that tight U-shaped kitchen space. A long wall now held a counter running over the oven, below a shiny new microwave, pushing the fridge into the unused corner where our table used to sit. The dining room table and family room, hidden on the other side of the wall, were reborn when Dad designed a pass-through opening over a built-in cutting board and updated dishwasher, bringing conversation and dinner plates more easily into the kitchen. He then added a sit-down counter, creating a beautiful place to cook and gather. Creamy white and wood-trimmed cabinets welcomed us more brightly into what is always the center of any home.

We didn't have Dad at home anymore, yet he lived in every space we inhabited. We could handle seeing and remembering him in that way. Much harder was seeing Dad's face randomly pop up on the nightly news, next to his killer's. Everyone we knew was affected. Neighbors and classmates didn't know what to say to us. Piteous faces and respectful distances stood at every turn. I was grateful when summer break cut off the stares at school.

My longtime friend Holly and I hung out most of the time. We shared a name but not a school. Like family, she was easy to be around and didn't expect me to be anyone other than myself for her. Though I turned sixteen at the end of May, I had no immediate intention of getting my driver's license. Doing so would not help me navigate the hard roads I was already traveling. Meanwhile, Heather graduated high school. I sadly have no memory of it. John was sleeping and gaming away his pain. We might catch sight of each other in the kitchen over a glass of milk. Mentally I wasn't there for anyone, including myself, and slices of that time have peeled away.

Early summer I tried working a couple jobs. I hung out with a few people here and there, dated a guy with a family produce store for a few weeks, and did some babysitting at the end of the street. Both John and I slept in and ate a lot of Hostess products in that beautiful kitchen. Lost in a dizzying fog of emotions laced heavily with adolescent hormones, I responded more by instinct than intellect. No great plan for my future was in the works, no internship or study program lined up. Entering summer with little else to focus on than all we had gone through, tomorrows came with a peculiar disposition.

During these months after Dad died, I learned a lot about the authenticity (or artificiality) of others. Hesitant conversation-starters, sideways stares, delayed laughter, and disingenuous attentions stood out to me glaringly. Sensing and disarming uneasiness became my superpower. If I kept smiling and laughing, the people around me, naturally uncomfortable with my situation, became more comfortable. Big emotions are hard on folks. When friends fell silent or fell away altogether, my goal was to put myself at ease, so I pushed down the anger that sprung up when people inevitably said, "I'm so sorry"—empty words to me. Locking sadness into a box, I preempted awkward silences with jokes, masking my true mission of making an unbearable situation easier on me.

As a recovering "pleaser," I employ this same tactic to this day, without thought but with sincerity. Like Mom, I always have been a people person who really enjoys meeting and discovering new people. In the late 1980s, though, new was especially nice. Unfamiliar faces didn't already know my story. More rare was meeting someone who didn't let that story lessen who they became to me.

ON AN EARLY SUMMER EVENING in June 1987, we welcomed someone new into our living room on Grossepointe Lane: Pat Minarcin, the nightly news anchor and managing editor for WCPO Channel 9 in Cincinnati. Having been in contact with him for weeks as he sought information and photos of Dad, Mom was not surprised when he asked to visit. Minarcin walked in with his sympathies, dressed casually, capped by dark hair graying at the sides, thinning on top. His resonant voice spoke plainly and carried a tone of respect. WCPO's producer, Ed Wilson, had already

reached out to Mom asking not only about Dad, but more generally about our time at Drake. By now she had an inkling of a
larger story in the works. Minarcin's visit cemented that, and finally
revealed the results of his ongoing reporting.

Sitting with Mom, sharing the unbelievable and heinous details
he'd uncovered thus far, Minarcin could see her emotions rise. He
agreed to explain to us kids what he'd learned.

Cornered on our sofa, the reporter wove an unthinkable tale. A
widow and three teenagers listened intently as Minarcin spoke of
the strong possibility of more murders committed by Donald Harvey at Drake Hospital. He shared that he had been pursuing this
idea ever since, two days after Harvey's confession of Dad's murder,
the news of an arrest was aired for public consumption. Minarcin,
the evening anchor on April 6, turned to Cyndee Benson, a reporter covering the story who was seated at the desk next to him, and
asked whether Harvey might have committed more murders in the
past. Benson said that "it didn't appear so." The skeptical look on
Pat's face stayed with me. I remember watching it then, and have
since seen the video and read other accounts, and am truly as-
tounded that Minarcin was the only person to raise that possibility,
that probability.

Immediately following that evening news report, anonymous
sources at Drake Memorial Hospital began contacting Minarcin
by phone, encouraging him to keep looking. The unnamed callers
persisted, increasing in number. Minarcin kept digging.

Hearing that Dad's "mercy killing" was only one knot in a
string of wrongful deaths left us unmoored. We were adjusting to
euthanasia, to the belief that tenderness or humanity of some sort
was at the heart of Dad's death. What kind of person commits
murder once, let alone repeatedly, to people victimized by accident
or disease? No human we knew could do this, and yet—didn't we
now know a cold-hearted killer?

Minarcin then shared that nurses and aides had tried to voice
their concerns for months, to no avail. Higher ups at Drake weren't
listening. The police weren't asking questions; Minarcin was, and
at their request. We three teens, speechless, took in as much as we

could. Mom's tearstained face, full of concern, held us to reality, as did Minarcin's steady voice and eyes. Carefully stepping around Dad's memory, he went on to say he hoped to have his investigation completed soon. WCPO would be airing an extensive report about his findings, laying out all the leads that, according to his sources thus far, police had failed to follow.

With apologies for bringing such news into our home, and sincere wishes for our peace, Minarcin walked out the door, promising to keep us posted.

Unknown to us until then, seven months of chances were squandered that might have altered our family's course. For seven months, nurses had reported disparities to their superiors, noting deaths inconsistent with the illness at hand. For seven months, the length of Dad's entire convalescence at Drake, a yawning cavern of concern had run silenced through those halls. Ignorant of our proximity to its edge, we were destined to fall in.

The dogged reporter continued to work the facts, inquiring about statistics and gathering sources to support claims.

JAN TAYLOR, THE TOP ADMINISTRATOR at Drake Memorial, penned a letter to Chief Larry Whalen on June 3, stating the challenge of Minarcin's repeated requests for information. In return, Chief Whalen responded with a letter to Taylor concluding their investigation June 12, 1987; the letter was documented in several news articles.

Meanwhile, a pattern of increased and potentially unnatural deaths began to emerge on Ward C-300, overlapping with periods when Donald Harvey had been working there. When Minarcin felt he had more than sufficient evidence to raise a flag, he referenced the story he was investigating, producing and planning to air, in a call to Harvey's attorney, Bill Whalen. Soon after that call, Whalen made his way to the County jail downtown to visit his client and told him there was going to be a TV news story suggesting he had

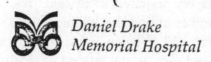

Daniel Drake Memorial Hospital

June 3, 1987

Board of Trustees

Jean C. Corbett, President
Robert A. Pierce, Vice Pres
William R. Dally, Secretary
Joseph M. DeCourcy
William V. Finn
Emma Johnson, R.N.
George M. Lockwood
Norman A. Murdock
Robert A. Taft II

J.C. Taylor
Chief Executive Officer

Chief Larry Whalen
Cincinnati Police Department
310 Ezzard Charles Drive
Cincinnati, Ohio 45214

Dear Chief Whalen:

We continue to be challenged by Mr. Pat Minarcin to provide additional
information regarding patient care activities here at Drake Hospital. Mr.
Minarcin has related that during a conversation with Donald Harvey there was an
admission by Harvey of involvement in more than one death. Minarcin further
relates that he is developing a report about multiple deaths in this case and
alleges that Drake, which implicates involvement of the police and the coroner,
is involved in a cover-up to preclude his story. In my association with the
police and the coroner the facts we uncovered did not indicate multiple deaths
had occurred as a result of Harvey's actions. We realize not all information
was shared with us, and this is as it should be, but we would appreciate
reaffirming the single death situation.

I would appreciate a letter from you indicating that a thorough investigation
was made and that there was no effort on our part to cover-up any information.
I recognize the demand on your time that this request creates but Mr. Minarcin
has caused concern on the part of too many people that are not privy to all the
information. He has gone so far as to report his theory to the husband of a
woman who died here during the same time frame and that really created
emotional stress.

Our board members and the County Commissioners would appreciate knowing, in
writing, that we have done everything feasible to make the facts in this case
available to the appropriate authorities.

Please know that should you wish to investigate any further the allegations of
Mr. Minarcin that we stand ready and willing to cooperate.

I look forward to your letter.

Sincerely,

J. C. Taylor
Chief Executive Officer

CC: Frank Cleveland, M. D., Coroner
    Michael Hawkins

JCT/ljb

151 West Galbraith Road   Cincinnati, Ohio 45216   (513) 761-3440

killed others. Whalen then asked Donald Harvey the obvious question.

According to his own book, *Defending Donald Harvey*, Whalen knew he was in trouble when Harvey hesitated, softly said "Yes," and then had to estimate the number of previous killings for his attorney: "around seventy," Harvey said. Whalen, in his position as Harvey's defender, felt shocked and torn. In the interest of sparing his client's life, Whalen decided to help Minarcin without violating his client's confidentiality.

Pestered repeatedly by Pat Minarcin's calls, Whalen chose not to hinder the WCPO investigation, walking a fine line in order to accomplish the two goals of protecting his client from a sentence of death while advancing the truth. We didn't know it then, but Bill Whalen discreetly supported the reporter's research, as Pat sought a wider angle on the story. Before the full picture could be exposed, it became another secret for our family to keep, another wall of silence isolating us from others.

Not long after his initial visit to our home, Minarcin called Mom to let her know that on June 23, he planned to break this story in a special report on the evening news. He wanted us to hear this preview directly from him, knowing it could be hard to bear; he explained there would be photos of Dad, and that viewing the broadcast might spark strong emotions for us. We felt indebted for the care and sensitivity shown. A strange anticipation lit in me, not only for seeing the full report and its validation of the Drake staff's concerns, but for finally not having to hold another secret among ourselves. Once the story was out there, we would be free to share with our extended family and friends the incredible burden we'd been enduring on our own.

Anchored behind his desk, armed with irrefutable facts, Pat Minarcin of WCPO-9 News broke an extraordinary story the night of June 23, 1987. The station aired a half-hour segment dedicated to the Drake Hospital Investigative Report, without a commercial break (unheard of at the time). Minarcin, the seasoned journalist, laid out for the rest of us the information he could not ignore. Charts, images and video effects were used to clearly illustrate the pieces of his investigation. Dad's name and photos laced the story, as Harvey's one known and confessed murder victim— begging the question of others who may have suffered the same fate. Harvey's work shifts. Times of patients' deaths. Numbers of deaths from other wards in Drake, where Harvey hadn't been on duty, compared to the alarming mortality statistics of Ward C-300: they were significantly lower.

Minarcin had invited local officials, including those in the Hamilton County prosecutor's office, to attend in the studio during the broadcast, to view his report first-hand. He spoke with medical experts and forensic specialists from other cities, too, who all confirmed the need for further investigation. Anonymous Drake Hospital sources, disguised in digitized shadows and with vocal distortions, spoke freely on camera about concerns they had held for all those months prior to John Powell's death. They recalled how their supervisors had ignored all the warning signs, and worse, how Drake administrators had asked the nurses and aides to keep their suspicions to themselves.

Cincinnati had seen its share of sensational crime stories, but never anything like this. Ten years' experience as an Associated Press reporter had given Minarcin the tools to uncover the inconceivable, but it was his humanity that allowed people to come forward with what they knew, all pointing to two questions: Could Donald Harvey, currently indicted for the murder of one of his patients, have killed others? And if so, could any of those deaths have been prevented?

Our family, gathered on the couch, watched the broadcast live on our living room television. Emotional as Minarcin had warned us we'd be, appalled at the numbers on screen, we were moved by the hidden faces with voices we knew, people risking their jobs to do what was right. Shocking as the truth was to hear, we were not caught off-guard, having been thoughtfully prepared. I cannot imagine how many families over the decades have been deprived of that small courtesy.

The day after the report aired, officials scurried to catch up.

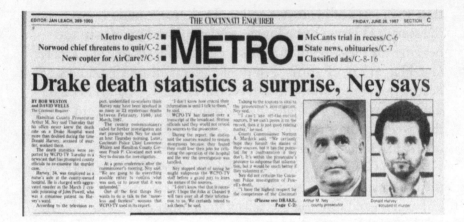

EDITOR: JAN LEACH, 369-1003

THE CINCINNATI ENQUIRER

FRIDAY, JUNE 26, 1987 SECTION C

Metro digest/C-2
Norwood chief threatens to quit/C-2
New copter for AirCare?/C-5

METRO

McCants trial in recess/C-6
State news, obituaries/C-7
Classified ads/C-8-16

Drake death statistics a surprise, Ney says

BY BOB WESTON
and DAVID WELLS
The Cincinnati Enquirer

Hamilton County Prosecutor Arthur M. Ney said Thursday that his office never knew the death rate on a Drake Hospital ward more than doubled during the time Donald Harvey, accused of murder, worked there.

The death statistics were reported by WCPO-TV Tuesday in a newscast that has prompted county officials to re-examine the murder case.

Harvey, 34, was employed as a nurse's aide at the county-owned hospital. He is charged with aggravated murder in the March 7 cyanide poisoning of John Powell, who was a comatose patient on Harvey's ward.

According to the television report, unidentified co-workers think Harvey may have been involved in as many as 23 mysterious deaths between February, 1986, and March, 1987.

The county commissioners called for further investigation and met privately with Ney for about an hour Thursday morning. Later, Cincinnati Police Chief Lawrence Whalen and Hamilton County Coroner Frank P. Cleveland met with Ney to discuss the investigation.

At a press conference after the commissioner's meeting, Ney said, "We are going to do everything possible either to confirm what was said, or to prove that it was unfounded."

One of the first things Ney wants to do is talk to the "nameless and faceless" sources that WCPO-TV used in its report.

"I don't know how crucial their information is until I talk to them," he said.

WCPO-TV has turned over a transcript of the broadcast. Station officials said they would not reveal its sources to the prosecutor.

During the report, the station said the sources wanted to remain anonymous because they feared they could lose their jobs for criticizing the operation of the hospital and the way the investigation was handled.

Ney stopped short of saying he might subpoena the WCPO-TV staff before a grand jury to learn the names of the sources.

"I don't know that that is necessary. I hope the folks at Channel 9 will turn over all of their information to us. We certainly intend to ask them," he said.

Talking to the sources is vital to the prosecution's investigation, Ney said.

"I can't use off-the-record sources. If we can't prove it on the record, then it is just good relating matter," he said.

County Commissioner Norman A. Murdock said, "We certainly hope they furnish the names of their sources, but it has the potential for a confrontation if they don't. It's within the prosecutor's province to subpoena that information, but it would be much better if they volunteer it."

Ney did not criticize the Cincinnati Police investigation of Powell's death.

"I have the highest respect for the competence of the Cincinnati

(Please see DRAKE, Page C-2)

Arthur M. Ney
county prosecutor

Donald Harvey
accused of murder

Minarcin's investigation inspired me to research, to dig—but always to be human in the face of dedication, drive or ambition. That report, so scrupulous by today's standards, was only the beginning of a bigger story that gave meaning to Dad's murder.

14

grasp [grasp, grahsp] *noun*
1. one's power of seizing and holding; reach
2. hold, possession, or mastery
3. mental hold or capacity; power to understand
4. broad or thorough comprehension

HEADLINE IN *The Cincinnati Post* on Wednesday, June 24, 1987: "Police couldn't tie hospital aide to other deaths." From the article by Bob Musselman and Sara Sturman: "Cincinnati Police Chief Lawson E. Whalen has discounted a news report alleging suspicious deaths at Drake Hospital. In a June 12 letter released today by Hamilton County Commissioners, Whalen said police had investigated the allegations. But, he said, 'at this time there is no reason to believe that additional deaths can be connected to Donald Harvey.'"

The Cincinnati Enquirer the same day headlined, "Review of Drake deaths urged," as David Wells and Kevin Washington write, "WCPO, however, quoted unidentified Drake co-workers as saying... hospital officials, including Administrator Jan Taylor, warned employees not to talk about their concerns."

The story goes on: "Jack Leach, spokesman for the coroner's office, said the report contained no new information. 'We had all of those figures and we determined that they were not significant... There is nothing pointing to this being a string of mercy killings,' Leach said. The hospital staff was interviewed by investigators from the Cincinnati Police homicide squad, Leach said." End of article.

Still, the Hamilton County commissioners called a special meeting on Thursday, June 25, and Art Ney, Hamilton County's top prosecutor, agreed to take another look at the case.

Clearly prompted by the WCPO special report, Ney launched a full-scale investigation two days later, promising in a press conference to "get to the bottom of it," despite the fact that then-Hamilton County Coroner Frank Cleveland had announced on camera that "no new news" had come from the media probe. According to Cleveland, and to spokesman Leach, the coroner's office had been monitoring mortality rates at Drake, and saw no discrepancies or unusual patterns. As far as they were concerned, there was nothing to investigate—until evidence to the contrary, compelling enough to force Ney's hand, was on the Channel 9 evening news.

J. Sanders, RN, a relief nurse at Drake Hospital who had known Powell since his admittance, reported to Sergeants John Jay and Ron Camden on March 26 in a police interview that "the last medication she gave to John was about 1 p.m. on March 6, 1987. Three days before his death he had been conscious to the degree that he cried, she saw tears coming down his cheeks and this saddened her greatly."

On page 5 of the Cincinnati Police psychological consultant's sample material on Harvey's killing of Powell, Walter Lippert, PhD, goes on to say that J. Sanders was a very sympathetic nurse who had become quite close to John Powell. In talking more, she brought new information to light, saying that "an orderly by the name of Donald Harvey had had conversations with her in the past. He had told her about working at Veterans Hospital and being involved in unexplained deaths at Veterans in the past. She recalled he mentioned this to her more than one time."

In Harvey's confession on April 4, he stated that on Monday March 2, he obtained the poison (he would later administer to John Powell) during an autopsy in the Drake Hospital lab. In his statement, he also indicated that he himself was suicidal and may have intended the poison for himself. Waiting until Saturday March 7 to use the cyanide, Harvey said he arrived at work around a quarter to seven that morning and that at five past seven, he gave John Powell enough poison to kill an army, and then went to a floor meeting.

Harvey said he went back later and Powell was dead, or nearly: "Well, he still maybe just a little twitch." Such detached, unempathetic statements, from someone who moments before, on the record, said he loved John Powell and didn't want him to suffer. Mercy killing? Was it merciful to cause fifty-five minutes of suffering, a slow, suffocating death? John Powell was given the poison at 7:05 a.m., according to Harvey himself. The nurse indicated respiration ceased at 8:00 a.m., with the doctor calling Dad's death at 8:05. Knowing Dad suffered his final hour in pain, in fear and alone, is a heavy burden to carry.

Though I consider myself an observant, inquisitive person, I'm not a professional detective—and yet, I see red flags everywhere when I read through Harvey's confession. "Enough to kill an army"? Why the need for such an excessive dose? How could he know a lethal amount, versus too much, unless he was well-versed in toxicology? Was there a reason he'd used so much cyanide to kill John Powell? Could it be that Harvey had made past attempts on Powell's life, or others, that hadn't been successful, necessitating the overdose? Hindsight helps, though it seems plain to me that when detectives asked if he had done this to anyone else on April 4, common sense would follow up his unsettling answer of, "I can't really say."

Holes were all over his statement, unconfirmed details about where and when he had gotten the poison, saying he had more at home. More poison at home? That's concerning. Questions also linger around how he said he disposed of the poison. Police detectives could have contacted law enforcement officials in Kentucky, where Harvey was from, and where in 1975 he had been arrested and admitted to other killings. They could have contacted his former employer at the VA hospital, another possible window into Harvey's sordid work history.

THROUGH MY EXPLORATORY PROCESS, I have discovered tragic

failures throughout this case, which must lead to teachable moments.

First, at the county level: There needs to be a full understanding
of Hamilton County officials' duty to protect public safety. Trans-
parency and review are essential, and foresight is required, to keep
citizens safe. Hamilton County Coroner Frank Cleveland, who
for years was a paid expert in all manner of wrongful death cases,
both civil and criminal, called the mortality data revealed in the
WCPO report "insignificant," with no unusual patterns. This type
of certainty in the face of irrefutable evidence seems inconsistent
with the coroner's charge. Granted, the field of forensic science was
less advanced then, with fewer known examples of serial murderers;
we can't expect county officials in 1987 to conjecture, as we might
today, on the diabolical scope of Harvey's crimes. We can only be
grateful that Dr. Lehman in the coroner's office used his olfactory
senses, his intuition and training to determine that cyanide had
been used to kill my dad. Without that essential revelation, none of
what followed would be known.

Next, investigation and charges. Glaring failures within systems
of justice occurred when homicide detectives didn't immediately
pursue a second investigation outside of Dad's murder. After their
first confession from Harvey on April 4, detectives admittedly
needed to focus on the conviction of Harvey for Powell's death.
However, anyone reading the transcript of that confession can see
a need for further questioning. CPD detectives involved have since
said they did not want to let a murderer walk free on an insanity
plea. Law enforcement procedures now allow for simultaneous,
separate and ongoing investigations. This is not a Fifth Amendment "double-jeopardy" situation, and after cases such as Harvey's,
new statutes and stronger legal precedents exist for holding one
person accountable on multiple charges.

Timing. The actual chronology of events in this case is at odds
depending on who you ask. Harvey's confession on April 4 concluded investigations inside Drake, per the nurse's statements. Minarcin's investigation began April 6 when Drake Hospital nurses
heard him question Cyndee Benson about multiple deaths and the

nurses began to call him. Chief Whalen, in a letter to Jan Taylor on June 12 concludes the investigation. Then, on June 23 WCPO airs its report—with the ensuing frenzy of confusion among county commissioners, prosecutors and other local officials. These dates are irrefutable, historical facts to this case, however much some involved considered the media's work a hindrance. This was not a "bullcrap story," as Hamilton County prosecutor Joe Deters claimed years later, in a Fox News interview in September of 2019. Even Art Ney thanked Minarcin for the report that spurred his investigation. To suggest otherwise demeans the real heroes of this story: those nurses who, despite their legitimate fears of retaliation at work, came forward with the truth.

"Telecast stirs suspicion about 23 patient deaths," reads a headline in the *Mansfield (Ohio) News-Journal* on June 24, 1987. The report goes on to say that "Mike Hawkins, lawyer and spokesman for Drake Hospital, said the administration pledged to cooperate. 'As soon as the news media raised the question of additional deaths, the hospital administration immediately notified the coroner's office and the police,' he said. 'We've been advised by police that as of June 12, there was no reason to believe that additional deaths can be connected to Donald Harvey,' said Hawkins."

More important, as we unravel the timetable here, is the Homicide squad's own chronological account of the investigation, where investigatory activity drops precipitously after April 6, only to intensify after WCPO's report, June 23. Not to mention twice-repeated admission that an investigation was *not* ongoing. In an *Enquirer* article on June 25, 1987, Michael Hawkins, attorney and spokesman for the hospital, is directly quoted as saying, "According to letters exchanged between Taylor and Chief Whalen, the police chief was aware that WCPO-TV was asking questions. Chief Whalen, in a letter dated June 12, 1987, assured Taylor that "a complete investigation was conducted by the Cincinnati Police Division, the Hamilton County Coroner and the Hamilton County Prosecutor's Office." Chief Whalen wrote that no one involved in the investigation had reason to believe that Harvey and other deaths on the ward were connected.

Officials to begin Drake death probe

BY BOB WESTON
and KEVIN WASHINGTON
The Cincinnati Enquirer

Hamilton County Prosecutor Arthur M. Ney Jr. will meet today with county commissioners to launch an official inquiry into televised reports of 23 possible mercy killings at Drake Memorial Hospital.

Commissioners want Ney to work closely with County Coroner Frank P. Cleveland and Cincinnati Police Chief Lawrence Whalen in the inquiry.

Tuesday, WCPO-TV said the suspicious deaths occurred at the hospital between April, 1986, and April, 1987, on the ward where Donald Harvey worked as a nursing assistant.

Harvey, 34, has pleaded innocent to aggravated murder in the

cyanide poisoning death March 7 of patient John Powell. Powell, 44, was comatose after a motorcycle accident last July.

Harvey is in the Hamilton County Justice Center awaiting trial July 27.

Joseph M. DeCourcy, president of the board of commissioners, said commissioners want Ney to determine whether Powell's death and others were linked. Ney was out of town and could not be reached for comment.

"We hope Channel 9 (WCPO-TV) will provide him (Ney) with the names of the Drake staffers who were their sources for the suspicions they aired in their special report," DeCourcy said.

WCPO-TV News Director Jack Cahalan said he would provide Ney's office with a transcript

of the 30-minute news broadcast and a dub of the videotape. He wouldn't say whether he would provide names of sources for the report.

Commissioner Robert A. Taft II said county commissioners also want to know the extent of the investigation by police and the coroner's office into the Drake deaths.

Commissioners were upset that Drake's chief executive officer, Jan C. Taylor, failed to tell them that WCPO was investigating the hospital deaths.

Commissioner Norman A. Murdock said Taylor had promised to keep them abreast of any developments growing out of the Harvey case. The hospital is owned by the county and all of the commissioners are ex officio members of hospital board of

trustees.

"I am very disappointed that he did not tell us anything about this — and that's as civilized as I can say it," Murdock said.

Echoing Murdock's sentiments, DeCourcy said, "I believe we should have been informed immediately (about Channel 9's investigation) and to this date, I don't know why we weren't."

DeCourcy emphasized that none of the commissioners was implying that the hospital administration was involved in a cover-up.

"I do not intend to overreact to one report," he said. "You do not approach this with the presumption that someone is guilty till proven innocent."

(Please see DRAKE, Page D-2)

Joseph M. DeCourcy
... wants Channel 9's sources

Drake

CONTINUED FROM PAGE D-1

Commissioners said they would insist that Taylor respond to questions about the Drake deaths, so long as he did not undermine the prosecution's case against Harvey.

Jean Corbett, chairman of the Drake trustees, drafted a letter to Ney saying she concurred with county commissioners' request for an investigation of the deaths, according to Michael Hawkins, attorney and spokesman for the hospi-

tal.

To alleviate worker concerns, Corbett and William R. Dally, board secretary, sent letters to the hospital staff Wednesday asking them to contact administrators if they had any questions or information.

According to letters exchanged between Taylor and Whalen, the police chief was aware that WCPO-TV was asking questions. Whalen, in a letter dated June 12, 1987, assured Taylor that "a com-

plete investigation was conducted by the Cincinnati Police Division, the Hamilton County Coroner and the Hamilton County Prosecutor's Office."

Whalen wrote that no one involved in the investigation had reason to believe that Harvey and other deaths on the ward were connected.

During an impromptu press conference Wednesday morning, Hawkins said hospital administrators have kept mum because the police

and coroner's office told them not to talk about the investigation.

Oral updates on the investigation were given to trustees during meetings, Hawkins said, but police never disclosed all of the details.

"It would be fair to say that the board wanted everything investigated," Hawkins said of the board's involvement in the investigation of additional deaths. "Mr. Taylor was fully cooperative with the police and coroner's office."

The Cincinnati Enquirer *article June 25, 1987 by Bob Weston and Kevin Washington*

Literally waiting for the police or Drake administrators to revisit their concerns after Harvey's confession for John Powell's murder, nurses knew no further investigation was ongoing at Drake. With their jobs threatened for seven months by superiors, where else can a person go if police, who are supposed to investigate crimes, say they have already, or won't? Again, Chief Larry Whalen (no relation to Bill Whalen, Harvey's attorney) had stated on-camera, and in a June 12 letter to Jan Taylor at Drake, that Cincinnati Police had completed their investigation at the hospital, with no further suspicions of Harvey. Drake's attorney Michael Hawkins affirmed it. County Commissioner Joseph DeCourcy stated the same, eleven days before Pat Minarcin aired his investigative report.

On June 26, the Metro section headline in T*he Cincinnati Enquirer* reads, "Drake death statistics a surprise, Ney says." Bob Weston and David Wells again write that "Ney did not criticize the Cincinnati Police investigation of Powell's death. 'I have the highest respect for the competence of the Cincinnati police and the coroner's office. It must be borne in mind that Harvey was being investigated only in terms of the death of Mr. Powell,' he said."

WCPO's special report changed that. Without journalistic efforts, John Powell's death would have remained, in the eyes of many, a solitary mercy killing. How many more victims might Harvey have claimed, then, before his guilt was uncovered? We'll never know.

Next, the importance of fact-checking. Almost every newspaper report available about this case lazily repeated the erroneous claim that Dad, Harvey's first known murder victim, was "comatose since a motorcycle accident July 8th, 1986."

He was not. Do the research. Interview first-hand witnesses. Ask the questions.

Anyone at Drake or in our family, had we been asked, could have accounted for the fact that John Powell was not comatose the entire time he was recovering at Drake Memorial. Nor was he soporific or comatose before he was poisoned. He was certainly gravely ill, and there were unnatural reasons for that.

Our collective family energies didn't go into proving each reporter or news agency wrong. Following suit, reporters simply kept reporting what others had. Whether or not Dad was in a coma must have seemed an insignificant detail, unworthy of further research for accuracy—though new photos of Harvey's face seemed to be of unceasing interest.

We really had bigger things to manage, as it was all we could do to stay afloat on the ebb and tide of our own emotions. Experiencing the loss of a man we loved in big and complicated ways, we were also recovering from his hard-fought eight months since the accident, putting the rest of life on hold through his miraculous progress, and on to his death. What's more, we were still processing Mom's layoff, the discovery that Dad had been murdered, all the secrets we were forced to keep. Finding out that he'd been taken at the hands of a caregiver we knew, in a place we had trusted to heal him, and that others there had been killed… It was a lot.

The news became something to overcome or avoid each day, as friends and neighbors equally either poured out sympathies or averted their eyes when finding the right words proved impossible.

On August 20, 1987, *The Cincinnati Enquirer*'s John Kieswetter reported, "After Harvey's day in court Tuesday, Hamilton County Prosecutor Art Ney told reporters that police and coroner investigations had been looking into other Drake deaths when Channel 9 aired its story linking Harvey to twenty-three Drake deaths. Ney admits that he was without any leads. Minarcin's story provided the who, what, where and when; and allegations from anonymous Drake employees that had not been heard before. Minarcin's legwork before the broadcast also brought him to William P. Whalen Jr., Harvey's attorney. It was only after Minarcin's visits that Whalen thought to ask his client if he committed other murders at Drake. 'Channel 9 did hurry it along, they accelerated it,' Ney said."

Here, Ney admits that Minarcin's report on Channel 9 "hurr(ied) along" the investigation that was considered concluded on June 12, with Chief Whalen's letter to Jan Taylor. Somehow the story changed from June 25 to August 20, when, after being caught with their pants down, officials insisted that "investigations were ongoing."

Kiesewetter's report went on to bullet-point the timeline of events initiated after WCPO Channel 9's report. He described how the investigation continued under Cyndee Benson, Tom Regan and John Matarese at Channel 9, and that everyone at the station was involved. He writes, "As an Associated Press writer and editor in New England, Minarcin covered Ted Kennedy's negligence resulting in a drowning after a drive over a Chappaquiddick bridge. At CBS News in the early 1970s, he wrote stories about Watergate, the Hearst kidnapping and the fall of Saigon. As editor of *Pennsylvania Illustrated*, his 1980 reporting on Three Mile Island resulted in a national journalism award, the Clarion from the Society of Professional Journalists. The Harvey story is far from over for

Minarcin. Channel 9 has a large master plan. Next, comes the fate of Drake Hospital's management, which ignored employee's suspicions about Harvey a year ago. Then comes the civil court suits from the relatives of Harvey's victims. After that comes the station's entry for a George Foster Peabody Award for distinguished broadcasting, the industry's equivalent of the Pulitzer."

Pat Minarcin, the anchor, reporter, and managing editor of WCPO Cincinnati, along with news director Jack Calahan, and executive news producer Ed Wilson, were deservedly credited with a Peabody Award in 1987 for this groundbreaking journalism.

Bizarre, the reluctance of anyone involved, whether prosecutor, or police detective, to accept and respect the various other roles played in this case—contributions as flawed, sometimes, as they were necessary. My dad's life was taken, and without Mom's autopsy decision, a strong nose at the coroner's office, nurses risking their jobs, and untold others doing their part, a serial killer would not have been stopped. Police investigated, and found a killer. Minarcin investigated, and uncovered a serial killer.

Justice is not at odds with news reporting; it often relies on it. Police officers rarely walk a beat, as they did decades ago, and they keep a very different finger on the pulse in each community. Trust is an issue. Then and now. Even when cops used to walk those streets, communities didn't always turn to the police with information. Journalists, who develop sources, are vital gleaners of truth in our society, often telling the "other" side of the story, sharing the viewpoints you don't get from an official press release. The "I-Team" of "9 on Your Side" is a perfect example of reporters uncovering information, exposing scams and schemes, to protect citizens and consumers. Other mid-sized media markets have their own teams of journalistic investigators, but their ranks have been drastically thinned in recent years, as has been the case here in Cincinnati.

Worthwhile lessons must be taken away from this case, more than bragging rights or finger-pointing. Ego, I am convinced, is at the heart of every corruption of truth.

That summer of 1987, after the WCPO report ended and an official investigation started, the city learned, and families endured the discovery, of a significant number of patient deaths at the hands of a killer employed at Drake. Donald Harvey's attorney Bill Whalen negotiated a plea bargain: Harvey could keep his life if, in return, he gave up information on the lives he took. Families struggled at first to understand the necessity of such a deal, but were finally convinced that only then could all families truly know what had happened, and to how many. In a twelve-hour videotaped confession on July 9, before a grand jury, a composed and confident Donald Harvey detailed the varied means used to kill his victims, from poisoning with cyanide and arsenic to smothering defenseless patients in their beds.

In order to verify Harvey's outrageous and unbelievable story, the bodies of those who had been killed by means still detectable after death were exhumed from their resting places. Letters were sent to families of thirty possible leads detailing, by grand jury order, an investigation with a possibility of exhumations. This brought hardship on families who'd made their peace with grief, believing their loved ones died of natural causes. Nothing was natural about the way Harvey killed, brazenly, preying on the weak, without remorse. To confirm the real causes of death, this was the only means available to prosecutors. Doing the unthinkable in order to solve his multitude of crimes was the only way to seal this murderer's fate behind bars. Typical of a murder investigation of this kind, at the time little information was given to anyone, including the families of the deceased. The coroner and prosecutor's offices had no comment.

A grisly midsummer search went on, substantiating the victims that Donald Harvey claimed as his own. If his information proved true, this plea bargain would stand, and he would be spared the death penalty.

Hearing / 151

15

hearing [heer-ing] *noun*
1. the faculty or sense by which sound is perceived
2. opportunity to be heard
3. an instance or a session in which testimony and arguments are presented, especially before an official, as a judge in a lawsuit
4. a preliminary examination of the basic evidence and charges by a magistrate to determine whether criminal procedures, a trial, etc., are justified

LATE AUGUST OF THAT SAME YEAR (1987), rather than celebrating their summer wedding anniversary, Mom had a date at the Hamilton County Courthouse with the memory of her husband. Not unlike other Augusts here, it was an unmercifully hot day in downtown Cincinnati. The sun burned into the low 90s, making surfaces and skin sticky like glazed buns. The windows in Courtroom Four, which still lacked air-conditioning then, were opened, and fans moved humidity about the room. Few of us would breathe easy that day. Crammed into the chamber were my mother, brother and sister, and many other victims' survivors. Sons and daughters, wives and husbands sat sweltering, waiting for the proceedings to begin.

Emotions were palpable. A wiry energy tinged the room—a mix of boiling anger, heated agitation and deep sadness. Reasons that sat each of us there varied wildly from seeking justice, finding closure, or feeding the rage that survives. Witnesses all. Our microcosm of victimhood testified to the final chapter of the story as we knew it then. Collectively we longed for an ending that could put meaning into our reason for being there. We had a right to hold space in that room, a right to represent our families. We had an obligation to John Powell. We wanted to see justice done.

Hamilton County Prosecutor Art Ney and assistant District Attorney Joe Deters met privately with the four of us in a small conference room a few minutes prior to the hearing. They met with each victims' family to briefly explain why there would be no trial that day: Harvey had waived his right to a jury of his peers in lieu of the plea terms that needed to be met. The plea guaranteed Harvey's life would be spared. He'd been given the chance to meet the agreed-upon terms by detailing more killings, thus avoiding execution himself.

Our family and others were only informed of this arrangement upon entering the courthouse. Some arrived expecting a full-blown trial; some wanted a death sentence for a killer. Entering into a plea deal would secure the total number of victims and their specific causes of death, so all victims' families could have some kind of closure. Harvey's cooperation, his sharing of first-hand knowledge of his killings, would ensure these crimes were counted. However, if Harvey lied, or if the Prosecutors ever caught him in a lie, all deals were off, and he could be charged with the death penalty.

A man who loved to kill, feared his own death. This was his motivation to confess.

HEATHER AND I WERE sweating under our dresses. It takes time for a courtroom to assemble, for families and the press to situate. Chairs were set up in addition to the benches, and they began to fill. Heather's face paled as she managed the thick air in the room with an asthmatic's lungs. Escaping into the restroom, I grabbed handfuls of paper towels from the dispenser to run under cold tap water, laying them across Heather's forehead and neck to cool her. When we returned, the room had swelled in number and tem-

perature. The jury box filled with chairs and their occupants (not
jurors); court staff staked out places against the walls; photogra-
phers set up shop, and attorneys talked quietly over tables. Mom
had been squeezed into a single chair behind the prosecutor's table,
near the wall, while my brother stood behind her with a long-distance diagonal view of the defendant's table. Not one person stood
or cleared a space so that our family could be fully seated.

County Coroner Frank Cleveland sat comfortably back on the
chair next to us, facing a huge presentation board refuting what on
June 25 he had called "no unusual pattern of deaths." Mounted on
easels, for all to see, was a looming catalog of Harvey's murders.
(Joe Deters had a family member help put the boards together.
Such placards, easily ordered online and quick-printed today, took
some effort in 1987.)

The dead were each present and accounted for, if only and
boldly in block letters. Their full name, method of murder and date
of death were spelled out for even those in the back row. Each
victim was individually recognized, but by little more than their
involuntary attachment to their killer. Their own names were the
only facts on the storyboard that Harvey had not altered. There, in
memory and name only, was my dad, John Powell, listed among
his fellow victims, facing a defendant who would seem, to all of us,
unaffected.

Donald Harvey, clean-shaven in a brown suit and tie, was led
into the chamber. His attorney Bill Whalen, wearing a tan suit,
made space for him at the table. Two sheriff's guards stood in dark
blazers pinned with star badges behind the defendant as he sat, and
they remained throughout.

Judge William S. Matthews sat on the bench. As his honor entered the court, the bailiff instructed us to rise; we all rose, respect-
fully, until Judge Matthews motioned for us to sit. He would decide
nothing that day that hadn't already been decided.

John and I stood during the hearing at first, giving Heather,
who seemed faint, that tight squeeze next to Mom on the chair.
Soon though, overheated and exhausted, my young knees knelt
down on the floor next to her. Mom sat upright and strong, cra-

dling Heather, frail and uncomfortable. Occasionally we were moved to tears, except for John, standing protective above us, his mind processing what his heart could not. Mother and daughters, we held hands across Heather's lap as we wrestled to understand our first experience in a courtroom as something so deeply personal, yet ostensibly public.

On went the names, the numbers, the methods of deaths. On went the cameras clicking, the nearby sniffles and tears flowing, the perspiration of the crowd saturating every bench and crease. Donald Harvey had his day in court yet felt no fear. He appeared immune to the terror we felt at his expense.

There's a video clip of Bill Whalen whispering to his client at the defendant's table that day, often replayed afterwards to further illustrate the lack of remorse in this killer. Whalen leans over and says something quietly to Donald, with a smirk; Harvey openly laughs, as if they were sharing secrets at a picnic. It happens quickly, and just as quickly, the defendant regains his solemn face. It is a sociopath's privilege to enjoy his proceedings while perfecting his performance.

Disorienting, the steady rhythm of decency and decorum as the hearing unfolded, laid over an off-kilter track of devastation. Turns taken, each number and name on the board had their moment to claim grievance. As names were read, families owned their connection with outward emotion. Dad's name was near the end, as one of the final victims of the man sitting just across the room. Sinking into a stupor, I could hear the names, I could recognize the pain in the room around me, but I couldn't attach to it. Surreal, the scene— being part of something so monumental, that would change so little. The heat and lack of suspense both felt unending.

Some sense of stillness had overtaken the room. Perhaps only my mind quieted, or an awareness slowed things down. The wave, pulling back from the shore before a sudden crash against it—this was my feeling, edging closer to Dad's name on the board in such proximity to his murderer. Becoming hyper-alert, I waited for his turn, receding, as I waited for John Powell's name to be heard, before it crashed. Waiting for his life to have mattered.

His name was read, but there was no crashing wave. No court-room became saturated in justice; no resolution washed over us, only joined hands tightening and my face quivering as the tears came. Little John in a polo shirt stood expressionless behind me. He was the man of the house now.

Photo © Ed Reinke – USA TODAY NETWORK (with permission)

ART NEY GAVE a rousing speech on that 18th day of August, about justice being done, knowledge now attained for the families. *The Sioux City Journal* reported, on August 23, that Ney explained in court, "He's no mercy killer and he's not insane. He killed because he liked to kill."

The next day, *The Record* of Hackensack, New Jersey headlined, "Ex-hospital aide given life term for 24 murders." Continuing on page 18, under the title, "Jailed," the article went on to quote Ney, speaking of Harvey: "He's got a compulsion to kill like some of us have a compulsion for cold beer."

The Atlanta Constitution reported on August 19, 1987, that in the courtroom Art Ney described Harvey's impulses: "He builds up a tension in his body, so he kills people." Ney called Harvey a cold-blooded killer who "enjoyed his hobby," and felt no remorse. The Hamilton County Prosecutor described the killer's own list of names, found behind a picture frame on Harvey's wall in his home.

With the guilty plea and deal for sentencing entered, there would be no surprises, yet a courtroom demands theater, and Art Ney directed it. Climactic statements were made with dramatic intonation, attempts to make narrative sense of otherwise senseless events. The show was presented for us, the family members and media present, so we all could know the prosecutors would hold Harvey accountable for his crimes. And they had, really. In the end what more was there to do?

The Judge ruled on Harvey's fate in this, the ceremony of due process: the killer would serve three concurrent lifetimes in prison. At 35, Harvey wouldn't live long enough for even one of them to fully count. I supposed he got one lifetime for half of the board of names, and another for the other half. I'll claim one lifetime for John Powell, the victim who posthumously uncovered all of Harvey's crimes.

No one else could be found guilty of not doing their respective jobs that day. Court recorder, guards, bailiff, attorneys, the judge—each were in place performing that which we in polite society call justice.

Misery sank my knees into the courtroom floor, as sorrow held them. Though I didn't fear for myself in that courtroom, there was fear in that moment.

I'd like to tell you exactly what I was feeling that day.

I'd like to wrap it up in a neat little bow for you.

Come to think of it, the only box that opened for me that day had no bows or ribbons—just plenty of trappings. What filled me then, and continues to overflow in me still today, is the lack of clarity on any one point of feeling, but rather the burden of experiencing them simultaneously, stacked, layered and weighty upon me.

Anger seems appropriate, but wasn't at all what I felt. Maybe terror is closer, now that I have time and space to access what that feels like. Terror. Rupture. Like a severing of one reality split into new things to loathe and fear that were previously unimagined.

Since that day in the courtroom, I've lived to witness the Black Monday stock market crash, the exposure of the Iran-Contra affair, Operation Desert Storm and the Los Angeles riots of 1992. On a restaurant television in 1994, I watched O.J. Simpson's white Ford Bronco trailing dozens of police. In 1995, the same year I was married, I cried fiercely over the televised aftermath of the Oklahoma City bombing. I saw Lady Diana chased to her death in 1997, the same month my first child was born, before we were all to blame for Monica Lewinski's mass-media shaming over Bill Clinton's infidelity. The news showed us the U.S.S. Cole bombing in Yemen, and the countless ships, planes and cities bombed since. My family moved into Cincinnati just months before the 2001 police shooting of Timothy Thomas sparked six days and nights of nationally publicized civil unrest. I wished I'd never needed to see the creamy entitlement in the face of a murderer kneeling on the dark-skinned neck of George Floyd, yet I did. We all desperately needed to see it.

We have all witnessed the politicization of murder. We felt the danger and loss in Benghazi and the ensuing assault on our tax dollars. Sick to my stomach, I learned of the waste of children's lives against legislated gun protections at Sandy Hook Elementary in 2012. "Je Suis Charlie, aussi," during the Paris attacks of 2015—and I can still see that car barreling through peaceful protestors in Charlottesville, Virginia, in 2017, killing Heather Heyer. Terror struck again at Marjory Stoneman Douglas High School in 2018, and at the Boston Marathon, and at a street concert in Las Vegas, and at Robb Elementary in Uvalde, Texas; it strikes again and again in countless places of worship, and in nightclubs, and in grocery stores… anywhere America's out-of-control arsenal of hatred can reach.

Nor can we escape Nature's terror, with escalating disasters flooding our feeds: wildfires, heatwaves, rising and sinking water lines, earthquakes and landslides rocking communities with rising death tolls, human and animal alike. These last two-and-a-half years we have felt the wrath of the COVID-19 pandemic, with 629 million humans infected and 6.58 million killed worldwide (as of October 2022)—as with climate change, a natural threat made more deadly by our own failed response.

War, too, constantly threatens our world and leaves us numb. We see endless fights over territory, religion, oil—and the mass migrations, starvation and other humanitarian crises that follow. We discover mass graves of Indigenous in Canada, civilians in Libya, and more Holocaust victims in Poland. Ukrainians go to bed on a quiet night in February and wake to Russian bombing. Loss of civilian and military lives resounds across history. We are the trauma-causers. Lousy with the number of terrible, terrorizing, plaguing acts that have occurred during my lifetime, we, collectively share in this derangement.

How can humanity handle this barrage on our hearts and minds? Not being personally or directly affected by a cataclysmic event does not reduce evidence of our trauma response. Anxiety and suicide are both on the rise in a world that feels closer to home yet further from the comfort expected there.

Panic and horror shocked readers and writers everywhere this past week, August 12, 2022, when Salman Rushdie was stabbed repeatedly in front of an audience at The Chautauqua Institute, for the enduring power of his words. Three months prior, Rushdie spoke at the PEN World Voices Festival and said, "A poem cannot stop a bullet. A novel cannot diffuse a bomb… But we are not helpless… We can sing the truth and name the liars."

I am writing my truth.

WITHOUT A DOUBT, we live in violent times. A magnetic draw pulls us to attend to tragedy; any train wreck, no matter how drawn-out or quick, fascinates. Tragedy invites us in.
I experienced that allure in the courtroom. Like any hair-raising or

abhorrent event, there is an element of intrigue, of giving yourself over to it, of becoming lost in it.

The only other event that comes close to what I felt that summer day in 1987 was the tragedy of 9/11. It is not a comparison I am drawing; I lost no one personally that awful day, though I mourn them all. But my feeling in the courtroom was the same: it was the chill that comes from witnessing something unimaginable, a life-altering event beyond mass death, a toll greater than the sum of lives lost or left behind. Encapsulating so much more than murder, the events of 9/11 cracked honor, broke trust and ripped through the heart of a country. Sadly it was only a beginning, or in retrospect a continuation of mankind's terror campaign. No peace has come, no resolution, even with the killing of Osama Bin Laden in 2011 and other Al-Qaeda leaders since; as Americans, we can never return to our pre-9/11 sense (illusion?) of safety.

This is the best way I can describe how I felt that earlier day, face-to-face with my dad's murderer. The world stopped for me in that courtroom, as it did for the families of 2,977 victims, and for much of the rest of the world, on that sunny September Tuesday in 2001. And when time began again, I was somewhere else—in a world where justice can never be served, for a loss so profound.

Were it not for my dad's death, others might still be dying at the hands of Donald Harvey. And I knew in that courtroom that unless I was sitting there, enduring this event in such proximity to my dad's murderer, more could be dying that very moment.

Penetrating knowledge weighs heavily on a young mind; it couldn't help but shape my future views. Without evil, there can be no goodness; without senselessness, there can be no purpose; without death there is no life.

No relief or resolution came when Donald Harvey was walked back to his cell. No rulings made in court that day would undo what had happened. Nothing could. I wish we'd learn to start better at our beginnings before such tragic ends.

Returning home drained, we faced another school year.

✦

HERE IS WHAT I know.

All humans breathing this shared air, walking this planet, each of us count for something. Humans are hugely flawed, and our behaviors and decisions impact others, and yet, each of us has a right to live our days with dignity. From a first breath to a last, from the most selfless saints to the most heinous criminals, humans are born into a story already in progress, often written into the margins or forced into a horror they cannot escape.

Systems are flawed. Some are sacrificed for others in systems meant to protect that actually protect only some. In war, those without special skill are first offered up to the front lines. Repeatedly slipped into cracks or wedged into legislation, if you don't have money, or can be labeled into a group, our systems likely won't serve you well.

Because I believe these things, I am against the death penalty—was before and assuredly have been since that day in court. Seems strange to have such certainly around that then, but I did. Driving with Mom once in downtown Cincinnati, when I must have been about fourteen years old, I saw a message scrawled in black spray paint on an overpass near Fifth Street and Elm or Plum Street, that read, "Killing those who kill does not teach others not to kill." This urban scrawl put into words what, for me, had always felt true. Perhaps the message was a response to gang violence, or a plea to city police at that time in the late 1980s. Maybe someone else felt as I did, that a result cannot be achieved by claiming and utilizing its very opposition as a platform. The dichotomy always gets me: Building a stronger military to ensure peace. Keeping secrets to avoid mistrust. Chaining some to gain freedom for others. Yelling at an already upset child to stop that child from crying. Charity given to an institution through a checkbook or tax deduction, but not extended to your fellow man on the street. Denying a right or privilege to a person, and then blaming them for not "pulling themselves up by the bootstraps."

Believing that exceptions prove the rule does not make sense to me, and seems to make a situation worse. If "killing those who kill" were a successful tactic, it would have proven far more effective over the hundred millennia we've employed its terror.

There are models worldwide for how to reduce and even prevent crime. Here in America, our cities and states, we look away from proven concepts, almost priding ourselves as Americans for our righteous exceptionalism and for reinventing the wheel.

Perhaps it is our own wheel that needs retooling.

The Bill of Rights offers no specific human right to safety, though I'd like to assert that the pursuit of happiness is difficult, if not impossible, without it.

IN APRIL OF 1990, Jim Fiehrer's Political Issues class at the University of Cincinnati was discussing the death penalty. Fiehrer approached a victim's support group to find guest speakers; the group leader reached out to Mom and me to consider talking to the class. My mother and I found ourselves on opposing sides of the death penalty question, and it was believed that we'd offer a unique perspective, given what our family had been through. Professor Fiehrer wrote a sincere thank-you letter to us, enclosing a stack of writing from his students about how they'd received the talk. The students were kind in their assessments, describing how revealing it had been to learn more about victims' struggles and needs for support, and speaking as much about how Mom and I were dealing with our tragedy as about the death penalty per se. Despite their individual views on sentencing for capital crimes, all were made to consider the actual justice of our American judicial system, and the importance for individuals and societies of working through pain.

One student wrote, "I admired their courage, it took a lot to talk to us as openly and frankly as they did about something so personal. It made me understand how much the survivors of such hideous crimes have to go through and how they are affected."

"They mixed the facts of the murder with their own feelings well," another young woman recalled. "It also made me think more about the effectiveness of our justice system."

Mom and I weren't there to persuade or change minds; we had agreed to speak on behalf of our support group when asked. We didn't have speeches prepared. Casually we sat on stools at the front of the class. I remember tall windows filtering a late-morning sun into the room and students at desks leaning into us, engaged. Mom and I answered some thoughtful, though at times naïve, questions.

Ambassadors of grief, that is how I can best describe our role. We weren't being drilled by reporters, weren't part of a think tank. We were lending our time personalizing a lesson around systems of justice. None of these students had been through a homicide. We shared what we knew. In that spring of 1990, we knew about surviving, for just over three years, the murder of a family member.

We don't all ask to be specialists in the areas we become one.

As much as we were in that college class to discuss the death penalty, any good discussion goes to the side, and the students' own concerns became obvious. The young people couldn't imagine living through a loved one's murder and wondered how we were handling it. Relating the impact of our own healing and the importance of seeking support, I shared how hard I had worked with therapy to get here, and how talking helped more than it hurt. Mom said her faith and caring for her children helped her through. I could feel the genuine interest, the empathy emanating from those young people. Actually, it felt rewarding, to think that my words might bring some value to others. It was empowering to think that some-one may walk away understanding something they hadn't before, simply by hearing about our experience.

Finding honest and engaging conversation very stimulat-ing, I really don't have taboo topics. Conferring on difficult issues comes naturally to me. I do not prefer safer shallows, and at times I've repelled people in my pursuit of depth, but these students were interested. They cared to know how I stood against the death pen-alty and for the benefit of therapy. Mom and I balanced each other well; she in her softness, no less staunch in her views, countered and complemented mine.

At this point in our lives we had moved through the tears or upheaval that used to accompany any conversation of Dad's death. Three years had passed, and I was a young woman who had learned to communicate openly about death, dying and murder. These students before me, most my own age, at that time, hadn't had to overcome so dark an experience. Times have changed.

Scientifically we know that the body and mind are connected—in action, in wellness and illness, they are proven to act in concert. How then can we so easily dismiss the power and care of the mind? Today, there are myriad scientific proofs linking past trauma to negative health outcomes, showing the importance of psychological wellness for physical vitality.

For our families, for our communities, and most tragically for the suffering individuals themselves, the result of unaddressed, un-treated trauma is always more trauma. We are the ripple effect on each other. How many times do we have to learn this lesson before we take what we know, dig in, and deal with the root causes of our society's pain?

16

aftermath [af-ter-math] *noun*
1. something that results or follows from an event, especially one of a disastrous or unfortunate nature; consequence
2. a new growth of grass following one or more mowings, which may be grazed, mowed, or plowed under

Police Statement of Joseph Suesz:

John Powell and I were close friends for 22 years. Prior to the accident we would get together approximately twice a week. We enjoyed playing volleyball, camping, riding motorcycles, home improvement projects and building trailers. John was a very skilled motorcycle driver. He had been riding a motorcycle since 1967 and was always alert, very natural and at home on a bike. I have been riding a bike for 20 years and during that time have never met a more skilled driver – John was tops.

Subsequent to the accident, I went to the hospital every day until John was moved from University Hospital to Drake Hospital. After he was admitted to Drake Hospital, I visited him approximately every other day, at least three times a week, until his death.

Immediately following the accident, John's condition was critical. He suffered from severe head injuries, his head was swollen to twice its normal size, he was paralyzed on the right side, blinded in his right eye. He was in

a coma for four months. In November he came out of the
coma mentally impaired.

As time went by, John began to improve. He had periods during which he was alert and able to stay up approximately one-half hour before drifting off to sleep. John was
able to move his left arm, leg and occasionally his right
foot and hand. His left eye would make contact with you
and look around the room.

I believe the brain damage John suffered was repair-
able to an acceptable level. Over time there was definite
improvement. During my visits I would tell John funny stories from our past and he would smile and open his mouth
as if to laugh. In January we had a birthday party for John
and you could see in his face that he was getting some
enjoyment out of it. He was able to communicate with me
by slightly nodding his head to yes or no questions. John
was regaining his personality.

Physically, it is very difficult to assess the pain John
experienced because he was in a coma for four months. I
believe he was comfortable most of the time until he began to regress. At one point, he was able to propel himself
down the hall in his wheelchair. In January, John began to
regress. He was experiencing, what the doctors believed,
problems with lung infection – pneumonia. John was
transported from Drake Hospital to University Hospital
for testing and treatment. After a few days at University
Hospital he would stabilize and return to Drake Hospital.
After his return John would again have a setback and have
to return to University Hospital for testing and treatment.
Again, John was able to stabilize and was returned to
Drake Hospital. This occurred approximately three times
before the doctors decided that John would remain at
Drake Hospital.

I believe the setbacks John experienced were caused
by cyanide poisoning administered by Donald Harvey. John

was able to recover and stabilize while at University Hospital, but upon his return to Drake Hospital, would again have a turn for the worse. John was given a fatal dose of cyanide and died on March 7, 1987. Living through the experience has devastated John's family and friends. His stepdaughter, Holly, is undergoing therapy and his mother was admitted to the Psychiatric Ward of Christ Hospital.

I have read the above statement which consists of two pages and it is true and correct.

Signed 10/26/1988 Joseph T. Suesz

CAGNEY & LACEY WAS a popular television show in the early to mid-1980s. From the sofa's edge, our family used to watch the two clever women detectives every week as they "got the bad guys," uncovered crimes and solved forensic mysteries. Before that, shows like *Dragnet, Hillstreet Blues* and *Magnum, P.I.* addressed crime-solving, however, this television series was the first police procedural I watched. It was the comparison I could draw to our situation in 1987 when suddenly, it seemed, I was living inside an episode. Since then the world has seen twenty-two seasons of *Law & Order* (so far), numerous iterations of *NCIS,* and countless other shows and movies about killers, criminal psychology, forensic science, interrogation techniques, courtroom theater and all the late-night televised edge-of-your-seat drama a body can stand or society can covet.

Over the years I've watched plenty of these shows, and for a decade-long phase I read creepy books steeped in murder, death and the darkness in our culture. Before turning twenty I began to devour books by Dean Koontz, John Saul, Stephen King, Thomas Harris—any shadowy scenario that would paint the world as dark as the depths of my mind. Equally fascinated by both victim and

killer, having sat with both, I dove headfirst into the pits of hell.
I think I watched the film too young, and the Jaws movie shark terrified me as a child. Fear stays on the tongue; I became accustomed
to its bitter taste. Sucked into countless psycho thrillers as a late
teen, I've since enjoyed blockbuster movies rampant with violent
action, along with the rest of you. I'm not a prude or an advocate
for removing violence or death from our purview. I'm not in denial
of death's trance or deep historical pull over our society. I merely
question the prominence and glorification we allow killers, over
their victims.

We Americans thoroughly enjoy making someone famous,
however briefly, based on all manner of talent or flaw. Our entertainment has shifted to meet our collective longing for ridicule,
death and mayhem. There is a reason the new Netflix series *Dahmer*
is on the tip of many tongues and why *Tiger King* became so swiftly popular in 2020 when we had nothing else to do during the pandemic lockdown. There are reasons that true-crime podcasts have
deep fan bases; *Rolling Stone* magazine describes the twenty-five
best true-crime podcasts of all time; YouTube has millions of views
on videos of brutality, beheadings and police shootings.

We can't look away. And there are instances where we absolutely should not look away, knowing justice is often only derived
by video evidence. Society lives within a split atom of morality.

Despite my own sensitivities, I understand that murder itself is
a fascination. Death and dying are natural, inevitable stages of life,
and therefore universal causes for concern, ceremony, and reflection.
Our body politic is centered around war; veterans live the violence
integral and ceremonial to our culture. Artists create around the
topic, authors feed readers the concept of dying at a safe distance.
Seeking thrill or catharsis, streamed or in print, we seek a world
most of us would not choose to actually live. Death and violence
are intriguing and deeply rooted in our history. There has always
been a crowd at a public hanging.

Immediately following Dad's death, I trudged through paralyzing dread and situational anxiety, consumed with worry that more family members would die at any moment. This kind of state is a common post-traumatic response. Dreams and reality make irrational, inseparable companions. This strange and stress-filled apprehension recreated my world then, regularly spinning benign events into darker scenarios in my young mind. Brains are not fully developed until our mid-twenties, though I'd wager that many of us, despite advancing years, are consumed by manifestations of fear. Envisioning repeated responses to another loved one's death or murder, I'd wake from a nightmare tormented by projections of how I might handle a personal attack. Outwardly, I could manage most days, but inside I was delving into a territory I didn't want to explore. The more I tried to ignore my lingering angst, the more panic-filled I became. My family could not escape the storm of emotions as I tossed between shores of safety and sanity.

Deep-seated anthropological issues of attachment, abandonment, entrapment, or regret plague many of us. I tasted each of these bitter pills for a time and laced them with a healthy dose of hospital paranoia. A doctor's office or hospital is a classic stressor for patients, acutely felt by those of us whose loved ones were murdered inside the supposed safety of protected healthcare. As you might imagine, these issues I was experiencing also troubled my loved ones.

Heather turned eighteen one week after Dad died. There was little in the way of celebration. My own sixteenth birthday, which I remember vividly, was understandably forgotten by my family at the end of May. Sappy words soaked my journal at 12:03 a.m. as I began my first day as a sixteen-year-old in 1987, sulking, wallowing in what I know now to be minor disappointments.

The treadmill of life kept moving, but we had each lost our footing by finding out how Dad died. As we attempted to find sleep, routines or excitement that would numb or at least dull the pain, there was inevitable upheaval within my family and myself.

Home life became more difficult to bear, with each of us

kids stuck in our own corners, picking which opponent to fight through—at times, choosing to fight each other. Mom had to be the referee. I sought escape from the ring often, through friends and drinking, parties and boys. I hung out with Deanna, a high school senior and a friend. During my sophomore year, she and her car could drive me away from all those pesky emotions, left waiting like unsolicited callers on a doorstep, to be dealt with later. During my fifteenth and sixteenth years, as I struggled to make sense of what had happened, avoidance was an easier choice, but it made me easily upset and quick to anger. Turmoil boiled beneath my surface for months, heating me through the holidays.

In early January, 1988, Heather and I were bitching back and forth, fighting over who knows what. Siblings fight, some more than others, but before all this went down, our dust-ups rarely got out of hand. Twenty-two months younger, I am the older sister by temperament. A foil to Heather's shyness, I could talk without embarrassment about dating, periods, sex or politics. Occasionally, though, Heather claimed her rightful place and the true older sister came out.

Bickering that day turned to yelling, then finger-pointing, then all-out screaming, which was not typical for us. My voice strained. Trembling in my throat, that last screech started digging into the back of my neck, a chink tightening. A monster of a headache settled in behind my eyes. Doors slammed, opened, then slammed again. Our small house forced close quarters; rooms squashed up onto each other's walls were no match for the sound. There was simply no place to go to get away. Though we were both at fault, Heather was better at getting her mind off her chest. She heaved it onto mine.

This fevered argument quickly heated the air, and enflamed my face. Usually, I overcome heavy things better when I can get someplace alone. My flight instinct was kicking in, and although I wanted to simply run, winter waited outside the door. I plotted leaving, yet didn't drive. If only I could step out of the fray and into some quiet place to think. My mind factory doesn't easily shut down, but with all the yelling I couldn't think straight, and could not understand or be understood. We all duel our truth. Fighting and screaming is not in my nature. I'm the middle child who craved imaginative play and time alone, who grew into a diplomat, who made signs to calm the family down with my "count to ten" campaign, on pretty pictures taped to our wall. I didn't respond well to this level of anger and finger pointing, not that any of us do. I'd had it, was maxed out. The world started closing in.

Wanting nothing but quiet, I balled my fists tightly, shaking them at the air and yelled one last time at my sister to "LEAVE ME ALONE!!!"

Where could I go? Nowhere. Maybe this was the only place I was ever going to be. No long-range future could be seen in that moment, only this current suffering. Having left all those emotions waiting back at my doorstep, I couldn't discern sadness from anger, or grief from powerlessness. I was in misery, and I couldn't even be alone to deal it. Anger and injustice rolled over me and knocked me flat. I could run away; I'd done it before. But that time a friend drove me to another friend's house. Where could a teenager immediately go with no money and no car, in the freezing cold? I felt trapped.

Not wanting to hear anything else from Heather, Mom, or anyone ever again, I shut myself in the bathroom and locked the push-knob door. Grey and white tile boxed me in, amplifying the pulse in my head, keeping beat with Heather's fists pounding the door. Old, cracking grout disgusted me. I must have said something to worry Heather because eventually she stopped pounding and started yelling for Mom. John, deep in his own gloom, stayed downstairs.

My head wouldn't give up the fight as Heather's yelling through the door pressed in on me. I stopped responding. Pacing like a caged animal in the tiny space, I saw in the mirror a version of myself I didn't recognize. In that bathroom, even my curling iron was shared. What did I even have that was truly mine? What I needed was silence, complete and utter silence, and I knew if I had it, my head would stop hurting and everything would be okay.

No intention entered or crossed my mind other than finding

quiet in this storm, nothing beyond wanting to diminish the pain. Tears streamed from eyes that hadn't decided to cry. I reached for the Tylenol bottle on the counter, and with shaking hands struggled to open the child-proof lid.

No wish was made other than for silence. Heather was still yelling and Mom was calling and the door handle was jiggling and I popped the top open and poured some white tablets into my hand. How many I do not know.

I just needed it all to stop.

Heather, who had apparently been working with a bobby pin, picked the door lock open just then, startling me as she slapped my hand spilling pills out and over the floor.

This was proof to Heather that I was trying to kill myself.

She yelled for Mom to come see and say so.

I realize there are worse things than a concerned sister. While I can honestly and thankfully say that I have never intended suicide, that day or since, who knows what I might have done in that state. I do know how it appeared to Heather and Mom.

For me, it was actually the complete opposite: Death was a fear faced daily, a reality too close to home after Dad's murder, and I never sought solace in it—only from it. However, it is possible that with my strong desire to silence the world that day, in extreme distress, I could have been a danger to myself. Too much Tylenol, though not a fast track to death, could have made me sick or damaged my liver or other organs. Though I had not exhibited any other self-harm behaviors, we cannot know how far a trapped mind will go to be free in that moment. How far can we be pushed under, before we succumb? This was what both Mom and Heather decided needed to be addressed. I only pushed past far enough to get to my room.

This entire incident had blown up out of nowhere, something from nothing, and yet it prompted discovery. Pressured and forced far enough, I had demonstrated a problem, and in my case, thankfully without doing any irreparable harm. Mom took it with seriousness. It was obvious to both of us that I needed help I could not find alone or at home.

In this awful time of tough love and hard choices, Mom worried for her child while still grieving herself. I was just one of three that she carried that level of concern for. Still, she pulled her resources together, made a few calls, and was able to get me a spot immediately in a psychiatric care facility for adolescents with behavioral, emotional or addiction/chemical dependency treatment needs. That is not exactly how it was described to me.

This was the 1980s. Seeing a therapist to talk through your inner troubles just wasn't commonly done, and hardly understood or perceived as it thankfully is now. Parents were simply parents then, not also the entertainment coordinators, armchair psychologists, educational tutors and career managers we've become now—but Mom knew her three children were in pain. Being the most verbal and expressive of my siblings, my own needs stood out and loudly. Mom offered me time away from home with mental health professionals. I thought perhaps they could help sort out the demons that had taken up residence in my head. Thank goodness facilities did and still exist to help troubled minds evict them.

Emerson North squatted impressively on Hamilton Avenue in College Hill, a historic village of Cincinnati. Originally built as the Cincinnati Sanitarium in 1873, it once sat lavishly with ponds and gardens on thirty-two acres, a respite and retreat for troubled souls. Later, around 1956, it was renamed for Emerson Arthur North, a specialist in psychiatry at the University of Cincinnati. By the time I arrived in early 1988, most of the grounds had been swallowed by pavement and progress, but the stately old structure had held onto an acre or two, along with its historic character.

Though I had agreed to go and to stay at this institution, mostly because I couldn't stand to be at home, nothing in my sixteen years could help me understand what I had just signed up for.

❖

I must insert this disclaimer here...

Unless you've spent time in a behavioral health facility or psychiatric ward, provided or undergone intense individual therapy, I cannot ask you to fully comprehend this part of the story. I believe it is more important to empathize and accept than to completely understand. It's essential to hear how others have stepped forward in their shoes, just as it is crucial to feel heard and seen through your own experiences—but another's truth or salvation is not axiomatic. I'm sharing this process, this part of my healing, not as a professional, but as always, in the hope that any part of my story could help others.

Every individual meets a hard edge somewhere in life, whether through trauma or circumstance. Low points narrow options. Manifesting stress and anger, our body prompts more serious health concerns and costs. Therapy, communication and emotional expression create awareness of self and others. By reducing stigma around mental wellness, we can encourage more people in need to seek treatment. Connecting better overall health to empathy, through knowledge, we can discover and increase helpful approaches to troubles commonly held among us.

With that said, I'll continue.

WINTER SUN HAD SET as we parked in the lighted lot at Emerson North. Pulling this year's Christmas gift, a leather bomber jacket, tight against the cold, I stepped through a portico alongside Mom. Impressive doors opened into a warm entryway where a receptionist, stepping out of her small office off the lobby, welcomed us into the manor. High ceilings and ornate woodwork defined the room. Asked to be seated on worn leather sofas, we discussed with the admittance person in charge, rather openly, that I'd been struggling with anger and some negative behaviors. These were facts I could not deny.

Uncertain as I was of being any better understood here than I had been at home, anything seemed better than going back. Yet, contemplating a stay in this place scared me. After that fight with my sister and the desperate feelings that followed, my options had narrowed. This, my mom gently asked me to consider, might help.

Working through emotions, participating in group discussions, meeting peers who were going through similar issues—this was the pitch from the staid lady at registration. Begrudgingly, I agreed to stay over. Mom was met with a professional demeanor and the right catchphrases from the on-duty staff, assuring her in the decision to admit me. Soon papers crossed her lap, signatures landed on lines.

The woman then looked at me directly and asked to search through my bag. What could I say, as I hesitantly shrugged compliance? She reached forward, opened my backpack, and began to rummage through it. Unnerving, her touching my things. An invasion. I watched her remove several items and hold them up to me, referring to them as contraband, and laying aside. Somehow a shaving razor, a hairdryer and curling iron were now forbidden to me. These items were fastidiously placed in a large plastic bag and handed over to Mom. Then, standing up, the woman in charge politely and firmly asked my mother to leave, now. Ripping the band-aid off quickly.

Unprepared for such a sudden goodbye, I felt uneasiness set hard upon me. I had not often stayed away from home, in unfamiliar places, and Mom's departure signaled something about to begin that I already regretted. Moments before, I was ready to be rid of Mom's company; now, acutely, I feared abandonment. My fear and inexperience protested. The lady insisted this was the best way to move forward, encouraging Mom to go. As she headed toward the door, Mom looked back quickly, uncertain. Then with a soft smile, she said everything would be okay. Mom told me she loved me, and promised to be back in the morning. It was a promise she wasn't allowed to keep.

Shortly after arriving, silent shock settled in as I followed a counselor, whose name I couldn't remember, up to the fourth floor where my room waited nearest the girls' bath. Here I was informed I would not be allowed a razor to shave my legs or underarms, no cough drops, belts, over-the-counter syrups or pills, mouthwash, shoestrings, or freedom. Dangling electrical cords, sharp or dull edges, and too much unstructured time apparently weren't healthy for kids like us. Feigning indifference, I nodded acquiescence. I didn't know that mouthwash and cough syrup had alcohol in it, or that belts and blow-dryer cords had been used by desperate teens in attempts to strangle their own young necks. I only knew I wasn't in Kansas anymore. Well past dinnertime, I hadn't eaten, but the feast of eyes on me from the other teens gathering deterred me from complaining.

High ceilings opened the space and a pale yellow attempted to cheer the walls that ran the length of the common space, pointing to a counselor-staffed reception desk waiting at the opposite end. Doorways branched off the main space into the girls' wing. My bedroom had originally been two smaller rooms, but at some point, a wall had been opened between them. Across the open doorway, a twin bed lay beneath a window, and a small desk was tucked just inside the room. Those were to be mine. Two unoccupied beds and desks cornered a further compartmentalized section of the room. That first night in Emerson was endured alone, shivering beneath a thin blanket, too spiteful to ask for another, too angry to sleep, too tired not to. Settling in bed against the window, I withdrew into my thoughts of escape—but to where? The hell at home, or this new hell? I waffled as the night passed.

The next morning found me tired and wary. I took little comfort in the other captives, who didn't look all too different from myself. All wore regular "street" clothes, with the exception of shoes with laces, because as it turns out, we literally might choke ourselves with them. Teens of all backgrounds wandered around in jeans, sweaters, sweatshirts, tees, and slippers or zipped shoes. This "hospital" environment seemed more like a dorm or rooming house. I'd brought very little with me, not knowing I'd need more than two changes of clothes; I made a note to ask Mom to bring things, even while I seethed for needing to do so. Several of the girls around me put effort into looking nice. Waking early, they show-ered, applied makeup and curled their hair. This was a co-ed facility, after all, and we were teenagers. Lists hung on clipboards to check out curling irons and blow-dryers with monitored time limits (they had cords, after all). A few young ladies seemed to care to a worry-ing degree about their appearance—not trusting their plain faces without the made-up mask, hiding imperfections only they saw.

That first morning I absorbed the place, studied routines, noted fluorescent-lit paths the other kids walked toward rooms they called home. A prisoner feeling out the level of her constraint, I searched for weaknesses. Pulling a counselor aside that early after-noon, I said, "I'm ready to leave now. I really don't need the kind of help you think I do."

Politely, I was informed that I was not free to go. I did not have the right to leave, having been signed in as a minor. This place of sanctuary, which had I sought for a day or two to straighten out the lines of my thinking, now might impound me for weeks or even months of treatment. Once admitted, I would remain until the doctors and counselors agreed I was healthy enough and ready for release. I couldn't even leave my assigned floor or go outside, unless I was with a counselor. I was trapped, again. With no way out. I had no control; no choice was afforded me. At home I could bargain, have the comfort of my room or the outdoors anytime I wanted, but this type of confinement—I was completely unpre-pared.

I didn't think to ask what "healthy" meant. I didn't think to ask who these people were or how they got to decide what "ready" for release looked like for me. If they told me anything else helpful, I didn't hear it. Choking back anger, swallowing it down indignantly, I asked them if I could call my mother.

No. I could not. Not yet. I would have to earn the privilege to use the phone.

Anger boiled tears threatening to spill, confusion and fear of further retribution restrained me from screaming. Seeking any vulnerability in the cage closing around me, I told the counselor I didn't know this when we signed in, that our family had been misinformed, and surely my mom would not have done that to me. You'll see, if I could only use the phone for a minute, my mom will sign me out right away. Nodding in understanding, the counselor accepted my truth without buckling. You are here for a reason, they said. There's some things you need to work through, they said.

What I needed to work through was you, dammit!! But I didn't say that. I just took a deep breath and pressed every button I could. Without yelling, fighting or belittling me, the counselor' didn't budge. Then I remembered that I'd only packed for two days and didn't have everything I needed. "I need to talk to my mom," I begged, humiliated. "I don't have my stuff, I need to ask her to bring my things." I thought maybe, if I could just talk to Mom, I could slip in a signal for her to sign me out of this prison.

"How could I know what I'd need? I wasn't told I'd be here a long time, and I only have like one change of clothes!" I added indignantly.

"That's very common," the counselor assured me. They would call her for me—I could make a list of what I needed, and they would ask her to bring my things as soon as she was able. There went my hope of sending a secret message to my liberator. Just what I wanted, Mom rummaging through my bedroom.

She did bring exactly the clothes I asked for later that day, and again my bags were searched and approved while she waited downstairs. However, I was not allowed to see her. The first few days, all privileges of contact with family were to be denied. I had never considered these things a privilege.

Have you ever noticed how easy it is to blame yourself for shit when it won't help you, and how hard it is to accept responsibility for your actions when it may? Certain that Mom was at fault for bringing me here and keeping me trapped, I rebelled and plotted. Days later when my mother finally could visit, I took every opportunity to make her feel that blame most painfully. John and Heather were not allowed to visit those first weeks either, though I hurled plenty of anger my sister's way, too, thinking she probably needed this place more than I did. I seethed.

Days at Emerson were fully planned and overseen by dedicated professionals. Counselors, medical practitioners, doctors, nurses, psychiatrists, group and art therapists, kitchen and maintenance staff comprised the team. We patients ate downstairs, slept upstairs, and I spent most of my first weeks just shuffling between those two levels. I met a few other troubled teens that were friendly; we played nice until we didn't have the energy to. Any given moment one of us might openly cry, crumble, withdraw or, if needed, blow up. I got a roommate, then two. Then I was alone again.

I watched with interest the girl with the face painted heavily who would slowly and begrudgingly eat only one saltine cracker for lunch and then only two for dinner. I couldn't escape her stare as I ate heartily, not yet knowing a thing about disordered eating. One girl reminded me of Rizzo from Grease; she met a world she knew to be cruel just as harshly. Another petite girl with a thick bob of unkempt black hair kept her head down over a sketch pad, where incredibly detailed drawings took shape under her hand. She later informed me the images came from her dreams. I also checked out the resident males, in varying stages of height and acne. Half the faces were disguised under greasy curtains of hair, while others showed themselves unabashedly, ears sticking out under buzz cuts. There were at least two dozen of us in total.

Adults don't want to be subdued when riled up. Teenagers feel no differently, and have less patience for authority. Youth are often told to be quiet, to not talk back, to stifle themselves, even as a parent demonstrates the opposite by yelling at them to do so. These young men and women at Emerson, struggling against their own repressed anger, were volcanoes too long dormant. Sometimes kids just need to lose control—and they often do. How else can they release their frustrations with a world they have so little control over? When kids reached their limits in Emerson, when they "lost it" or "went off," they were placed on Unit Restrictions (UR), and at times were physically restrained.

A bout of screaming or yelling could erupt from a patient at any time, and a pair of counselors with firm but monotoned voices would ask them to try to calm down. When the calm couldn't come, and an episode pitched higher, the same two counselors would lower their voices, move in slow and close to give another verbal plea to calm or "pull it together." Troubled individuals may know what pulling it together means in theory, yet without tools in possession, it can be a battle to calm themselves. Chances were always given, options offered for taking a break or, as it was known, a "time out," or offers of going to talk with someone privately, quietly. Sometimes those offers were accepted. When they were not, another two counselors would swoop onto the floor, moving through the halls, calmly asking the rest of us to stay inside our rooms or doorways until otherwise notified. Unit Restrictions were used in times of individual upset or group distress. This always had one of two outcomes, either motivating a kid to calm down or inciting more destructive behaviors. Acting out physically, whether by throwing something, kicking furniture, or hitting a wall with their hand or head—there was no next request, and three to four coordinated counselors moved in to restrain the teen before they could harm themselves or others.

The first time I saw a kid "go off," I hadn't been "in" more than two days. It was a traumatizing scene. No matter where you are in life, if you have ever seen a fight break out, you know that tensions rise, crowds gather, and a collective heart rate climbs. By that time the only real fights I had ever observed were when Dad got mad at Little John a couple times, or when high school boys full of machismo were going at it in the hallway or cafeteria. This level of tension at Emerson was distinctively different from what I had ever seen in the schoolyard. To witness this one-sided fight, someone literally fighting themselves, with nothing specifically aimed at these counselors, was beyond my imagination. Intense, to witness such internal upheaval, to experience a heightened state of restlessness on a psychiatric floor full of young people all standing on their own precipice.

During this kind of restraint procedure, a young body would resist with a typical fight-or-flight response. Wrestling with the counselor team didn't last longer than a few seconds. These counselors were well trained, having done this type of coordinated subdual countless times. Systems were in place for quickly disarming a patient, safely holding a twisting body alive with unrest, even as feet flailed and cracked voices cried out. Bystanders all, we could only watch. With no time for staff to close all our doors, and a policy to keep them open until bedtime anyway, it was really hard to look away from that scene and not also become upset yourself, especially when it was one of your new friends. Streams of obscenities, yelling, tear-filled and strained pleas for release sadly became more common in an approximately biweekly event. Yells quieted as the tangled group moved their way down the hall. We all felt victimized and constrained right along with whichever kid had been taken, whether for several hours or overnight.

Atmosphere on the floor was altered afterwards, negative ions activated. Counselors remained on high alert for anyone else entering a dangerous place mentally. Spending time going from room to room, checking in on us, asking if we needed to talk. A piece of me stood in solidarity with my fellow patient and bucked the authority that had clamped down on them, but more often I found a larger part of myself glad that someone was there to prevent that young person from hurting themselves or anyone else. Boundaries set in my household were outlined in the spankings Dad had landed on me or Little John. Heather towed a straighter line, and was too frail as a youngster to stand up to a spanking. School paddlings and hallway fights—all these past scenes had a weak resemblance to what I was seeing and feeling now.

As difficult as being physically removed must have been for dented pride and mortification, these young adults appeared significantly calmer afterwards, following their episode of constraint. Not all, mind you, but many. I couldn't believe watching them joke with the care team about it after and move deeper into a state of their healing. Repeatedly kids progressed quickly post restraint. What a release of emotion it must have been, as well as a drain— probably the first time some of these kids had felt emotional exhaustion or discovered boundaries and consequences. As seen in nature, when pressure builds, a top must blow before the dust can settle.

I did not personally lose control or require any restraint while there, not that I wasn't irritable or outraged. I was asked to calm down twice; I had simply been able to choose calmer behaviors in those moments. But to say that I did not feel I belonged there in those first days, cannot be overstated. I honestly felt I didn't need what these other kids must, setting myself apart. What did I have in common with teens that "went off" regularly, kids who had suffered from incest, assault, severely impaired esteem, chemical imbalances, had eating disorders, abused alcohol or struggled with drug addiction?

Though not apparent immediately, it turned out we all had the task of being teenagers facing real problems, without tools to handle ourselves or situations in common. We were all seeking ways to cope with our traumas, which ranged wildly from feelings of inadequacy to significant mental or behavioral disorders, assault or abuse. Though the tragedy suffered from a loved one's murder was more rare, there was no shortage of trauma from death, rape, addiction, misguided family principles and miscommunication among my fellows.

Oh, I obtained quite an education inside, learning creative new ways to act out if I so chose. We are impressionable beings. I tried binging and making myself sick a few times after I got out; I drank a bit more at parties, but clung to control too much to lose myself in drugs.

Studying my peers at Emerson, eventually their stories and hardships became of profound interest and importance to me as I weighed and rated myself, my own misfortunes, my worth and value against others in that place. Judgment is more difficult to sustain when you have a person's face, name and story behind their actions or thoughts. Who could say which of us actually had it the hardest? After one week I was certain I did not. Still, I wrote pitiful drivel about my "lot in life" in journals and denied the role I was being asked to play in my own "recovery," whatever that meant. Keeping a lower vulnerability profile in Emerson at first, within a week I could no longer hide the fact that I was enraged. Trading what I saw as being trapped at home for being trapped here, I felt tricked into my stay and was so hurt that I became hurtful. I'd leave Mom to wait at length in the visitor room after her long days at her new job—once I left her waiting alone and did not come out at all. I inflicted pain to redirect my own. Aiming to drag her into my depths, I instigated, yelling "I hate you!" to the one person who genuinely wanted to see me whole, happy and well. Holding myself accountable or responsible wasn't an ability I'd yet acquired. Hell, most adults haven't acquired it. I was not in possession of the awareness, knowledge or words to understand what was happening. Lashing out was far easier. Easier is the way most people choose to go.

Hate. What a formidable, forceful word, one with abiding tenacity. Affected each time I hear it, I rarely, if ever, choose to use it now. Words matter. Ask anyone who knows me, I don't hate anything except willful ignorance, and I certainly didn't hate my only parent then. I just needed to say I hated her, as the only extent of measure I could think of to transmit my misery. Teenagers fling "hate" around when an inadequate vocabulary cannot share the weights carried. Deflecting from uncertainty, things become "stupid" when not understood or when worry and intimidation tell us that we won't be any good at them. We fling "love" around too, for things as overwhelming as lust or arbitrary as lip gloss and ice cream. Youth cannot know any better. Admitting that time and experience will be our truest teachers, would render meaningless the limited experiences of our teenage years. We're too proud for that.

Our parents bear the brunt of our words, as we have borne theirs. Extrapolate to imagine how society later bears the burden of a child without support. What is the totality of neglect? Society always ends up paying that cost.

I was fortunate enough to still have my mom. From an early age she was the only person I knew I could truly count on. From my earliest memories I sought comfort and aid from her. I trusted her to stick around, to withstand the tempest of emotions that damaged, but did not break her. Whether our parents can make things better or not, we look to them until we grow up, and oftentimes even blame them for our own adult shortcomings. Rarely do we see our parents as discrete people. I was in my early 30s and a parent myself before I truly saw my mother as a woman, daughter, sister, friend or professional. Before that she was simply my mom, and I was entitled in my mind to treat her however I wanted.

When I would cast hatred towards her in Emerson, unvanquished by my hurtful veneer, Mom would smile slightly, a tear in her eye, and say, "Well, I love you, Holly." Then, she would sadly turn to walk away, trusting others to help me when I wouldn't allow her to do so. My mother, knowing I was aching, did not rise to my fight, unintentionally laying bare the bluster of my stormy mind. To be mean, truly mean spirited, merely because I could, was not how I'd been raised. Confronted by my own anger in the face of such disarming, unconditional love, felt fundamentally wrong. Any immediate gratification in the wince I'd caused her was quickly lost and I was left craving another chance to prove superiority rather than deal with my own accountability. Any hurt I intended to inflict on her, blew back on me. Realizing Patricia Powell, decidedly without malice, glazed in tears and compassion, upright in her vulnerability and kindness, was far stronger than I, my admiration for my mother grew.

8:01 p.m. Sunday night 1-10-88

I just read this whole diary. It's pretty sad. I bet if my mom read it she'd cry. I have to stay in my room all the time now cause of UR (unit restrictions). I can't stand being in this room alone. I drew two pictures w/ markers explaining my fright and my isolation feelings. (…) Time seems to stand still in here. You don't remember what day it is and an hour seems like 3 or 4 hours. I think one of the reasons that I cry to my mom is cause I feel nobody wants to listen to my problems in this place. Or that I'm tired of acting hard & unfeeling around her & I want to be emotional and I want to be able to feel comfortable telling her how I feel. Maybe its both reasons. I'd really like to be closer to my mom.
—Holly—

From a diary of my time in Emerson North beginning January 3, 1988

ANOTHER WEEK PASSED, and routine set in. Withholding as much as I could from everyone for spite, left me emotionally and physically drained, exhaustion slowly sucking away any control I had. Inside of Emerson, my calm often remained elusive as emotions regularly swept me off my feet and landed me with a face full of tears in my room. We were warned to think carefully; our counselors reminded us that once we were "on the outs," or that after release from Emerson, choices would become more difficult. Staying calm became a decision. With this realization came the power of choice, one that I could make, if I wanted.

Relishing my other choice daily, of what to drink with breakfast, apple juice comforted me every morning, and "It's the little things" started to make more sense. School work was attempted if not completed before lunch, and we moved between art or music therapy around our psychiatrist appointments and group sessions. I found comfort in painting most afternoons. My dog, Matti, became my mental model for art class. I missed her the way you miss the only soul in the world who understands you. Eighty pounds of love, she gave more to me than I would ever give her. That pure, beautiful being whose face stayed lit for me in a dark place was so loved. Stored in the basement there is still paint put to canvas of that soft rusty brown fur wrapping her sweet snout.

Several roommates came and went while I was there, young women whom I easily would have passed unawares on any street had not our troubles brought us together. Several became confidants during that time, trading blue jeans and secrets with me after lights went out. Friendships forge fast and tight from immediacy of need and depth of vulnerabilities. It was as if I were in battle at Emerson and these peers were my allies. Bedtime conversations revealed our war-torn homes, where I learned about the good life I was only now discovering I had.

In the dark of our shared room my eyes were opened to the weight of my own wealth versus the pinch of poverty other girls felt. I saw first-hand the damage done by a dysfunctional family. I saw through a young woman's eyes the unforgiving mirror held in her hand and mind, that expanded her waistline, trash talked her looks and told her not to eat. My ears could not believe or understand the ravages and cravings of drug use until I heard about the desperate lengths a rich girl will go to feed a habit. These girls were victims too, though our perpetrators were vastly different. Common threads were found in the ghosts that haunted our dreams and the crushes that caught our eyes. Our shared frustration of not feeling heard fell on deaf ears, so we listened to each other.

What I heard was that my family, though fractured and sadly fewer in number, was not evil, twisted, or neglectful. They were not too wealthy nor too poor, and were significantly more supportive and structured than that of my peers. Obviously I found myself in a situation that I had taken for granted.

7:55 p.m. 1-14-88

I had my family meeting today at 3:30. I knew all I would talk about is how unfair I feel I'm being treated & that I want to go home. And I did. It was pretty bad. I cried and I was mean. I hate being so mean. I want to just be good and adjust partially. (...) I wish I didn't have to be here. But I wish I had a reason more than I do. I'm going to be real calm tomorrow the way I was in school today. I wrote 2 poems.

1987 – "Too Late" by Holly Brians

Did you ever have just one last wish
To tell someone you knew,
That you really cared enough,
And that your love was true?
To explain all your feelings,
As complicated as they are,
To let them know you were really near,
Although you seemed afar.
One never thinks ahead enough,
To see how things might be,
Who would of thought

That the day would come,
When you wouldn't be here with me.

—Holly Brians
For DAD

Required individual and group therapy sessions became less per-
functory, and mostly from boredom, I began to dole out a comment or two, surprised to find people actually listening. As days
crawled by, I contributed more. Caring, empathetic energy bounced
around the room, and when it landed in my lap, I passed it on.
We shared deep sadness in that space, and glossed-over eyes met
across our circle. There were kids here who truly had it rough, with
no cleared paths ahead. Grateful for experiences I did not have to
live through, I learned to empathize with unique issues and others'
concerns. Nobody knows what someone else is carrying or burying.
Maybe these teens had it way worse, but maybe we all had it pretty
bad. It began to dawn on me that it mattered little if someone had
it worse or better than anyone else, given how raw these feelings
were in each of us. Maybe just having pain in heart and mind was
our common bond, the world's bond.

By the time another week passed, I had made more friends.
Becoming aware of myself in a way I couldn't have otherwise, this
time and these people allowed me to view my chances in life very
differently. Home and family contribute a great deal to a person, if
we're fortunate enough to have both. Even so parents cannot teach
wider lessons when children are made the center of their world or
become an unnoticed moon circling their own troubled system.
Balance of parental and outside influence and experience must be
struck. My own mom's visits continued, and I learned I hadn't lost
her love despite my outward hate-filled display. She, the scarred
yet unbroken rock, exposed to the harsh effects of her daughter's
unpredictable climate, was all the more beautiful and loving for it.

Mail call was a welcome sight that not everyone on the floor got to see, as envelopes bearing my name were placed in appreciative hands with return addresses of grandparents and aunts. Gratitude grew for the family I was lucky enough to be born into.

Every bit of my independent self in many ways, even then, I rarely confided in others. Moving into a solitary place of decision-making, I learned to trust my gut implicitly. Nevertheless, I was becoming tethered to my peers, thinking of more than just myself, growing aware of my privileges or blessings as some would call them. There was comfort in knowing I wasn't alone in strife, but I still often chose my own company and sought my own counsel.

1–15–88 8:15 p.m.

Today I've been good. No saying "I hate it here". I don't mind being slap happy & fun cause I otherwise would constantly think about when I'm getting out. I'm going to be good on pass too. Mom and John are coming tomorrow afternoon. I'm going to just discuss our pass. I'm trying hard. Only cause I want to be home working and trying, not here. But what can I do. I'm in here (…) I can't make her get me out. She's determined that she's doing the right thing. I'm better accepting the fact that I'm in here but thats because I hate being so miserable and I have to do something. (…) Plans for Pass: Heather's going to come and we'll go out to eat. Then shopping (…) wherever they want to go. But I'd like to go home to see John & dogs. I miss them a lot. Living my life by the guidelines of getting out of here. I hate that!! Me.

8:35 p.m. 1–17–88 Sunday night

I'm back. It went great. No crying or begging to go home & lately I've not been quite so angry. I'm happier now. Maybe this place is doing me some good. I might only be here one or two more weeks.

8:56 1-20-88

It's been quite a few hours since I've written, a lot has happened. (...) My attitude has drastically changed for the better. I'm not angry anymore. I don't know why but I can just laugh w/ mom & I don't feel any anger towards her. Mom is very nice. I feel better about myself. I'm looking forward to this weekend's pass. Mom came to visit me tonight and it went really well. I won't be here much longer. Me.

Privileges, such as open or closed family visits and phone calls were earned, reinforced by what were deemed "positive behaviors." Arriving on time, opening up or sharing in group were called "active engagements"; when you provided a "lift" to someone else around the room, it was noted. My release date was all I could focus on, desperately wanting a specific date to hold out on a horizon that would fly me home. Anchored better into routine and making progress, I was no longer adrift on emotional outbursts or stormy fits, and found a calm in feeling somewhat stable.

Visits from extended family were finally allowed, and my siblings and I sat close on cornered sofas in the shared space on the main floor. Jealous and excited, we patients stalked each other's family and friend visits from further spots down the hall, waiting to see whether it was a rough or a good visit, or if we might even be called over to be introduced as new friends to their family. Bizarre how in each other's business we were. Soon phone calls were reinstated, and I awkwardly dodged other patients for privacy in the communal space where the phone cord and I rested tight against the wall. Familiar voices pushed through from the other end of the line in strings of friendly, caring, small talk, often threaded with a hint of concern. Some voices were unable to evolve along with me and lacked the words I most needed to hear.

Anne, the friend I was hanging out with junior year prior to my admission, was further down on my call list. We were thick as thieves, having spent a great deal of time together that fall, and I was impatient to tell her everything, especially about some of the boys I sort of liked or at least didn't mind looking at in Emerson. Finally, the day came when I was approved for this goal I'd built up in my mind to achieve, to call Anne and return to the safety of a friend's voice outside of Emerson. It had been weeks since we'd talked, and my excitement at just hearing her voice must have gushed through the phone. My jubilation was met with a strong indifference. Hanging out with some other girl now, Anne was friends with so and so, who she described as really cool. She even began sharing some of the fun things they'd been up to. Anne didn't appear to have missed me at all, and if she did, it was worth her mentioning how replaceable I was. No questions about my time away, my health or well-being came my way. Small talk died, leaving nothing to say. As tears filled my eyes, the sound of her silence choked me. I could not know she was flaunting her friend to sting me for leaving her.

Counselors helped me process that disappointment and told me about the flow of people that need to come in and out of our lives to heal. Some folks are simply not supposed to be with us for the long haul. Lessons learned from entrances and exits in life alert us to those who are meant to stay.

Passes home for eight-hour weekend visits were motivation to stay on task, to work the problem. The more I worked, the better I felt. The better I felt, the more people I was able to spend time with. An in-person visit from a dear friend followed, the other Holly, whom I've known since I was ten. There was a chalky pill of pride to swallow at first, being seen by her in this strange place, this psychiatric hospital. She met me with only love. Another lesson, moving through the pinprick of pride. True friendships meet without awkwardness and find us where we need to be.

Bathed in a halo of light from the small desk lamp, I bent over my journal each evening before "lights out." My one haven. On the pad of glowing paper before me, with each imprint of my pen lay entries for the person I hoped to someday become. Ink pulled the weight from my shoulders and laid it down. Sleep, another visitor I hadn't met in a while, dropped into my bed by the tall window on the east wall and shared several hard to shake visions in heavily draped dreams. Peering down, the moon painted recurring dreams on the backs of my eyes as it watched over me at Emerson. Uncertainty lingered between me and whatever was coming next.

During this time I began to identify the major players in my life. The red motorcar of anger raced up my spine and flagged my cheeks. The physical heft and doom of depression moved slow and thick like a fog through my head, slumping shoulders, sapping my energy. The shrill sound of anxiety in my ears could paralyze or make me jumpy, sicken my stomach, making breathing difficult. Panic boxed me in a sweltering tomb. Powerlessness tightened like a band cinched around my head, shrinking my options. Heartache left a gaping, aching hole in my chest, stabbing my solar plexus. Grief moved through my memory like a scissor cutting color and shape from my life, trimming sharp corners, dulling the finish.

Recognizing these unwanted companions physically meant potentially I could change the effect they had on my inner life. Without knowing how I was feeling it was going to be more difficult to work through emotions; I needed to name them, see them for who they were.

Calm, that steady beat allowing smiles to cross my face without effort, started to walk with me occasionally. Counselors took notice and began to rely on me to welcome and settle arrivals of newer patients. Lessons, strung on the ropes I'd just learned, tested out on weeks old versions of myself walking through Emerson's doors. Uncovered ears heard some new truths sing. Counselors began to have genuine, albeit professional conversations with me, trusting me to hear their own life experiences, snapshots of what most humans endure and survive. These people had fallen apart and put themselves back together, often repeatedly. What strangely seemed to drive them forward was working with someone like me. Selfless adults all, finding purpose by paying their pain forward, I found that I admired them for it. I got close to a couple of counselors, a man in his late twenties and a woman in her early thirties, who both had a relaxed energy, and knew how to remain steady when I was not. They did not escalate troubles in my mind. There was little they hadn't heard in their line of work; my issues became some of the least shocking things they had heard.

The freedom I found while confined was that I wasn't judged for my struggles and that I did not need to judge others for theirs.

1-22-88

I skipped a day Sorry. I'll tell what happened. I wrote Donald Harvey a letter in school & -- kept asking what was wrong, -- saw a couple tears, I pushed him away even though I didn't mean to. (...) I took a time out. Then I had Loss Support Group & we had to say goodbye to -- & --. I cried bad. (...) I've been able to talk to Dr. -- easier & --(counselor) saw the letter I wrote Harvey. Today I guess will be a good day.

All around me dwelled youth in different phases of pain. In new patients I could see the difficulty of their starting points. When I slipped, and I did, I could catch myself before I fell too far by taking a time-out for myself or seeking out someone to listen, whether it was my diary, the staff or peers. It was so much better than the unsatisfying exhaustion of being angry all the time. I'd moved through another stage of grief.

According to Dr. Elisabeth Kübler-Ross and David Kessler, those stages are denial, anger, bargaining, depression and acceptance, and at Emerson we were taught how to recognize them. (A psychological standard in 1987, the "Five Stages of Grief" are now recognized as limiting at best, much like outdated thinking on learning styles.) Though close to what I experienced, this is not the only way to process or understand our reactions to a traumatic loss.

We each go at our own pace trudging through grief, often getting stuck. Steps that might walk myself and my peers out of these antique doors became clear. Wanting that peace and freedom for them, and for myself so badly, to be deemed well enough to go home—honestly, it only occurred much later that by helping others, I was helping myself.

"Institutionalized" refers to someone who, having been living in a residential situation, be it for health or imprisoned for crime, has learned everyday conventions of survival, or in other words, the safe ways of functioning there. A reliance gradually develops upon systems which at first seem an affront, soon become a comfort and finally, are a barrier to fear of the unknown that lay outside the door. "On the outs" we called it, when one of us had been released or discharged from Emerson. Several kids left only to land right back in during my time there, unable to handle life on the outside. I would eventually come to understand that.

7:54 p.m. Saturday 1-23-88

Just returned from pass. I'll tell you about last night first. I'm on UR (unit restriction) again cause I was a minute or 2 late for A.C.. -- was supposed to wake me up. So last night was pretty bad. I cried cause I missed --(roomate) & cause I was afraid that I was going to forget all my memories of my step dad. A new girl came last night. I talked to --(counselor staff). She helped then we watched Raising Arizona.

1-27-88 11:03 p.m.

I was happy most of the day cause of my DC date (discharge). Got it Tuesday at my family meeting. As soon as she said the word discharge, I smiled so big, I couldn't help it. It's February 10th. The night of the Harvey support meeting w/ Bill Whalen.

The next fourteen days I rode the high of my discharge, entering a hierarchy among the few of us given such a date. Having for weeks looked in awe upon those with that certain distinction, I could now sense the same looks upon me. Leaving was all the motivation I needed to stay on track, to focus in school and in group. Strong and better equipped, I assured my doctor as such.

The day of my discharge, all packed and set to leave, I said my goodbyes. Leaving is a big deal, having experienced the joy and weight of it for other patients' discharges. Conflicting, knowing you want your friends to be well enough to leave you. I too, was both happy and sad to be going. Thanking my counselors, they advised me to keep working, to use my tools and to be well. Hugs and tears were allowed for a half hour before a discharge. Friends staying behind to work on themselves signed my goodbye book, just as I had signed theirs. Hopeful words, memories shared, and promises to write filled the thick pink construction paper pages bound with spiral wire. For those friends I would especially miss, I wished discharge dates soon. Encouraged by staff not to share our outside contact details (far easier back then without smartphones), they made statements contextualizing our resentment and attachments, saying it was important to move on from this time and these people as a lesson, not a way of life.

Baggage packed felt lighter in my hand as I waved goodbye and walked off the floor. Entering the "real world" after embracing the safety of being "inside" would at times be difficult, I knew, but I had the support of my mom who had stood by me through it all. Weeks after going through those front doors I walked out better understood and more understanding, feeling significantly more confident in my abilities.

Strange as it may sound, I feel pride for my time at Emerson North. I hope every life that touched mine while there is surviving and better. The building itself, by the way, was demolished; Cincinnati Children's Hospital now runs an adolescent psychiatric treatment facility in College Hill, exactly where Emerson North once stood. That parcel of land, it would seem, is ripe for digging deep into the wounds so often sown in hearts and minds.

For anyone reading this amidst their own struggle, please seek professional help for yourself or your children, and please be patient with yourself and them in the process.

❖

Mom ARRIVED IN THE LOBBY she had left me in nearly six weeks
earlier. Days clung to the light longer now, and we tightly hugged,
happy to see each other on this end. Steering away from Emerson
into the slow traffic of rush hour, we weren't heading home. First,
since I'd been insistent, we drove directly to the meeting planned
with other victims' families not far away, at Talbert House on
Reading Road. That very same day as my discharge, Bill Whalen,
Donald Harvey's defense attorney, was scheduled to speak to the
victims' families. Mom knew I wanted to be among those present.

A circle of mixed folding chairs filled in as I walked in through
the fading light of dusk, recognizing other victims' family members,
familiar faces met or seen at Drake Hospital or in that sweltering
courtroom. Mom and I found two seats together, and joining the
group added to polite conversation. Bill Whalen soon arrived in his
suit and overcoat with the dimming day, carrying a professional yet
cordial demeanor along with his briefcase. We got right to it. Slight
and balding, the attorney walked the inner circle and began with
a small thank-you and welcome statement. He agreed to answer
questions prompted by family members. To be clear, there were
no answers he could provide that would bring solace to a crowd
already emotional, and morbidly curious. One victim's son stood
out, the acrimony sharp in his voice. His grief appeared lodged in
the anger stage, and his emotions escalated. The rest of the group,
all wounded people who were easily agitated, followed suit.

In a strangely condensed display of all I'd just witnessed in
Emerson North, the participants in this group session seemed to
be in danger of "going off"—but these were adults! No mediator
was present. No thoughtful guide was taking us through turmoil in
turn, asking us to respect each other or suggesting we take a "time
out." Accusations, defenses and denial spun unhelpfully around the
room. Despite the combined lessons of almost six weeks of intense
therapy, spectator stress removed my ability to speak, leaving me
entirely isolated in the room. The group's passions rose and fell in
hateful and sorrowful waves, and I became caught up in the seismic
wave, overwhelmed. Unable to focus on anything other than my

own discomfort, I quietly excused myself before I drowned. Pain exploded in my chest the minute I stepped into the ladies' room; a sharp spasm tightened hard, making breathing difficult. Fear for my life roiled my stomach as my head pounded, gasping for air. Supported by cold stone, I slid down the wall, slouching, half sprawled on the floor. Clutching my sweater, I imagined I might be dying, adding to my paralyzing fear. Breath felt impossible. Mouth gaped open, my diaphragm strained and yet little to no air came in. Chest pain this severe must mean a heart attack, I thought. Decision abilities were unavailable; only pain and terror lived in me in that moment. After minutes that felt like eons, a woman who had come into the washroom for the usual reason found me on the floor visibly struggling for air, and ran for help.

My concerned mother was fast at my side, as an ambulance was called. Soon EMTs rushed into the bathroom, assessing me before the lift onto a gurney as they rushed me to the back of an emergency vehicle. Quickly on our way, my chest heaved, my throat dried completely as an oxygen mask was pressed over my mouth. A very worried Mom followed in our car close behind. Arriving at the hospital, my gurney was pushed through to a curtained area in the ER revealing new levels of anxiety, spiking high from being back inside another hospital so soon. I was surprised to be conscious. Doctors ran tests and asked questions which my Mom attempted to answer. After a while, a brown paper bag was pushed to my face, a nurse encouraging me to take slower, deeper breaths, until eventually constriction lessened and air began filling my lungs, slowing my heart. The agony in my chest slowly released its grip. I turned on my side, worn-out. Taking my pulse, a doctor determined I'd be fine.

Here is where I learned the true power of panic. No longer would I underestimate the influence the mind has over the body. There is little controlling panic when it decides to attack; only patience and reassurance can call it off a person. Not as well known then, anxiety is extremely common for anyone undergoing high levels of physical or emotional stress. I was prone to both by simply leaving that institution at Emerson, let alone insisting on attending such a highly charged meeting on the way home. More lessons in what we each can handle.

My mind holds this picture of a teenage me, experiencing this panic attack, wearing exactly what I wore to my Dad's funeral visitation. The same ensemble worn that sad and rainy night was also previously worn to an extended family wedding, I have a photograph of me dressed in it then. I cannot be sure if I actually wore that outfit to the Whalen meeting, the night I thought my heart might explode, or if somewhere in my mind, the association or depth of memory has me reliving the tragic moment of standing at Dad's casket, realizing he was really gone. Armchair psychology at its best. Whatever I wore, that particular sweater and skirt stays in my mind as an outfit donned only for such occasions and has even dressed me in some dark dreams.

HOME FROM TWO HOSPITALS in one day, I finally walked through my front door, really happy to see my dog. Thankful to be with her, back in my room, my immediate relief was short-lived, though: Home doled out an anguish all its own, marked by memory and sadness. Life carried on amidst languishing grades and the social suicide of trying to explain six weeks of absence to schoolmates. Holly, my longtime friend, was a true companion. Attending a different school, she was removed enough to be undeterred or unconcerned with what others thought; she simply cared for me and what I was going through, which placed no barriers around our friendship. Having visited me in Emerson North, she made sure to come see me right after I was "out." Most of my other friends at school, though, were not in a place to understand or offer support, so I often suffered alone with my family, and they with me. Returning to school was a challenge but one that presented a continuing education. Nothing in life was certain, anything could easily change—and so could I.

Forced treatment and contemplation turned out to be the

greatest gift I ever allowed myself to receive. Life, at times, forces us to stop in order to repair parts broken or in need of reinforcement. Choosing to act on the repairs or not, both are decisions we get to make. Walking away with the knowledge that my life is directly affected by my own reactions was powerful, though it took quite some time to adjust to. There is no magic pill to prevent downfall or despair. Emerson taught me to do the work of facing emotions, confronting things about myself that I didn't like or weren't serving me well.

The level of impatience I possessed then, is something I still work on today. At times irrational, I'm led to unreasonable expectations; a need to fix things immediately. Be it an argument or confrontation, I live knowing that in the event someone dies before either of us apologize, I will have to live with it. Fear of regret is, for me, a far heavier burden to bear than the discomfort or indignity of foregoing pride, convention, ego or shame. This urge to confront is what motivated me with my father years later and has saved or challenged other relationships. Inexplicable control issues were harder to tame or explain away, but these are the bags we claim and must carry on a journey such as this. Somehow, I grew stronger by exposing my vulnerabilities. After all this time, it has become clear to me that we need both strength and vulnerability to fully heal ourselves and others.

My family has also evolved through their pain with varying degrees of difficulty. Despite our shared and individual struggles, I am truly proud that we all came out the other side without hatred and bitterness in our hearts. Still, it took decades, hard decisions and much soul-searching to stand where we do today.

17

help [help] *verb* (used with object)
1. to give or provide what is necessary to accomplish a task or satisfy a need; contribute strength or means to; render assistance to; cooperate effectively with; aid; assist
2. to save; rescue; succor
3. to make easier or less difficult; contribute to; facilitate

DESPITE THAT PIVOTAL TIME at Emerson North, nothing felt right for too long. Second semester of junior year, 1988, was a blur of distractions. Though I had acquired better tools, I still struggled to make sense of the fear that crept up on me, a defeating anxiety that prevented even small tasks from being accomplished. That spring I missed more and more school days. Nightmares paralyzed me; I'd often wake with a terrifying fear that Mom was going to die. Harvey's face could haunt my dreams with clarity as Dad's face began to fade. Scarce sleeping intensified. Insomnia slithered into my bed and even as of last night has not left.

My mood was often hijacked by benign reminders, street signs bearing the name "Harvey" or the inevitable recurrence of anniversaries, birthdays and holidays without our full family. I began to dress in myriad shades of black, craving The Cure, The Replacements, Erasure, Depeche Mode and the Eurythmics, Simple Minds, Thompson Twins… more empathetic music, now referred to as Emo, that better suited my angsty mood. In order to overthrow the power of my mind, I continued to consume myself with books by Ben Johnson, Alice Walker, Sinclair Lewis, Nathaniel

Hawthorne, George Orwell, and even more of my dark friend Poe. I found a few new friends, people who were easy to be with. A group of skater boys became a fixture in my weekends, and we would hang out in Cincinnati's emptied center, on Fountain Square. In charge of the boom box, I'd flip the cassette tapes over as trucks and boards clunked on concrete around me. I sipped my first Mad Dog 20/20 and Boone's Farm on rooftops in Clifton, and drove around with guys I barely knew, who weren't sober. Zooming around bends and along the tree-lined ridges of the West Side, Rybolt Road sent us flying over the unknowns of narrow blacktopped hills at night. I wasn't doing anything most teenagers don't try and parents deny, but I wasn't fully functioning in all areas of my life. Schoolwork took a backseat, as I spent my energy on anything other than studying. Soon even these diversions didn't hold, and I had to admit I needed more help.

By the end of junior year, tapped out and fearful, I'd stopped going to school at all, insisting that Mom call me in sick. Every day I passed at home made the prospect of returning to school the next day that much more difficult to face. Worried, Mom tried to do what she thought was best. In the end neither of us could deny a school policy on absences that added up to truancy, or the clear fact that I needed more support. I agreed to be admitted into another psychiatric residential program. Available beds for treatment in any city are limited for teens, and at this time Millcreek Psychiatric Center for Adolescents, had the only available bed, and was a vastly different environment to Emerson North in every possible way.

Upon entry, Millcreek certainly did not extend the warm welcome of a renovated Victorian manor; my first impression of this stay, compared to my last, was one of boxed sterility. The space felt overcrowded and disjointed to its purpose: punitive, not compassionate. Staff, with a few notable exceptions, seemed short-tempered, obligated by pay more than driven by skill or passion to help troubled teens. We slept in stuffy shared quarters that summer, with at least a dozen beds per room (each with a nightstand, no desks) providing little personal space or privacy. Some of the staff clearly lacked proper training to handle us, leveling verbal assaults, overstepping with inappropriate prying, and in several memorable instances, violating the verbal and physical boundaries expected of caregivers.

Shift guards walked the halls after nightfall, opening each door to check that nobody was roaming when they were supposed to be asleep. Flashlights pushed into darkness, sweeping the room, ensuring beds were safely filled and all inmates were accounted for. Searching the room should have taken ten to fifteen seconds, tops. However, those flashlights were held by twenty- to forty-year-old men, and their beams hovered for minutes on end upon each of us girls—girls who, in the heat of summer, wore less to bed or whose pajama tops or nighties wound up around their middles from restlessness. Insomnia had me often awake when they made rounds, twice a night, just past 1 a.m. and again after 4 a.m. The lit beams scanned our beds top to bottom, lingering on every enticing patch of exposed underaged skin. When the light found me, I always played dead with my eyes shut, interminable moments fraught with alarm; I lay frozen. Looking back, I wish I'd sat bolt upright and called out those pervs, but I did not. Teenaged girls rarely understand their power. Waves of insecurity incapacitate us. Dread washes over young women in the face of potential danger, especially where adult males are concerned. Choosing to hide rather than fight, I waited, attempting to blend into the swarm of girls by flying low. By the end of my stay at Millcreek, I woke each night at 1:21, the red digital clock announcing a warning that stayed with me for several years after.

At the end of May, I turned seventeen. Still a child in plenty of ways, I also felt too grown-up for the kids I resided with. More comfortable with adults, I mostly conversed with staff and counselors—as mentioned, several were exceptions, good people with caring hearts, making small dents where they could. They stand in contrast to what was an accepted norm at Millcreek.

Continuing my treatment, another unfortunate encounter with power and domination occurred. Around the grounds there was a male counselor, a strong guy with ripped muscles, shaved face and head. Not having him in my care team, I hadn't spoken directly with him, though I'd walk past him at least once daily. One late afternoon, as I made my way between buildings, out of nowhere, he advanced on me in an outdoor courtyard. Knowing I was walking alone, he took advantage, quickly grabbing my wrist and herding me toward the side wall, out of sight. I was shocked at how quickly I found myself squeezed between this man and the building I'd been passing, away from any windows. Pressing himself against me, full-body, upon the rough block wall, and still holding my wrist, he then placed his other forearm on the wall over my head.

We could not be seen from our location, a point I am certain this counselor had planned or practiced before. Terror held me in place as much as his strength did. Tending to laugh nervously (yes, at funerals or when my brother was spanked as a child), I did so then, lightly. He stared at me intently. To ease myself, I started talking, the way I always did when worried, saying something like, "Hey, I have to be at my next appointment and really have to go." Fighting against him would prove pointless, I knew. His goal was to intimidate me, to make it clear that he could take what he wanted, when and where he wanted it. With his free hand he touched my face and hair, then he started talking, saying how much he liked me, that he liked watching me, that he wanted to see me on the "outside." I could only assume he was one of the silhouettes with a flashlight at night.

His hot breath hovered close over my face. Trying to stay calm, I said something about having a boyfriend (which I did not), then thought to say again that I had to get to an appointment: "My doctor is waiting." Doctors didn't wait, there or anywhere, everyone knew that. People would come looking for me. Releasing my wrist, with his body still up against me, he stroked my arm, running his fingers slowly up then down the side of my breast and hip. Restraining my breathing, I met his intense gaze with all the indifference I could muster. Finally he pushed his body off of me, backed up slowly, allowing me to pass. Wanting to run, I moved slowly, worried he might chase his prey. Casually, he promised to keep an eye on me. And that he did.

Taking different routes around the hospital campus, walking

only accompanied, I avoided this predator as best I could. He must have gotten into my records, because twice he called my home when I was away from Millcreek on weekend passes. One such time while at home on an overnight pass, my good friend Holly and I went to dinner with her dad, Brian, a really fun-loving, good and protective man. I'd known him since I was ten, so I confided to them both over dinner about this guy at Millcreek who had touched me and had been calling me at home. Telling someone else how anxious this person made me, and how hard it was to feel safe at Millcreek, really took a load off. Afterward, the mood lightened, and Brian and Holly and I enjoyed the rest of our meal together. The three of us sang loudly with the windows down all the way home.

When we arrived at my house, still chatting, Holly and Brian saw me inside to say goodnight, and to say hi to my mom. Just as we stepped inside the door, the kitchen phone rang, and without a thought, I picked it up. Brian saw my face drop as I answered the call. He was quick to understand: this very same counselor was calling me again. Brian motioned with his finger at the phone and I slowly nodded, handing him the receiver. Brian raised it to his mouth, and said evenly, but with menace, "I know who you are. I know where you live, and if you ever touch Holly again, I will find you and kill you." Then he hung up the phone. We stood there silent, mouths agape, before our nervousness burst into frenzied laughter, defusing that heavy situation. Mom walked into the hall not having a clue what just happened.

Thankfully, Brian's warning worked. Though I received intense leers regularly on campus, that particular counselor never spoke to me again.

I am so grateful to Brian—indebted to him, truly, and sad that he is no longer alive to hear me say it. But he understood how essential it is for well-intentioned men, who are able, to step into the role of safeguarding young women from those with bad intentions, especially if there is no father to look to for protection. Beholden as I am to men who ward off the aggressions of others, what new levels of liberty would women experience if we lived without fear of encroachment by anyone? If bodily autonomy and respect were such well-established norms, that we could see our children safe from predators and raise our daughters to walk in the world without fear?

ENDURING MY TIME at another mental wellness hospital, in earnest I worked to recover my sense of self. Any child battling a world outside of themselves is waging a far more dangerous war inside. An assault like the one I experienced is just one of the countless obstacles that can stand in the way of recovery, on either front. It's also a relatively tame example of the barrage of sexual aggressions too many females have to endure. In hindsight, I wish I'd had the courage to report that guy: I might have a saved a string of other girls from his unwelcome attentions—and I'm sure there are many teens who left Millcreek bearing worse scars than mine.

Of course, people of all genders can be abusers of power, or their victims. One day in the break room, while I was talking with some of the other kids and staff, a female counselor who didn't seem to like me (or most of us, to be frank), started to interrupt. Jeering and making snide remarks, she seemed to be instigating a fight.

After letting a few of her remarks slide, I turned to her and asked, "What's the problem?" Now, it is certainly possible that my question carried a tinge of smartassery, but I was still undeserving of her answer. Walking right up to me, pointing a finger in my face, she said, with hate-filled eyes and a tight lip, "You are. You. Are. The problem." Forcing herself into my space, she poked my left shoulder hard with her finger, again and again, walking me backwards toward the wall. Exerting her brawn, she sneered, hissing out her curse: "You will never have any friends. Never. Not one girl will ever truly like you! None!"

Dumbfounded, I felt the heat of humiliation rising in my cheeks. Pulling her lips into a nasty grin, she shoved a finger into my shoulder once more for good measure, jabbing me back into the wall, and then she backed up slowly, smirking as she walked away.

From the wall, I looked back at the few male staff and patients I'd been talking to, their expressions revealing their own alarm and confusion. We had been laughing, talking easily about nothing important, when she leveled her attack. I couldn't imagine what I'd done to her to make her charge me like that. It took years before I understood. We women can be really hard on each other, faulting our delights and deficits. If we don't feel comfortable personally, we take it out on those who do, in a variety of ways. We have all experienced those people who feel stronger when they tear others down.

Enrolled in Millcreek school, I finished an Algebra credit that had eluded me until then. Preferring letters to numbers (have I mentioned math is not my strong suit?), I was thankful that a creative writing group and an art therapy class were offered. The leader of the writing session, a kind woman in her early 30s with premature gray in her long brown hair, encouraged me by publishing one of my poems in the flyer printed for the group.

There at Millcreek, as at Emerson, patients received counseling in both individual and group therapy. Once again it became increasingly clear to me that I didn't have the corner on tough problems; again, it stood out how fortunate I was to have my mom.

My psychiatrist, who didn't seem to enjoy talking with me, determined within one session that I needn't feel emotions so deeply. Within two sessions, and without any diagnoses from my time at Emerson, he attempted to medicate me with "provisional diagnoses" of depression or an unspecified mood disorder. He tried to convince me that my few sips of Mad Dog, one drunken night with Deanna, and a glass of champagne I'd downed at a family New Year's gathering, meant that I was a teenaged alcoholic.

Sadness and anxiety squatted in my mind. Unresolved anger that had led me to Emerson, better expressed through therapy, no longer lived with me. I woke each morning, found joy in art and music, and joined in with friends. I knew I didn't suffer from those particular disorders, because I knew kids who did. Almost every patient there was diagnosed and medicated. Was I emotional?

Um... yes? Prone to internal conflict? Absolutely—in large part, because that is who I am. My main issues of abandonment were not a result of a chemical imbalance; they were due to trauma I had experienced, and indicated a need for therapy.

Millcreek treated children who came from and found themselves in hard places. I cannot imagine the emotional fortitude it takes for any psychological professional to see young people day in and out, kids who are suffering in deep ways and needing your assistance. Yet in that place, in the absence of additional context, perspectives, resources or diagnoses, I felt boxed into what was a standard there. Feeling unheard by my mental healthcare professional, as I processed significant life events, I looked around in comparison to my peers for the care I felt was needed. With what I saw, I had to question before accepting, at face value, what they prescribed.

I was a grieving teen with symptoms of (if I can presume to diagnose my younger self) Post-Traumatic Stress Disorder, though perhaps they didn't call it that, then. My histrionics, lethargy, sleeplessness and anxiety were direct results of what I'd been through. Wanting so desperately to talk through things, I felt my true path of treatment would be found in writing, growing through reading, discussing and learning to understand myself and others. Checking the clock every few minutes, this psychiatrist clearly was disengaged, which discouraged me from talking. Sadly, he spent more time pushing medication than allowing me to discuss my troubles.

Medication absolutely has a place in mental healthcare. Prescribed therapeutics can save lives, create a more balanced mind, limit stress and allow for healing—but those prescriptions can never be one-size-fits-all, whether for youth or adults. What I speak here relates solely to my own personal treatment. Twice at Millcreek, I refused medication, trusting my gut, ready to put in the work of reflection—an evolution that I craved and was convinced I would benefit from. Though personally I did not utilize meds for mood or behavior, at Emerson or Millcreek, I know and trust the drugs' benefits for others, and I'm thankful these therapies exist, should I ever need them myself.

For me at that time, progress came more quickly after I turned down the meds and determined that I might be strong enough to handle life outside. Worry worn at home morning noon and night, leading into my stay at Millcreek, dissipated. I wanted to live my life, not cower in fear from it. Feeling stronger than ever, I began to make the best of my last couple of weeks there.

Radical realization, at seventeen, to find that adults don't have all the answers! Seeing adults who regularly abused their positions—it was as if a curtain had been pulled back. Young people naively think we will grow up to understand life, and from that Day of Enlightenment onward, we'll know how to live, within a framework of sound judgment. What a joke. "Adulting" is what we call it now. Often, our parents and elders seem to:

a) appear to have it all together, and maybe they do, or,
b) either make excuses, or allow themselves to be manipulated, or,
c) use power and intimidation to encourage compliance.

I learned my ABCs.

But no one has a handbook for this thing called Life. Adults mask fear with a show of knowledge and power. Millcreek granted me an awareness I didn't have prior, that adults often are acting out their own past traumas, and we kids were just in the wrong place at the wrong time.

That angry counselor truly did me a favor when she showed her insecurity. I've grown obliged for her warning. Her intention was not to be helpful, and still she prepared me for an inevitability I would face, that most of us face: There will be people who choose to hate or marginalize, rather than seek to understand.

I've used that knowledge to reduce negativity in my life, to extend grace and to bring strong, loving people in. Most hatred comes from a place of torment or uncertainty within. If I can suss out the root cause, then, more often than not, I can carefully sidestep, disarm, or maybe even help a fellow hurting human.

Gaining surer footing within myself, I started to see and understand weakness, and to admire true strength. One wise woman, a part-time counselor at Millcreek, helped me see that I didn't need to attribute others' actions toward me, as an indicator of my worth. Revolutionary! That former Ben-Gal—for all you football fans, those are the cheerleaders for the Cincinnati Bengals—was a lovely individual, a smart and empathetic woman, a petite powerhouse of motivation. We only got to see her twice a week, but in that time she reminded me to stay on the task of helping myself, not wrap myself into the drama of others who needed to learn to do the same. Invaluable, that lesson. Though no life is without drama, over the years I've adopted the airlines' "place the mask on yourself before helping others" policy: I would be no good to anyone if I weren't also, and first, helping myself.

Insecurity reigned among my fellow patient peers, and we ranged from indicted juvenile criminals or terrified depressants to manicky teens, living in the spaces between fear and sadness. We were trying to heal ourselves while simultaneously fighting a system using coercion, power, and fear to control us.

Challenges were overcome while at Millcreek, and I was able to pluck some hard kernels of truth out of those eight weeks. Conversant with new concepts, reaffirming and dismissing long-held thoughts and beliefs, I was awakening to my own abilities, while becoming aware that we humans were all lacking in some areas. For those priceless lessons, and for a few admirable adults I met during my stay, Millcreek wasn't all bad—that is, mostly, because I had survived it.

18

grit [grit] *noun*

1. abrasive particles or granules, as of sand or other small, coarse impurities found in the air, food, water, etc.

2. firmness of character; indomitable spirit; pluck.

W HEN I WAS FINALLY DISCHARGED midsummer, I found everyone at home struggling in their own ways. Heather, in a serious relationship, was losing ground at college and exhibiting some obvious anger toward me. Without my new tools, she couldn't explain why she was mad, so it took a while to figure out that she had needed me at home, and I hadn't been there for her. John was sleeping through the pain of his grief. Mom was trying to navigate our choppy waters while earning her real estate license. The summer ebbed, another school year loomed, and I was not sure how best to face it.

This is when I learned the art of the pivot. Oak Hills High School wasn't serving me well—or, better said, I wasn't taking advantage of my OHHS education, so I begged Mom to allow me a new start at a new school for the upcoming year. Supportive of my request, she re-enrolled me for junior year, a repeat grade, in an all-girls, Catholic school. In my class at Mother of Mercy High School, I knew no other young women, but attending a couple grades below me was Holly, my best friend with the same name, and I was glad that we shared lunch and locker times.

Boxer shorts under pleated plaid school uniform skirts signaled freedom that September. Off went the pressure of appearances as I saw strong young women around me, without the distraction of ogling boys (or them eyeing us). All the hands raised, all the answers called out, came from females of all stripes, from frilly to no-nonsense, athletes to dramatics. Every contribution came from young women, of which I was now one. Feeling apart from the whole nevertheless, as a newcomer, I found opportunities for self-identity and growth. Though some of my schoolmates showed kindness, with a smile or gesture, it was a slow road to friendships, since many of these girls had been attending parochial school to-gether for years, and cliques were well formed—but one girl in my grade named Kim was interested in the new girl, and we began to hang out.

Geometry was grasped far more easily than algebra, thank goodness. Literature class was full of participation, the teacher asking for our views on authors' works from the likes of Steinbeck, Shakespeare, Brontë and Dickinson. We read and discussed *All Quiet on the Western Front* and *The Crucible*. I suppose it was then at Mercy that I recognized I actually had a brain, and enjoyed using it.

Religion class was interesting. As the sole Presbyterian and religious challenger in the building, my researched topics for debate weren't appreciated by the Sisters, though I was only asked to leave the classroom twice.

Debate, I find healthy. For example, when we talk about how Moses parted the Red Sea, as the oppressed Israelites fled the Egyptians, was it a miracle? Some scholars recognize that "the Red Sea" translation could also be called "the sea of reeds," a wetland or lagoon which in that part of the world would dry up half the year—and there might have been a meteorological "miracle" or phenomenon around the time of that dramatic Biblical escape. My point is, these scientific or historical probabilities are either noted, ignored or actively denied, depending on one's education, and yet, empirical knowledge need not take away from religious or spiritual truth. Faith carries us into meaning. Affirming faith and challeng-ing it in positive ways reveals belief, which is rarely predicated on fact. Ignorance is not like cleanliness; it does not bring us closer to

God. At the time, though, the nuns seemed far from accepting any kind of inquiry or dissent.

Raised in a Presbyterian community, I was taught to believe in a power greater than any one of us, an all-knowing God with an all-encompassing plan. I took seriously the idea that we were all created in God's image. What a wonderful reflection, if we look at all those other images around us with love. It took me years to understand how divisive religion can be. The love I was raised with assured confidence in my fellow humans, not judgment, and empowered me to stand up for those who are not given the same platform. Faith can uplift us, even if that faith is placed only in each other, in the stars or in the ground under our feet. Faith is free will. There's something so beautiful in growing up knowing that every single one of us must be divine. I've held the conviction that no matter our gender, race, sexuality or faith, no matter where we are born, that we are beautiful and part of a plan. None of us has concrete proof; it is our traditions that set us on firm paths. Belief joins us to a greater purpose; it is an act of daring, to sense something shared in our existence.

Seeking connection and comfort, my spirituality has altered and grown as I have. I struggle to believe in anything that condemns others for who they are. The Christian faith of my youth seems now strangely political and diametrically opposed to Jesus' teachings. Jesus helped the poor, the sick, the hungry, the downtrodden. He overturned the tables of wealth; his currencies were hope and brotherly love. I strive to live by those sacred examples of my youth, to treat others as I would want to be treated. Finding solace now more in other people and in natural places, rather than in a pew, I anchor myself in those who choose love and dignity for others, at all costs. Seeking sanctuary in places that make me wonder at the power that brought them to be, I've put my faith in the natural cycles that have carried us from our origins.

Your faith path may be similar to mine or wildly different, firmly defined or open-ended, but I don't believe anybody's beliefs make another's faith, spirituality, or lack thereof, inferior. I don't feel it makes us less, to see things differently. We each cling to meaning by our own definition. If your faith works for you—and more importantly, isn't hurting or limiting anyone else—then I say, more power to you. If, however, your beliefs are bent on changing or oppressing others (by forcing abuse, assault or marginalization to stand), that, to my mind, is not faith; it is control. Those ideas come from man, not God.

Aside from my provocations of the nuns and my philosophical arguments against certain Catholic dogmas, Mother of Mercy High School (now part of Mercy McAuley High School in College Hill, after a 2018 merger) had my respect, and Mrs. Murphy, my Creative Writing teacher, was a true support. As I wrote about what had happened to my family only a year before, she not only empathized, she encouraged me to write it better. First quarter closed, and I posted strong grades.

I landed a part-time job at Video Town—remember video stores?—up the street on Delhi Pike. To add further wages to my gas tank fund, I then applied to join the front-of-house staff of a floating local theatre, the Showboat Majestic, moored at Cincinnati's Public Landing on the Ohio River. When I was a youngster in the 1970s and '80s, our family often spent time in that same stretch along the Ohio Riverfront. The concrete curves of the Serpentine Wall were completed in 1976, when I was five, and I can't remember our city without this distinguishing landmark. At summer day camps, my siblings and I cooled off in the water feature at Yeatman's Cove. From the Public Landing my family watched the WEBN fireworks, an epic display set to booming rock music (still a Labor Day Weekend tradition on the river). On summer days as a young teenager, my mother would drop me off at the Public Landing in the morning, and Holly's mom Susan might pick us up later that day. We didn't have cell phones, so a strict pick-up point and time were established. Holly and I shared each other's closet contents, swapping cut-off jean shorts, and brought our boombox and snacks. People-watching with a bunch of other young people we didn't know, we'd spend the day on the hardened waves of the Serpentine Wall, watching the murky Ohio roll by. It was a place to be, bigger than our neighborhoods, though of course today's downtown Riverfront boasts many newer parks and amenities. Back then, it was just cool.

The Showboat Majestic, built by Captain Thomas Jefferson Reynolds in 1923, was one of 50 traveling entertainment barges built in the United States between 1831 and 1929. With the Attaboy sternwheel tug towing it up and down the Ohio, a steam-powered calliope would announce the theatre's arrival into town. The Showboat Majestic had given up river touring years ago, but it was still a fun place to see a show—the perfect date night, with its intimate stage and starlit deck—as well as being a unique place to work. There, I met new friends: professional performers, boat crew and stagehands. Personable actors would chat as loved ones dropped them off for their performances. I worked there in 1988 and '89, in the box office for ticketing as well as setting up and selling concessions for intermissions. My friend Tara was interested in working with me, and we'd spend evenings after our shifts hanging out near my parked car on the slanted landing, or hanging out with John, the boat's caretaker, who lived upstairs. Young and silly, we lived on soft pretzels and mustard, and mooned more than a few barges passing by; when their spotlights found our rumps in the silky darkness, we were always rewarded with an appreciative horn blast.

A regular on the river, I felt more tied to that shore than to school. I watched the current and shoreline change with the seasons, heard the water gently lapping against the boat after a barge slid by, cheered for the ducks who paddled hard against the encroaching ice at the river's edge, in that chilly winter of 1988. In 2019, the Showboat Majestic was purchased by a private owner and moved west; though designated a National Historic Landmark, the vessel's future is uncertain.

I FELT MORE STABLE than I'd been in a long time, but I was a seventeen-year-old in a never-ending endurance run, jumping the hurdles I kept placing in my own path.

This fall was when Grams Clara revealed Jack's whereabouts, and Mom flew me to New England. Tara wrote me a letter for the plane ride, my first, and insisted I not open it until mid-flight. She understood that I'd spent my entire childhood conjuring a dream relationship with Jack, but along with her encouraging words, naivete accompanied me on that flight to visit my father.

Tight hugs from Jack and his blonde girlfriend, Priscilla, met me at the airport. From the back seat of his car, I held a beginning in Jack's extended hand, rough and worn with construction work. Layered with emotions, it was a memorable reunion. I felt forever changed, being connected to my birth father again. Having lost two fathers in seventeen years, I can't overstate the importance of gaining one of them back into my life. Jack seemed just as happy to have his Princess back, as he called me, and with no blame laid at his feet, soaked up the love and excitement I lavished on him.

Blame Freud or Mother Nature, but we daughters long for that special father-daughter relationship. You know the one, found inside bridal magazines and Father's Day cards. Without an offer of more, we will often take what we are given, whether or not it serves us well. Jack and I were more like old friends at a party than father and daughter, though I only found that novel and fun. We drove into New Hampshire to shop with no sales tax, ate and had cocktails at a Chinese restaurant he liked, and later sat around the table in his kitchen where he didn't mind pouring drinks for his newly found underaged kid.

This lady of his, Priscilla, recognizable from the photo I had found years earlier, was kind. She shared a life and her children with Jack, a grown son and teenaged daughter. What thought, if any, she gave to Jack's only now reconnecting with his daughter is beyond me. Perhaps in her relationship, she met Jack where he was and did not ask for more.

Her daughter Kellee was almost exactly my age when we met in the decent but darkened ground floor apartment. The amount of time this stand-in daughter had spent with my father was hard to take, when I thought about it, so I tried not to. Despite the immediate bad taste it left in my mouth when Jack sat us down and

taught us both how to drink Alabama slammers, I was eager to
be positive. Befriending her was the price to pay for acclamation.
We weren't dissimilar, both products of divorce, and Kellee was a
nice person; it wasn't her fault she'd had all that time with Jack.
In truth, I didn't know how to hold it against her, usually holding
things so well against myself. Perhaps Big John's daughters' example of kindness toward me helped me decide against resentment. I
was certainly aided by Mom's compassionate parenting, and by our
church's reminder to turn the other cheek.

Still, that visit left a dark mark on me. On my last night, Jack
released Kellee and me to a high school party in town, with classmates of my new friend. Unknown faces partially masked by Solo
cups filled an apartment with no parents at home, a fractal of every
other high school party. After sipping a bad beer in hand, one
particularly bulked-up football player named Luke handed me a
colorful drink.

The cup's concoction tasted like a sweetened punch. Within
minutes, I blacked out from its contents. Apparently, Kellee had
placed me in a darkened bedroom. I roused to find myself being
dragged upward off a coat pile by the same hands that had given
me the cup. Then things go dark again. I have no memory of being
walked, pulled or carried through that apartment full of thirsty
teens. No memory of walking out the door without my coat in a
thin turtleneck on a chilly New England autumn night, though
many in the small apartment, including Kellee, would have witnessed me passing unsteadily for the door. I have no memory of
the cold night air hitting my face when I was taken outside. I have
no memory of being walked across a wide parking lot up the curb,
through the mown grass, before being pushed down into the copse
of trees on the opposite side of the asphalt, where no one could
easily see or hear me.

My memory picks up again on cold damp ground, where I
woke to find Luke on top of me, my blue jeans pushed to my
ankles chaining my legs together, as I tried to wrap my slow and
flailing mind around what was physically happening to me. Saying
"No." Saying "Stop." Pushing and squirming to no effect. My body

betraying my will, my fuzzy mind betraying my body. Unable to resist invasion, my body crushed deeper onto the bed of jagged rocks
and rotting leaves of fall.

Finished, Luke pushed off me, zipped up, walked away and left
me there. Struggling to stand, formulating slowly what had happened, for some reason I yelled out to no one in particular that I
was not alright. This invader was already across the parking lot at
the building door before turning back to me and yelling out that I
was the best he ever had.

His form faded smaller into the light of the glass doorway that
closed him inside. Shaking, I stood, holding onto a thin-trunked
tree, awkwardly pulling my pants up. Stumbling out of the trees,
slowly walking across the long lot to the door, I yanked the handle
before realizing it was locked. After knocking, to no avail, I hugged
myself and sat on the freezing curb outside, waiting for Kellee.

I didn't call it rape then. I didn't call it anything. I tried not to
think how many others he had done this to. Who the last "best"
was. Angry at myself, for being in this situation, for being here, for
accepting his fruity drink, for coming to this party, for not having
a friend to look out for me, for the damp leaves twisted into my
hair—denial insisted that to spend time on what had happened
might mean I would look weak, stupid or worse, and that I would
miss out on time with Jack. Mom would never let him see me
again if she knew. The cold concrete beneath me numbed the parts
I wanted to deny existed. When, nearly an hour later, Kellee finally
came looking for me, she assumed I was just drunk—and I didn't
correct her when I asked her to grab my coat and take me home.
I didn't want to talk. I didn't know or trust her enough to tell her
what Luke had done to me. Shivering, I laid my head against the
cold car window, pretending to sleep. Still fuzzy and ashamed, I
quickly told Jack goodnight as I walked past him, before I got under a hot shower and into a cold bed. My head pounded excuses for
the force pressed into my skin, pounded blame on myself for the
bruises forming along my spine and neck, damage that the power
of entitlement and testosterone had left on me.

As I kissed Jack goodbye at the airport the next morning, wincing quietly at the pain from his full hug, I knew I wouldn't choose to hold that or the assault against him either. He was, after all, the only father I had now. Overpowered, overruled, my silence let everyone else off the hook. Alone in my window seat, I allowed the pain and sensitivity I sat on to squeeze me uncomfortably into the box that carried me home.

As I arrived back home to Cincinnati, that Princess part of me, newly thrilled to know my father, lingered for a little while. Dreams don't easily die. When, weeks later, I heaved relief at not being pregnant, and months later, when I at last fully acknowledged what had happened to me in Massachusetts, I understood, for better or worse, just how incapable Jack was of being responsible for a teenager. The rape wasn't his fault, nor did he prevent it. He operated his life without thought of consequence, treating me more like a pet or a pal, never seeing past my pretending to be okay. I saw Kellee again when I was nineteen and tried to tell her what happened, but she thought maybe I was remembering it wrong—so again I shut the memory inside, doubting myself, doubting her. We stayed in touch for a while, but I couldn't get past how she had let me walk out the party's door into danger that night. She hadn't looked out for me. It wasn't her fault, but she didn't prevent it.

My mom became the hero for sending me, for trusting me to go, for welcoming me back, for knowing something very wrong had happened (Mom's intuition never failed) and loving me through it, without demand for answers. She knew I couldn't betray Jack then, or for several years after—and what's more, I couldn't make her doubt her decision to send me. She would not have sent me into danger, and Jack simply didn't know any better. Besides, how could I blame him, when I carried enough blame for all of us?

Exposed (again) was a man's ability to take something from me. Exposed was the hard reality that Jack could never be the father figure I had grown up with, and lost. Exposed was the truth that no one could ever be as cool as Elvis. That autumn when I went to visit Jack, a year and a half had passed since Dad died. I began to think of his efforts very differently then, still holding myself accountable for what I'd taken for granted in our relationship. Dad started to visit my dreams as Jack faded. I'd survived another trauma, but I refused to let go of the guilt that dined best at my table.

Jack and I would continue to call a half dozen times a year, to chat and reminisce about a childhood that wasn't great and a visit that carried vastly different memories for the two of us. Even as my awareness grew, I didn't let him believe that the illusion was bust. He still called me his Princess, so I learned to accept our relationship as fantastical as that.

After returning from Massachusetts, walking the halls of an all-girls' school felt safe. I buttoned down, contentedly, into a more boring routine. Far less focused on boys, I participated in discussions in class. Holly's wonderful Grandma Helen lived close by school, and we often walked over there, sunk into her soups, hung on her laugh, gleaned her wisdom. Most weekends would find us singing and laughing together on sleepovers at my house or hers. Both Susan, Holly's mom, and Pat practically became adoptive moms to the other Holly, we saw each other so often.

I stopped hanging out as much with my older friend Deanna, from Oak Hills, when I tried to tell her what had happened to me in Massachusetts and she also suggested I was probably remembering it wrong. Our culture, rape culture, is rough. Even our friends doubt us. I started hanging out more with Kim, my Mercy friend, and her boyfriend Nick, who didn't mind me being a third wheel as we hung out with movies and popcorn. Nick drove us around town as we matured, considered concepts, and aspirational, looked at houses, imagining adulthood. Holly and I also became friends with Peggy and Nancy, some other really great people at Mercy doing normal teenage things like shopping and laughing. Holly and I watched and cried to the classic friendship movie *Beaches*, sang our hearts out to Anita Baker, and knew inside-out the words to every Tracy Chapman song. Choreographing our own dances to Madonna hits, we dabbled in liquid blue eyeliner, made up strange snack foods, and walked malls. We joined the school production of Annie, with my dog Matti making her own stage debut as Sandy, and ate Grandma Helen's home cooking. As I turned eighteen, ordinary came back into life. That spring I built a backbone.

As HARD AS I could be on myself, I refused to live in fear—something I had learned at Emerson or Millcreek, or known within my bones. I went out, I hung out with friends, I talked myself through choices. I got smarter with my safety and stopped my high school drinking altogether. A licensed driver now, I ferried myself and female friends everywhere we went, becoming a security warden for them as well. When I did date a nice guy later that spring, my own car and my own money took me. I shared what had happened to me, and he treated me kindly. I clawed my power back by living in the moment, by learning to overcome fear, and by loving the idea of being loved—and I got stronger.

Already a writer and chronic journaler, I saw a pathway to a career in front of me that I hadn't considered before. My grades were holding steady, and as senior year approached, I began to focus on the future. The world loomed large for a legal adult with options. Artistic dreams replaced nightmares, and I begged my mother for an audition to attend the writing program at the School for Creative & Performing Arts (SCPA) in downtown Cincinnati. With her blessing, she signed me up.

Being admitted to SCPA injected confidence into my soul. It lent support for skills I needed to hone. For half of my senior year of high school, River Road carried me, between Delhi township and downtown Cincinnati, for a far longer school day, with my paychecks filling the tank. Listening to WEBN classic rock or 97X alternative music on the car stereo to and from school, I'd hear the DJ's joke and promise the next reason to stay tuned. I'd also pop The Cure, The Replacements or Guadalcanal Diary just as easily as Tracy Chapman or the Eagles, Fleetwood Mac, James Taylor or Elton John into my cassette tape deck. Interesting classes fueled my imagination, as SCPA shone a brighter light not only on learning, but on the importance and beauty of uniqueness, and on the unequivocal life-sustaining power of the arts. Being a student there was often like walking into a scene from the movie Fame, with singing and dancing all through the halls and a rarely empty piano bench in the cafeteria.

A beacon hangs over those months, a brilliance obscuring faces and names, offering confirmation that I was indeed a creative being, holding place among expressive talent in the world. What a wonderful view the garden of our differences can provide if we aren't seeking sameness.

Unfortunately, my time at SCPA was cut short. While I was a senior there, stress mounted, until my chest tightened with panic, that familiar and unwanted visitor. An autoimmune disease indicator also appeared on a blood test, and conquering my anxiety felt like a full-time job. The longer school day proved too much to maintain my wellness, while managing homework and my jobs at the Showboat Majestic and Video Town. When it all became too much, I reduced my work hours and decided to change schools. Again. It was hard to leave SCPA, a special place, but I had learned to face my own needs.

Though SCPA didn't provide many lasting friendships, I encountered only friendly faces while there, and was encouraged by my teachers to follow my talent for writing and art. This came with an awakening inside that I truly wanted to do so. Today, I'm proud to still be a part of that artistic school and community, and to say that one of my own children found her place at that school and recently graduated, with her own mystical, musical path ahead of her.

Leaving SCPA mid-senior year, sad but determined, I returned to Oak Hills High School. Late January found me an Oak Hills Highlander again, but a changed one, traveling full-circle around my high school experience. With a shorter day, I was able to find time for work, study, and play. Interested in the Drama Club, similar to the Thespian troupe I had joined while at Mother of Mercy, I found a great group of like minds and hearts there. My class schedule allowed for photography and journalism electives, both of which I adored for the remainder of my senior year. Heather was at a local college; I visited her dorm a couple times, and for the first time considered attending college away from home. Motivated, I sent my application to Ohio University's Scripps Journalism program, and was promptly denied. No ego plunge followed. I knew that despite any recent efforts, my school records weren't stellar, with all I'd gone through—and I owned that. At this point my studies hadn't prepared me to matriculate with such ambitious aim.

At Oak Hills, Tara, who carpooled with me, lived up the street and shared some of my quirkiness and independence. With a passion for note-writing and a skill for passing them under the teacher's nose, we kept up a lively classroom correspondence and spent time after school together at Drama Club. Finding solace in black-bottom raspberry cheesecake, we ate dinners at Zino's in Clifton and aged ourselves drinking coffee at night in diners and coves there, near the University of Cincinnati campus. Student directing came easily to me, and I enjoyed helping my new friends, Mark and Aaron, shine onstage while supporting from the wings. We hung out with that group of students and a couple of relaxed college-aged guys as we worked together at the Showboat Majestic.

Tara and I also hung out with Valerie, who was way too much fun. Those few months of senior year we grew into the messy business of becoming strong women, making missteps, falling flat and getting up again. The conclusion of high school nearly achieved, I'd sliced off a bit of a typical teenager for myself.

Accepted to Wright State University, the only other place I had applied outside of my first rejection, the campus seemed a good option close to home, and Mom took me on the tour for new students shortly before my graduation from Oak Hills.

A FUTURE WAS TAKING SHAPE that summer with college ahead, when a missed period led to a positive pregnancy test. Shrinking into a new and narrowing box, my restless mind contorted. My fractured self resorted to fears I had once carried, and I clearly lacked the mental or emotional capacity to become a parent. Whatever your beliefs, pregnancy forces irreparable changes on women's bodies, lives and minds. Motherhood, a cherished opportunity for some, also cuts off opportunities for others, then as it does now, as it always has.

The U.S. Supreme Court ruling of *Roe v. Wade*, decided in 1973 (upheld in 1992), held that the Constitution protected abortion as a basic right. With determination, at nineteen, I made my choice. One in four people who become pregnant choose abortion, for myriad meaningful reasons, for their own wellbeing and health, for their safety, for their family's makeup and resources, or because of financial hardship. To this day I have only gratitude for my choice, made by myself for myself, which allowed me to determine my life's path, leading me to my healthier self and my beloved, intended family.

On June 25, 2022, the Supreme Court overturned *Roe v. Wade* and *Planned Parenthood v. Casey*, stripping fifty years of a federally protected right in the *Dobbs v. Jackson* decision. Some believe this ruling will protect life. Whose lives, and at what cost, is still in question.

Wright State had over-admitted freshmen that year, and dorms were unavailable to many new students. The choice was that I could live in a hotel lobby for at least one semester or, on the recommendation of a boyfriend, I could apply to a different school, a couple hours north, Bowling Green State University. I started classes as an Education major that January.

Reflecting often on my needs for attention or isolation, I continued to tackle things on my own. Projecting power felt important, though I lacked insights into my own. Wrestling with countless vulnerabilities, away from home, in a relationship, I kept my actions and responses close, honest only with myself. College and a steady boyfriend brought alcohol back into the mix, with a few foolish alcohol-induced evenings.

I think that work at Emerson, which had afforded me the space to assess, took a back seat then. Young love, relationship navigation, uncertainty and college drinking don't make for the best healing practice. Powerlessness forced me into darker places; a creature of habit, I chose to walk there alone. My three years at university didn't roll up neatly into a diploma. BGSU instead led me to meet my future father-in-law. I think the world of that institution, and remain close to it.

Rocky roads we journeyed, Heather and John on their own hard paths. Thankfully our mother set aside her own needs regularly for the three of us, to find and deliver the help and support we each needed.

My story of struggle during high school and beyond is not an uncommon one. Daily, students battle demons, real or imagined, at home and in classrooms. Like toddlers at bedtime, it matters little whether adults can see the monsters under the bed; acknowledging how real they feel is the first step in conquering them.

Homelife, school life, social life—so much of it can feel inescapable for teenagers. Now, as a prepared parent, it is easy to see how our culture, our now fast-paced digital culture, laid over undeveloped minds, ensnares children into unsafe behaviors and life-ending scenarios. I've seen it so many times: one blunder, omission or misstep, and kids feel they have failed. A heavy burden to carry, the possibility of disappointing your parents forever. Forgetting the instability of our own young minds, and the minefields we walked in them, parents don't always realize that children cannot be made to feel worse than they already do.

Silence and worry represent uncertainty on both sides of the parent-child equation. I've subtracted and added to that. I try to understand the autonomy my children seek by remembering my own youthful quest for it. Even in the face of unconditional love, it is difficult for a child to ask for or to accept help. I couldn't ask for it from Dad or Jack, or even Mom some days. I'm thankful she saw my needs, and allowed weakness in me without ego around her own parenting. Unfortunately, most families are unable, by awareness or income, to assist in seeking outside support. This is when teachers and counselors can be a student's lifeline to tomorrow, to graduation, to life outside of institutions.

I was so fortunate to have compassionate professionals standing by for me, alongside some of the darkest waters I traveled. Lighthouses all.

19

support [suh-pawrt, -pohrt] *verb* (used with object)
1. to bear or hold up (a load, mass, structure, part, etc.); serve as a foundation for
2. to sustain or withstand (weight, pressure, strain, etc.) without giving way; serve as a prop for
3. to undergo or endure, especially with patience or submission; tolerate

noun
1. the act or an instance of supporting
2. the state of being supported

O VER TIME, WE ATTENDED more meetings with other families who had suffered the loss of loved ones at the hands of Donald Harvey—none as charged as that first meeting with Bill Whalen, but still, tough sessions. There was little healing to be found among such raw wounds with those families, the anger and sadness refusing to scar over so we might better tell our stories. Simmering resentment raised the temperature in the room. Anguish among us was extensive, contagious in proximity.

Murder victims' families, unwilling as they are be where they find themselves, carry understandable anger, pain and bitterness. To question a loss so deep, so intolerable—at times only rage or destruction can fill the void where love once lived. Twice traumatized, some families were newly learning of Harvey's murder of their loved ones during grand jury testimony that summer of '87. We understood their pain, having had only two weeks ourselves to grieve a natural death before we discovered how Dad had actually died. Survivors can't help seeking answers; we desperately want the truth, but murder is a problem all its own to work out, leaving "natural" and "normal" out of the equation. Loved ones deserve the certainty around cause of death, and closure through justice sought. This awful knowledge was assured to deepen bereavement and dispense a double dose of heartache. I cannot say if some of the families wished they had escaped gruesome facts, preferring to remain ignorant to how they sustained the loss. It was not lost on me that Dad's death was the only reason all those other people knew just how their family member had died.

Ready as I was to work past my own outrage and sorrow, I could not benefit from those meetings. The whole of our victim-hood was so overwhelming, we sliced off our piece of pain to more slowly digest all that was laid before us—and still it was too much. Moving away from that group for self-preservation, we took a recommendation from the staff of the police department to try another group, Parents of Murdered Children, thinking members there could be empathetic to our loss, but not so entangled with our personal situation.

Therapy is expensive and time-consuming for a family; with four of us in need, these groups afforded a chance to heal without draining our financial resources. Mom encouraged us to attend a POMC meeting in the bland, multipurpose basement of a church in Kenwood, a northern suburb of Cincinnati. Again, seated in a circle of support, folding chairs and hearts open, survivors shared dates of the killings with names—first their own, and then the name of the wife, husband, friend, partner, sibling, son, or daughter they so deeply missed. Easy to bleed for each other there, and holidays, anniversaries or birthdays were the worst times for many. Dark seasons of sadness lingered over the souls in that room. Speaking of how their special someone had been ripped away, others focused on what might be, if only they were still here.

Professional group therapy, familiar to me by now, provided a trained leader to guide the conversation and move us forward. A safe place for misery to make friends. Well versed in its effective-ness, I participated and felt for the other tear-stained faces around me, a circumference of shared loss.

"My name is Holly. My dad died March 7, 1987."

"My name is Pat. My husband John Powell was killed March 7, 1987."

Mom has unlimited reserves of compassion, but was wise to seek support for her family in countless ways; understanding that our pain exceeded her scope was the first step. Parents don't have all the answers and can't solely "fix" their kids on authority. Mom could not repair or even plumb the damage we were sustaining. Outside help was better than sinking or standing still.

"My name is Heather. My stepdad, John Powell, died March 7, 1987."

In the best of circumstances, the death of a loved one can take years, even decades to mourn. Accidents happen, people die, and though intent to harm isn't implicit, there is usually a place to lay blame, whether an icy road, an unsafe product or an impaired driver. That kind of loss feels sudden and senseless. Conditions such as cancer or heart disease have been called "killers," justly, since an invasive disease forces (yet at times allows) a goodbye. The face of cancer is the pained face of its victim.

"My name is John, and my dad John Powell was killed March 7, 1987."

Actual murder, by a known or unknown culprit, puts another face on death—a visage that survivors work to avoid but cannot help focusing on. It overshadows and contorts the victim's features, the face we love and cling to. That stubborn, murderous name and face take up residence in our hearts and minds, crowding out loving expressions and cherished memories. Energy we no longer have, spent richly on someone so undeserving... It's infuriating.

Murder further complicates death, encompassing violent loss and violation with disturbing thoughts and recurring nightmares. In waking hours and in sleep, we play out levels of terror our loved one endured in their final moments. I still struggle with that. Death, that natural inevitability, feels forced past mortality or morality in murder, setting everything off-kilter. It spirals grief further out of control. A sacred trust is broken in stealing days with our loved one. Viral strains of media coverage and conflicting criminal or judicial components attach to homicide. Survivors often lose their privacy, too, on top of everything else: because murder (particularly serial murder) is a crime against society, the deaths of our family members are considered public property, and so is our grief.

This particular group session was hosted by an organization founded in 1978 by Robert and Charlotte Hullinger, whose daughter, Lisa, was murdered at age nineteen by her ex-high school boyfriend, six months after she broke up with him. Both young people were in Hamburg, Germany at the time, on a work/study abroad program through the University of Cincinnati. Lisa's killer, unsatisfied that she wouldn't take him back, lured her to his apartment and brutally beat her with a hammer. She died from her injuries thirteen tortuous days later. He served only sixteen months in Germany for killing Lisa, and returned to the States with no criminal record.

Several months after the death of their daughter, Robert and Charlotte met with a Catholic priest known for bereavement counseling, who put them in contact with three other parents who were grieving similarly devastating losses. What began as simply convening to find comfort and support for their individual tragedies, soon grew into much more. Having gone through the worst, others sought comfort from their experience, and the Hullingers found a calling, a purpose to their pain, by providing that same level of support to others. Parents of Murdered Children was born.

Now with dozens of local chapters in twenty-two states, POMC works to provide a community of emotional support to those who have endured a homicide within their family. The criminal justice system can be daunting; the media gauntlet around any high-profile killing, even worse. POMC offers education and resources to navigate those rough waters. This incredible organization, still headquartered in Cincinnati, was suggested to us nearly a year after Dad died. There, we received a level of support few others could extend, knowing we weren't going through this type of tragedy alone.

The Hullingers knew too well the ongoing assault of murder on a family's grief. In an awful, and not unpredictable turn, Lisa's killer killed again in 1997, when a woman in Florida tried to break up with him. Recognizing the man as the murderer he was, a jury found him guilty and he was sentenced to death in 2002. The Hullingers were forced to repeat the horror of losing their daughter to a sociopath's rage. Justice may finally have been served, but there is no compensation for the ravages of a killer.

The Hullingers are a great example for us: Selfless action in the face of grief, can create purpose through the incomprehensible. How we share the love we lost allows that love to live on in the hearts and minds of others. Their response to murder is the exception, most of us don't choose to stay so close to such a difficult thing. It is a challenge to do that in any kind of a healthy way.

And yet, here I sit, by choice, in this emotional cesspool, darkness amplified by the isolation of my disturbing search, scratching and clawing my way out by putting these words on paper. The irony is not lost on me, that this story of my healing might surface wounds for others—people I care about who went through this nightmare, or strangers who've experienced any terrible ordeal. Compelled as I am to share in depth this part of our family history, my fervent wish is that someone else can, through these pages, examine their own pain, and find healing. Revealing this intimate portrait with you, reader, and with my own grown children, who were robbed of their grandfather—I hope others will feel less alone.

228 /MET THE END

20

retrospection [re-truh-spek-shuhn] *noun*

1. the action, process, or faculty of looking back on things past

2. a survey of past events or experiences

MOM LOVES TO hang on to things. We both do—I simply hold onto them differently. Mom's things had a habit (she's made great headway) of turning into piles that over months moved into bags and then bins that after years pushed into closets and cupboards. Decades of newspapers with Cincinnati history or listings of events long past were saved. Hundreds of church bulletins and pharmacy receipts wedged within stacks of invoices, statements and social memorabilia. Paper scraps with names to remember, important records, weighty stacks of glossy bound *Woman's Day* and *Redbook* magazines for the working mom were harvested whole for safekeeping, with plans to get to them later. Even *Birds & Blooms* magazines, her two favorite things in one title, were among the landslide of litter.

In late fall of 2016 and early winter of 2017, I spent a good deal of time at Mom's place during one of her surgical recoveries. With that uninterrupted time together, we decided to pare down her material life into something more organized and enjoyable. We opened dozens of bags and bins holding the evidence of her life. Priceless original artwork from our childhoods, and memories captured on film or in print, were lodged together with expendable paperwork, coupons and periodicals.

Every handful of paper headed for the trash bag was met with Mom saying, either aghast or in jest, "Oh, Holly, I might want to look at that later!"

"We can't keep it all, Mom," I'd say, firmly or playfully. "Soon we will be buried here, stuck under all the things you want to look through!" Her face and shoulders would relax, and a smile would cross her face as she said, "I know," and we'd throw more waste into the bag.

We never took the job too seriously, but make no mistake: It was a big job. For years now we've been organizing the incredible amount of paper she's amassed in this life, and the process is no longer new to either of us. With more flexible work commitments, I was the child able to help her sift through the accumulation. We found synergy in reconciling her life. Packrat extraordinaire, her gift was innate—but in fairness, busy as she was most days, her priority was saving memories, not purging them. Humor carries us through; she finds a reason to smile, effortlessly laughing at herself, making it painless for the rest of us to laugh.

We easily tossed or recycled well over a dozen large trash bags of the unwanted past that wintry month in 2017. Hidden for nearly thirty years, pieces of this particular story were brought to light. Additional boxes were hauled in and opened up, with more souvenirs filtered and sorted. Calendars and datebooks, dotted with thoughts, crossed out time; dull pencil-embossed names and dates on the backs of old photographs cross-referenced vague recollections. Notepads too numerous to count stacked to teetering on the bed, boasting list upon list penned in Mom's characteristic hand. Funeral programs, sympathy cards, letters and well wishes driving memory to a finer point of clarity—one that only experience, time, and this remarkable quantity of reminders could bring.

Later the same winter, Heather uncovered a sticky old three-ringed photo album filled with dated and yellowed news clippings that had been hibernating for decades amongst Mom's boxes, stored in Heather's house. Unbeknownst to us, our mother had carefully maintained this album during those late 1980s. Stuck under each layer of plastic sheeting were clipped headlines of the day, ballpoint dates and details in her loopy hand on news articles chronologically following the newsworthy path we were then on. Dad's gunmetal gray, lightweight lockbox, filled with the business of his life, was also there keeping important things together: check stubs from child-support payments to Little John's mom all those years ago, his union card along with his NRA membership card, among other various statements and receipts. The detritus trail of a life.

Given my interest in ancestry and history, I am a keepsake caretaker in our family. Most families have someone carrying this mantle. Uncle Stan laid the groundwork, with family research digging into the lineage on my maternal side. He exposed a fascination for genealogy and preserving what has gone before, that has continued with me. I've found that sometimes the most mundane details can be precious, an intriguing window into my family's past.

I fully understand how fortunate we are to have these records. Enslaved or Indigenous peoples, forcibly taken from their homes and cultures, often had their ancestral artifacts burned, stolen or destroyed, making accounts of family history much harder to pass down. (At the National Underground Railroad Freedom Center in Cincinnati, you can see some extraordinary African-American story quilts, and learn about other ways historically marginalized people have preserved their legacies.) In today's world, endless man-made conflicts and natural disasters have left countless refugees without family records or mementos of any kind. But for those of us with document privilege, archival evidence of our forebears such as census records can provide names, timeframes, countries of origin, places of residence or job titles. Ancestral and immigration records provide context; land titles and DNA analyses cast a bloodline to claim.

Alone, though, these dates, addresses, careers chosen or molded to, shops owned, places born or buried, are simply facts in a ledger. Combining research and folklore into family legend—that's when stories are created, to be shared and retold. Long-forgotten faces with familiar features beckon in a sepia-toned photograph; outstretched ancestral arms call to me when a name joins a face.

Generations are captured on black-and-white film, on Kodak paper or in Polaroids, tucked inside hope chests and steamer trunks to discover, to remember. Newspaper articles or thoughtfully hand-written cards, dated and stamped, teleport us to those moments, connecting one solitary life to a shared human history. These treasures, these buried belongings, are the closest thing we humans have, as of yet, to a working time machine.

Uncovering parts of this story long forsaken has made me nostalgic, emotional and amazed at the power of time bend-ing itself over any story. Perhaps when we die, we time travel to all-knowing places, or across the chronology of our lives to destina-tions of all-encompassing love. I am certain the dead leave memo-rable pieces of themselves in the time capsules of their loved ones. Perhaps in this case, with two father figures lost to the living, I've become the time travelers' daughter. Three decades and more feels like a lifetime, until a photo surfaces of me and Dad, and sudden-ly I'm transported back to a time when he was alive. Seeing our younger faces on film returns me to my youth, bearing me back to the days when we were a whole family.

Personal effects, old cockeyed furniture, antique bindings around musty pages, post-industrial glassware, mismatched silver-ware and stacks of letters tied with string typically end up in my care, and so that winter of 2017, when Heather gave this old album to Mom, it was then handed off to me. Those trapped articles and headlines have been begging me for release since landing heavy in my arms. With the sense that an eon had passed, as the thirty-year anniversary of Dad's death approached, I felt a build-up of longing to write this part of our family history.

My siblings and I now live with families of our own, branches off our twisted family tree. We gifted nine wonderful grandchil-dren to Mom, "G-Ma," or "Mamaw," as she is now known. While actively engaging in helping those children grow, she's also stayed active with her friends and involved in her church community. No one replaced John for her; she remains unmarried. Raising toddlers into teens and adults, we three siblings have worked, struggled, gathered, laughed, and cried, passing time. Years fade pain, easing loss into a more reflective mindfulness. We've grown into now. And in early 2017, I felt interested in facing the past, considering again if it were time to put it on the page.

Exactly three weeks after that landmark thirtieth anniversary, a wound was reopened: On March 28, 2017, Donald Harvey was severely beaten in his prison cell, by another inmate.

In order to cope, I began writing, pouring the story that had been waiting out.

THE WAY I FOUND OUT about Harvey's beating that day was not ideal. Rather than a preemptive or concerned call or text from a person close to us (which would have been appreciated), a Facebook post brought that bit of news and trauma back in the harsh ways that victims' families know too well. Hurt, by a post I decided was careless, I suppose at the time I felt that a thoughtful gesture ranked lower than the rush to deliver news to a wider audience. And yet, careful attention looks different to each of us anyway. Harm was not intended, I knew. But I can tell you that while shouldering weighty news, a lack of consideration (in any instance) becomes something to also overcome. Grief can become easier to manage over time, moving through hard emotions, in varying and enigmatic ways, with contradicting capabilities... But when life suddenly, unexpectedly forced us to revisit this tragic event, no matter how we had first processed it, faded pain felt very fresh again.

Then, as now, I am reminded of other people's interest and attachment to newsworthy, sensational information. My private pain is a public story. This book will create new stories through the lens of each reader.

Harvey's unwanted name and persistent glare returned to us as fragmented faces roiled over a sea of memory. Wanting to withdraw into myself, I felt denial wash over me like the wrath of a storm I had already weathered. Once you've survived something, it's easier to sink back into old habits that got you through the first time. My shelter was found in writing, which compelled me to collect any memories and findings that might give meaning to the events surrounding my Dad's death and record them here.

Thankfully years erode the sharpest edges of mourning. Time, that terrible trickster, still brings aches all its own. Living to see years that Dad could not achieve, is disorienting enough. Sharing the loss of his life once, then again (after learning how he died) and now reliving it again, three decades later, resulted in some very emotional conversations with my brother, sister and mother. Hard as it is to talk about what we went through, a large part seems unreal if we do not.

On March 30, 2017, Donald Harvey died from his wounds.

My mother and sister and I were actually all together when that notification from a local news station alert popped up on my smartphone. Oddly, we were sitting in a hospital room, as Heather was undergoing a minor medical procedure at the time. John was working on a job site. Texting him immediately, I shared the news, saying that we were together, and though he wasn't in the room, that he was with us too.

One of Heather's friends happened to be at the hospital with us and asked what we thought of all of this, and of how Harvey had died. My answer came naturally: "I don't wish for any person to die a violent death."

His face registered confusion—this was not the expected response. But it's the truth. I don't wish violence on anyone. Conventional wisdom seemed to be that our family must be happy that Harvey was dead, and even more so that he had been beaten and killed, having "gotten what was coming to him." I am not ignorant to that celebratory "ding-dong, the witch is dead" mentality pervasive in human culture. Persisting on assumptions and mob mentality, it was the overriding and unwanted theme in social media commentaries that day.

I didn't react with glee, or even relief, to the news of Harvey's death. That wasn't the response of anyone else in my immediate family, either. We don't revel in another's misery; it will not restore anything we've lost, and is unlikely to bring us peace or resolution. On the other hand, I begrudge nobody their feelings. This is my story, and while I have personally found a lightness in living without hate that I cherish, I recognize that anger is part of healing, and that everyone handles loss and regret differently. So, be angry—no one needs my permission. My only hope is that you can get it out in ways that are helpful and healthy to you and your loved ones. I hope you can move through it. Anger is a road I've traveled, but never a place I choose to stay.

Harvey's death played in national news coverage as a major event. New reporters dug up old newsreels of my family: younger versions of ourselves, along with the other victims' families, packed into a crowded courtroom in late summer in 1987, managing the surreal task of simply sitting or standing through tears and anguish. That week of Harvey's death, photos of a face I had no choice but to know kept flashing across my screens. Haunted still by the intensity of disaffection in Harvey's eyes, I was alerted to the countless times his sociopathic stare has plagued my sleep over three decades.

One video clip ran beneath the headline, "From the Vault: 'Angel of Death' case was unlike anything seen in Tri-State/WCPO helped crack hospital serial killer case."

I saw my teenaged self, my family as we were in the courtroom then. Confronted by current headlines, upset by old footage, we hunkered down, hid in our homes and checked in on each other. Only a very few friends who knew our story sent texts or called me, offering comfort.

News anchors of the late 1980s, some still seated in their newsrooms, stoically reminded viewers of the crimes Harvey had committed. Banners waved along the bottoms of screens describing what we had lived then, newly newsworthy now. In our digital age, every news story ever told, whether in print or on video, can be retold, revived, repackaged with contemporary relevance. Disturbing, seeing my younger self in videos, across the courtroom from Dad's killer, reminding me of all the work put in to forget that particular hell.

·I haven't quite been myself these past few years since Harvey's death in 2017, since the writing began. Or perhaps I am more myself, acquainting with the newness of me. Slow trickles of words slipped forth, then poured down in torrents, ebbing only to flow again, a strange tide pulling me into whatever this story is becoming. While the task remains for me, a necessary one, straddling time and perspective from 1987 to 2022 is disorienting, draining, rewarding, and isolating.

Writing helps me conquer this vivid nightmare not easily forgotten at dawn. An experience that rarely feels real, these words prove that my reality is not just some parallel passage buried deep in a book I once consumed, so realistic in the telling that the memory and textures have become my own.

Screen capture from WCPO video clip of courtroom, August 1987, rerun on March 30, 2017

21

bound [bound] *adjective*
1. tied; in bonds
2. made fast as if by a band or bond
3. secured within a cover, as a book
4. under a legal or moral obligation
5. destined; sure; certain

"I've met you before. I am the daughter of John Powell, one of your murder victims. I can't know what made you do all the things you did to innocent people who meant you no harm. All I can do is find out all that I can about you and all the circumstances surrounding the murder cases. ...I feel betrayed that I trusted you to take care of my dad and then you poisoned him. I didn't really trust people easily to begin with but now I'm afraid to get close to anyone for fear of them dying on me. I guess I'll never really get any answers to all of my questions, but at least I'm learning to deal with the fact that you've done what you have and I can't change it, only myself."

—Holly Brians Ragusa, age 16

From a cathartic letter to Donald Harvey written January 21, 1988, and never sent

WRITING THIS STORY has become such an important part of my life, and a necessary part of my healing. Recognizing the deep necessity of discovery gone unfulfilled, even my teenaged self (who couldn't grasp all facets in the midst of such grim circumstances) knew I would need to write this. My work has become a salve for my pain. Research feels steady and grounded in something true; breaking through questions with answers seems to topple mountains into hills I can actually climb. To lay these experiences down, my brain worked, disjointed. Formulating a plan, I made public records and archival requests, obtained my dad's birth and death certificates, searched our own documentation, notated, scanned and saved. I Googled and took notes, watched old videos, and called WCPO for footage.

Searching for a compass in the myriad directions this story could go, my first attempt for an interview reached out to Daisy Key on April 20, 2017. Head nurse on the ward when Dad died, I had remembered her name and wondered what she might tell me. This being my first step on the project, I was just grateful she took my call. Not expecting much, three decades after her tenure at Drake, I wanted her to know that we remembered her after all this time, and that I was finally writing about what had happened all those years ago. The phone was answered by a man; I asked for Daisy Key and gave him my name. My heart raced until, to my surprise, she took the phone and said "Hello?" I rushed right into my polite introduction, saying I hoped she was well, then laying out an explanation of who I was, what I was up to, and how I felt she could help. I asked her if she remembered John Powell. She hesitated.

Key seemed taken aback by the question. Clearing her throat, she kept it short, saying, "At ninety years old, I still remember Harvey, but I don't know anyone else from that time now." I mumbled some understanding comment, pressed lightly again; then she paused and told me, "I am sorry, but it has been so long, and many went their separate ways after all that business." A bit astonished, but allowing for her age, I didn't press harder. My first attempt at an actual interview, on this subject—I was shaky. Without all my facts under me, I thanked her, reminding her this was for a book I was writing to help process everything that had happened. I got the distinct feeling that, unlike me, she didn't like to reflect on that time of her life.

Months later into my research, I would discover that Daisy Key was the supervisor who completed an employee evaluation on Donald Harvey on May 5, 1986. As head nurse, she was the person repeatedly receiving open concerns from staff on the ward—concerns about mysterious patient deaths, intimating that Donald Harvey was the cause. Nurses who cared for Dad, and others on ward C-300, went to higher-ups with what they knew were wrongful deaths, up to seven months before my dad was murdered, before John Powell fell victim.

Daisy Key was the nurses' direct superior.

Attempting to make a difference in the lives of their patients, nurses spoke up to their managers only to be told to stop talking, stop searching for what was going wrong. It must have been disheartening for those healthcare providers, invested in palliative care, yet wanting to keep their jobs. How can you continue to care for patients while, under pressure from above, unwittingly participating in a cover-up?

In possession now of facts, testimony, convictions and lawsuits, I better understand why Key didn't want to reflect on that time. Being the supervising nurse, she would have asked those junior nurses to quell concerns, at the direction of Drake administrator Jan Taylor. Sources close to this case have acknowledged that Daisy Key liked and even favored Donald Harvey, who had ingratiated himself with the head nurse.

Early in my research process, though, I wasn't aware of Key's specific friendship with Harvey. In discovery mode at the time, I only knew she was a central character to this case, someone I remembered at Drake when I often visited Dad. My intention in calling Key was to see what she remembered of Dad or our family. She knew our struggle intimately during those seven months. Her reticence, age, and as I later learned, her problematic role in the situation, made it difficult for her to give any answers. Sensing her clamping up, I knew more wouldn't be said. I simply thanked her for her time. She wished us all well before I hung up. Knowing now that Key withheld the opportunity for months of early inquiry at Drake, delaying investigation into multiple accusations made by her staff, is a difficult thing to grapple with. No wonder she didn't want to talk openly with me.

How does a nurse charged with the well-being of her patients not attempt to get to the bottom of something so obviously troubling to her staff? Had Daisy Key actually listened, or seen the importance of investigating these claims, how many lives could have been saved? Even just one?

Still, she's an old woman now, and I am not an angry person.

This veteran caregiver could not have imagined the atrocities one unassuming orderly might be capable of, before all was revealed. No. In all honesty, my phone call with Daisy Key probably wouldn't have been much different with that knowledge. The Drake administrator failed in his responsibility to the county, perpetuating these deaths—and eventually he was held accountable. What kind of burden must Nurse Key have felt after discovering the depth of Harvey's crimes, and her own heedless complicity?

Looking back, though mourning, we were always a grateful family. Thinking in March of 1987 that Dad had died of natural causes, we felt a strong bond to the staff, as if we were in it for the long haul with Drake for Dad's care, recovery, even his death. Mom sent a letter shortly after he passed away with our love and intention to see others benefit from our experience there.

To learn later that the hospital staff we cared so much about had participated in hiding known issues since the very month Dad arrived, was such a blow to our already grief-stricken family. Realizing then that because they didn't investigate one of their own, Dad had died, along with many others… Eventually there was a lawsuit that couldn't possibly settle accounts for any of the victims' families left behind, couldn't possibly compensate for such a loss of life and of public trust. Those who hindered discovery of the truth, ignored concerns or were negligent—I imagine they've been living

Letter of appreciation from Patricia Powell to Drake Hospital staff, March 1987 with their own personal trauma. One thing is clear: No amount of hatred, questioning, resentment or ill will could change actions made at the time. Nothing can bring back our dad or give my mother back her husband.

These events have touched countless people. I can almost see ripples reaching far across to the shore where Dad met his end, spreading to victims, their survivors, stretching ever outward to extended family, investigators and personnel on each side of this story. People were greatly affected in lasting ways.

Events at Drake Memorial Hospital serve as an abiding lesson for any county official, healthcare administrator, human resource officer or journalist, that who you hire, how you interview or choose to represent, vet, or report about another person truly matters. The questions of accountability and responsibility dive deep into the heart of this case. After the truth came out in Cincinnati, bureaucratic norms changed; new checks and balances were put in place. The reforms in protocols, training and oversight went far beyond one county medical facility, and had an impact on the next generation's system of justice.

History has been set. Let us all hope that we have learned from it.

22

casualty [kazh-oo-uhl-tee] *noun*, plural cas·u·al·ties.
1.   any person, group, thing, etc., that is harmed or destroyed as a
     result of some act or event

M Y DAD IS NOT the only person in my family to have been
killed by Donald Harvey.

The same Aunt Lori who recommended Glen Whitaker, married Jeff Vetter in November of 1983. I was twelve then, a junior
bridesmaid in her wedding party with a lovely strand of pearls
laying across my neck. Little John, in a tie and coat, handed out the
printed programs, and Heather and I sat very still at our grandparents' dining room table, as a stylist fussed over our hair and makeup. Growing up, we had idolized Lori. Babysitting for us as young-
sters on nights when Mom went out, Aunt Lori, as a treat, would
make my grandmother's Milk Mush recipe, a comforting blend of
milk, vanilla and sugar, to be poured over toast.

I am fortunate to have loving relationships with my aunts and
uncles. Aunt Debra and Uncle Robert, Aunt Karen and Uncle
Stan, Uncle Dick and Aunt Gayle, and Aunt Lori who married
Jeff, my loquacious uncle, a Computer Science professor who, after
thirty-five years, recently retired from Cincinnati State. Christmas
Eve and often Thanksgiving are hosted in their lovely home. They
love to travel and camp and taste wines and beers; we enjoy sharing
a drink and eating generations of family-favorite appetizers with
them.

On Lori and Jeff's wedding day, Jeff's dear parents, Marge

and Jerry Vetter, stood next to Lori's parents, Al and Kay Myers, pleased to blend their families that autumn day. We've shared celebrations together with the Vetters ever since—birthdays, weddings, holiday parties and more as the years continue to pass.

Jerry Vetter passed away this spring of 2022, at age eighty-four, and we all mourn his kindness. The youngest of five, Jerry had an older brother Howard, known as Hardy. Hardy married Marlene Hoeweler. Marlene had a brother named Carl. Carl was a hairdresser who owned a salon for decades in Mt. Airy (a neighborhood settled in 1805 on Cincinnati's northwest side). In those early days of courtship and marriage, Lori and Jeff would often see Carl with his date at Vetter family functions, along with Marlene's parents, Margaret and Henry Hoeweler.

Times being what they were in the early 1980s, being gay went largely unsupported among family and community and was not an open topic of discussion. Fortunately, in his family, Carl was welcome to bring whom he wanted to events, and he often brought his lover to family cookouts, holidays or funerals. Aunt Lori and Uncle Jeff, Marge and Jerry, would talk politely with Carl's partner.

Carl Hoeweler and Donald Harvey dated on and off for six years, from 1980 to '86, and lived together for some of that time.

According to a research summary by Elizabeth Sellers, Pannill Hedgecock and Melissa Georges, studying the life and crimes of Donald Harvey at Radford University in Virginia, Harvey killed his partner's father and his brother-in-law. Here are two entries from their compilation, from when Harvey was thirty-one years old:

April 25, 1983 (death: May 1, 1983) – Killed Carl's father, Henry   Hoeweler (WM, 82) by giving him arsenic. He died four days later due to a stroke and kidney failure.

Late 1983 - early 1984 – Accidentally killed Howard Vetter (Carl's brother-in-law). Donald had been using wood alcohol to remove adhesive labels and left the solution in a vodka bottle. Carl got hold of the wrong bottle and served

Howard a few drinks from it. He was sick for a week, and suffered a heart attack. His death was attributed to cardiac failure.

Upon learning of Hardy's death at the hands of Harvey for the first time from my aunt Lori in the early summer of 2017, I was incredulous. How could I not know this information, and why didn't anyone think to tell me? Aunt Lori was absolutely right when she responded by saying, "You all had a lot going on then." The Vetter family found out about Harvey's involvement with Hardy's death late that summer of 1987, with a notice of an exhumation for the Hoewelers. Though Lori knows she told her sister Pat at some point, about Hardy Vetter, maybe Mom either forgot or didn't think we needed more to absorb amidst what had become an onslaught on horrendous news. Making the call to contain the damage, Mom let her children process what we could.

Lori and Jeff sat across from me in a local restaurant and proceeded to tell me, over glasses of wine and beer, that Hardy, Jeff's uncle, had hosted a New Year's Eve party in either 1984 or '85 and that during the party that evening, Lori and Jeff both sat talking for three hours on the sofa next to Donald, whom, despite the history, Jeff can still somehow repeatedly describe as "a very nice and friendly man."

In a statement Donald Harvey later made, he said, "I liked Hardy. Didn't want to kill him. Hardy went to get Woodford bourbon. But I didn't want him to drink it because it had paint thinner in it for Carl."

Marlene Hoeweler's parents were both exhumed during the discovery.

Harvey's murderous need killed two members within my own family.

Having met, up close, a murderer, a man who poisoned Dad, one who is still remembered by my uncle as 'very nice and friendly', leaves me beyond restless in reconciling all manner of ill accomplished when masked in kindness. I have struggled to trust in people, knowing the human who could do such things with a smile. At times, I have even questioned my own kindnesses. Serious debates have played out in my mind over whether or not to discuss Harvey; the child, the man, the serial killer, the victim, the psychological study; at all here. As I have mentioned, to normalize, sensationalize, or fixate on a serial killer runs counter to my sensibilities. At the same time, I think it is important to discuss what led one life to take another's, to draw lessons from case studies that might prevent such devastating consequences in the future.

Evil isn't inherited or manufactured. It is grown in a young mind, a petri dish for love or hate, whichever condition is ripest for harvest. My fervent hope is that by connecting the pinpoints of trauma, we can intervene with care before drastic detours lead to tragic ends. Budding behaviors begin to bloom in children, and society must decide to act in youth to prevent serious mental wellness issues in adults. Only then will we find and help other troubled souls in our lives and communities, only then can we prevent unnecessary death.

We dwell in a modern reality, and most of you will have already typed Harvey's name into a web browser's search bar by now, so I'll summarize with context here.

SERIAL KILLERS ARE PREDATORS by nature, though their motives and methods vary wildly. The Federal Bureau of Investigation lays out serial murder in a behavioral context through the National Center for the Analysis of Violent Crime. Seeking to draw from data and fact, former FBI director Robert S. Mueller III opens with a message about the group of multidisciplinary experts who contributed to this body of work during a 2005 symposium. The dissertation explains that in 1998, a federal law was passed by the U.S. Congress, the Protection of Children from Sexual Predators Act (Title 18, U.S. Code, Chapter 51, and Section 1111). This law includes a definition:

"The term 'serial killings' means a series of three or more kill-ings, not less than one of which was committed within the Unit-ed States, having common characteristics such as to suggest the reasonable possibility that the crimes were committed by the same actor or actors."

The dissertation goes on to expose some commonly held myths:

Myth: Serial killers are all dysfunctional loners.
Myth: All serial murderers travel and operate interstate.
Myth: Serial killers cannot stop killing.
Myth: All serial killers are insane or are evil geniuses.
Myth: Serial killers want to get caught.

Seeking to better understand the mind of a killer, this FBI docu-ment informs law enforcement about the nature of these crimes. The National Criminal Justice Reference System (NCJRS) has no shortage of abstracts written for academics and investigators to make more sense of mass murder, separating it into categories of organized and disorganized crimes, to know whether killers are motivated by psychosis, abuse, anger, power or control, and how those tendencies manifest.

In one piece, "Profiles in Terror: The Serial Murderer" (1985), published in the journal Federal Probation, Volume 44, Issue 3, R.M. Holmes categorized killers into four types: the visionary type, the mission-oriented type, the hedonistic type, and the power/con-trol-oriented type. Donald Harvey would fit this last category.

Holmes' work on this NCJRS abstract was likely why he was interviewed two years later by Todd Murphy, a staff writer for the Louisville Courier-Journal, for an article on September 20, 1987.

In the report, "Donald Harvey: A Killer Without a Con-science," Murphy writes:

"Holmes says that he has found that almost all serial killers have a disproportionate sense of self-importance. 'They think they're... supreme human beings,' he said. When something hap-pens that most people would immediately dismiss, such as someone failing to greet them on the street, serial killers become consumed by it, Holmes said. They feel they have been brought down unfairly and must restore their rightful position, he said. So, 'he's going to prove he's really in control by going out and killing.' And although serial killers excel at fooling people, at getting them to trust them, they never feel compassion for their victims or guilt for their acts, Holmes said."

Murphy, in the same article, interviewed Harvey's mother, nurses at Drake and other experts—among them, Dr. Walter Lippert, who was one of the clinical psychologists who assessed and studied Donald Harvey in 1987, after he was arrested. Murphy's article quotes Lippert: "What does a killer look like?... We expect them to look like Frankenstein or even Jack Nicholson in *The Shining*. They don't. They look like you and me."

A psychologist is an important resource in any sector, and without doubt, necessary in any metropolitan police department, given the crimes that live on in the minds of police officers.

In an academic assessment titled "Angel of Death: An investigation of the life, murders and psychopathology of Donald Harvey," Dr. Lippert (the independently contracted psychologist for Cincinnati Police Department until 1995), examined Harvey, saying "I have personally interviewed Donald Harvey for several hours." Recounting jealousy of a younger sister and brother who Harvey was made to babysit, and the disappointments and perceptions of a father who rarely spoke to him, whom he did not feel close to, according to the CPD psychologist, one, Lippert notes that it was a grandmother that soothed young Donald and advised him as a teen.

Lippert's document then lays out what seems to be the groundwork for his own book on the case and investigation, including his thoughts that the media (Pat Minarcin and WCPO) did not contribute to the case, also claiming that Harvey used the media to his whims. Dr. Lippert, in this document, even made an inference that my mother had released the details of Dad's murder, stating "Mrs. Powell could not refrain from telling John's father about the suspicion... She had been instructed not to tell anyone," suggesting that this was when the "Cincinnati papers began calling."

Though I know that assertion to be unfounded, Mom (a rule follower) would never have tipped off anyone, and certainly not John Powell's deceased and long-removed father. Pat Powell simply sought support from her own father who picked her up from homicide late that upsetting evening, following many traumatic hours, and then shared a hard truth with her three teenage children after learning how her their father was murdered. Lippert goes on to misstate (to understate) that the interview process was a lie detector test for mom, at a measly three hours. Still, professionals get to make their assessments. This paper is Dr. Lippert's research, through his lens, his assessment.

Through police documentation, myriad news interviews conducted with his neighbors and printed and digital articles (from 19897, 89, and 2017) and available online sources, including Lippert's work, I will detail what have become widely known public facts about Donald Harvey:

Born in 1952 in Butler County, Ohio, and raised between the small towns of Booneville and London, Kentucky, Harvey attended Sturgeon Elementary School where Principal Martha Turner remembers the student fondly, as did many of the neighbors and adult community members. Hardworking, well-respected parents Goldie and Ray Harvey did the best they could to raise Donald to be a courteous, caring young man. As a child, Harvey had few close friends, preferring the company of his elders. Fellow students remember him as the teacher's pet and a loner. Apparently, according to several sources, between the ages of four and sixteen, Harvey was sexually molested both by his uncle Wayne and a neighbor, Dan Thomas. He moved out of his house at age fourteen and in with an older couple he knew. Transcripts show he dropped out of Booneville High School in Kentucky. According to a hometown acquaintance, Harvey applied for a position as a nurse's aide at age sixteen, without a high school diploma, and was denied. Harvey then moved to the bigger city of Cincinnati for a factory job that didn't last. Returning home to his family, Harvey spent his days at

Marymount Hospital in London Kentucky, visiting his grandfather who was convalescing. Nuns there became familiar with Harvey and asked if he wanted work as a hospital orderly, which he accepted. Within that first year he killed more than a dozen patients at Marymount.

Arrested for burglary in March 1971, at age nineteen, a drunk and disorderly Harvey spouted off about some murders he'd committed. Though police looked into his claims, investigators could find no substantial proof of homicide, and he got off with a small fine for petty theft. No follow-up is noted to have occurred.

Immediately after this incident, Harvey enlisted in the Air Force, only to be generally discharged after ten months. He returned home battling depression, and twice in the fall of 1972, he admitted himself to the Veterans Affairs Medical Center in Lexington, for depression and attempted suicide. While there, he had twenty-one electric shock treatments. His mother, Goldie, would later condemn the hospital for releasing him too soon without a change to his condition.

Several jobs moved him through hospitals in Kentucky until 1974, when he returned to Cincinnati and found employment at the VA Hospital there. He returned home to visit his mother several times a year. For ten years he fulfilled various duties in housekeeping, as a nurses' aide, autopsy assistant or catheter technician at the VA. Working night shifts mostly, he was given unfettered access to all areas of the hospital. He kept a journal of details about the fifteen people he killed while there.

His personal life demonstrated further depravity, through fits of jealousy and paranoia that deepened after moving in with his lover, Carl Hoeweler. A neighbor's dog died after Harvey cared for him, and neighbors were often sick or dying around him. Unassuming and well liked, Harvey would host gatherings where he repeatedly poisoned Carl and his family as well as their neighbors and friends.

By 1985, Harvey was suspected for significant damage at the VA facility, and he had been stopped on site for a violation, possession of a firearm. Samples stolen from the lab were also found on him, as were books on the occult. He was given the option to resign rather than be fired. After paying a $50 fine, Harvey left the VA empowered, with a clean record and no barrier to his next job at Drake Memorial Hospital.

❖

READER, AS YOU CAN SEE, this was a person with a history of mental unrest leading to serious personal and workplace behavior issues. Unaddressed and enabled, Harvey's problems intensified, passing from one place of employment to the next. With professional job records left incomplete, confessions made while in police custody not taken seriously, his charges and fines reduced and downplayed, Harvey's killings were permitted to go undiscovered for at least eighteen years.

From 1986 to 87, Harvey was employed at Drake Memorial Hospital, where he murdered at least twenty-four patients. (There were additional victims that the grand jury believed they did not have enough evidence to fully convict on.) The death of one of Harvey's final victims, my dad, John Powell, was discovered by Dr. Lee Lehman, an astute coroner, through his training and sense of smell during autopsy. Exposed not only as a murderer but as a serial killer by an intrepid reporter's work, Harvey was held accountable by the Hamilton County Prosecutor's Office in August of 1987, and sentenced to life in prison. Donald Harvey was tried and convicted in Ohio and Kentucky for a total of thirty-seven murders, though Harvey confessed to killing significantly more.

After his confession in April of '87, and between the grand jury testimony on July 9 of that same year, in interviews with expert psychiatrists and a psychologist's summary report from Radford University, Harvey admitted to killing other lovers and roommates and said he was sexually molested as a child.

It is widely agreed that Donald Harvey killed upwards of eighty-seven people, making him one of America's most prolific serial killers.

We are left with questions about his motives. A life that started out loved and well liked in small-town America ended scores of others. Could proper interventions, made earlier in life, have subdued such a troubled person? Did his ongoing molestation at such a young age contribute to his own mental decline, his secrecy and need for control? Did societal pressures add to his angst? Did the people placed in positions of care and power miss the chance to read his cues?

The greater questions: Are we doomed to deal with deranged minds, psychotics and sociopaths, as a general rule? Is murder bound to be a loose thread in the shared fabric of humanity? If so, how can we mitigate or reduce the impact of these inevitabilities? If childhood abuse is a contributor, what proven examples actively work to reduce those instances? We cannot change the past, and history repeats itself. Signs pointing to despair lead us to understand potentially dark turns ahead; let us strive to shed light on preventative outcomes.

What lessons can be applied to save future souls? When looking back at the whole of a person, can we paint a full picture? Can we pay closer attention to warning signs, to broken pieces and sharp edges as they emerge? It's not impossible—science, data and infrastructure are available—however, it would take a revolutionary new approach to mental health and wellness in our society to treat life for health, quality and prevention.

Harvey lived in a small town and was a lonely child who connected better with adults. He dropped out of school, worked and moved towns without friends. In context, being gay in the 1970s and '80s, living in the rural Midwest, certainly meant he lived a secretive life, repressing urges, likely under attack. He worked as a teenager with nuns and the elderly, never short of good examples, but then was arrested for burglary. While in custody he admitted atrocities, but was not fully held accountable for his crimes, as there was no concerted effort over the years to check out his claims of murder.

Joining the military rather than serve time in prison, he received an unspecified discharge. Shortly after, he sought treatment for depression and attempted suicide. He was known to be paranoid and jealous with his lovers, and those closest to Harvey were regularly ill and dying. Can we start to see the common denominator? Preferring to work around sickness and death, Harvey had a record of disgruntled-employee behavior. Acting out, he was suspected of causing $25,000 in damage at one workplace, and yet was neither censured nor fired. For another infringement, being caught with a concealed firearm and stolen lab samples, once again he was not fully held accountable. Let go with a small fine and no smear to his record, no taint or suspicion followed him.

Nurses had reasons to be concerned about Harvey while he worked at Drake. They expressed these misgivings to superiors in 1986, and tipped off local police as early as March of 1987.

Madness leaves traces, if people are willing to look for them.

23

obligated [ob-li-gey-tid] *adjective*
1. bound by law or regulation, moral principle, duty, etc.; obliged
2. (of funds, property, etc.) pledged, committed, or bound, as to meet an obligation

UNDER THE HEADLINE "County considers Drake probe, firings: Mediator plan meets favor," a *Cincinnati Enquirer* article by Bob Weston, from August 20, 1987, describes the Hamilton County Board of Commissioners coming to grips, sort of, with the unfolding Drake Hospital crisis. After reporting that one Hamilton County Commissioner, Norman Murdock, called for Drake trustees' resignations, Weston reports that the Drake leaders offered no comment and goes on to say, "But they were more enthusiastic about his (Murdock's) idea that the county form a board of mediators to come up with a formula for financial settlements with families of patients whom Harvey killed. [Norman] Murdock, a lawyer himself, said that would be the best way to avoid the legal chaos growing out of an anticipated 'wild flurry of lawsuits.'"

A wild flurry of lawsuits. Suits filed against a county hospital for criminal behavior resulting in at least twenty-four murder victims, in a care facility paid for by taxpayer money. Most of the plaintiffs, the flurry presumably, would be surviving families like mine.

The commissioners clearly were shaken by the scale of this tragedy, but even more so by the scandal now left to them to clean up—without bankrupting the county. They started off right, with a mediator and a formula for considering settlements. It was a reasonable plan. Might have behooved administrators to actually carry it out.

As a side note: Elected officials really ought to choose their words more carefully. That statement by Murdock makes it sound as if there would be a free-for-all of legal filings entirely disconnected from the lives lost due to the mismanagement at Drake. Didn't families have a right to seek compensation, and shouldn't our interests in this case be regarded with solemnity? Where was the accountability? Shouldn't those in positions of responsibility show some decency and humility in making reparations, unprompted by lawsuits, but by recognition of a need to restore public trust and do right by grieving families?

Within four months, though, the county gave up any plans of making amends.

Associated Press wire services reported on Wednesday, December 23, 1987, printed in the *Dayton Daily News and Journal-Herald*, "Prosecutor won't share evidence." The article goes on to say that Art Ney "will fight efforts to share the evidence with victims' families who are suing Harvey. 'We feel strongly about this,' Ney said in court Monday, [citing] the confidentiality of county grand jury proceedings and the need to protect the privacy of patients' families."

Patients' families were the ones seeking damages. What this says to me is that Art Ney wouldn't share evidence against Hamilton County and also wouldn't allow several families of murder victims that Harvey confessed to, who were close to conviction, but just shy of enough evidence, to seek civil damages.

"Will Harvey Confession be aired?" asked John Kiesewetter on page 45 of *The Enquirer*, June 19, 1988. "Joseph Deters, chief assistant Hamilton County prosecutor, says that could happen."

Court referee Rory Clear has recommended the distribution. Harvey's attorney, William Whalen, has asked that the confession and Harvey's psychiatric report remain sealed," Kiesewetter reported. " 'I anticipate that it will be released in the very near future,' Deters says. Deters is prepared to have videotape copies made, if Morrisey (the appointed judge) accepts Clear's proposal... 'It just seems inconceivable to me that some reporter somewhere won't scrounge that up,' Deters says. 'Knowing how society is, I would be shocked if it didn't become public.'"

August 10, 1989 Drake, a county hospital when culpable, denies deaths with impending lawsuit, the Associated Press reports. "Drake officials made the denials in response to questionnaires submitted by attorneys for the victims' families, who are suing the hospital, the *Cincinnati Enquirer* reported yesterday (August 9 1989). 'We definitely are denying that,' said R. Thomas Moorhead, a Drake attorney. 'There is no evidence that he murdered these people. It is up to the plaintiffs to try to prove that.'"

The AP article continues, "Marc Mezibov, attorney for the family of Roger Evans, one of the patients Harvey admitted killing, called the hospital's position 'duplicitous,' and 'callous and cruel' toward the families of the victims."

Drake's day in court approached. Slowly. As one delay followed another, the lawyers for Drake knew time was on their side to defend the county-funded institution. Without a settlement agreement for the families, a trial finally was scheduled: Judge Robert Morrisey would hear the case March 5, 1989.

"The families are just so hurt, they think the county just doesn't care and hopes the elder spouses just die off," Paul Martin, attorney for eight of the victims' families, said in the Enquirer on October 29, 1989.

"We just don't think there's any proof of any of the convictions," said lawyer Leo Breslin representing Drake Hospital (renamed Drake Center Inc. by the county before the hearing). Associated Press reports in the same article, that if Morrisey denies a request for summary judgment (a decision entered by a court for one party against another without a full trial), then it would be up to jurors to hear evidence. Martin said, "I was surprised (Drake's) attorneys took the position that Donald Harvey didn't kill. The proof is there, already... In effect, Drake Hospital is asking the jury to hold that Art Ney is either lying or grossly incompetent."

One lawsuit, the largest, for $4 million, was filed a day after the courtroom proceedings on August 18, 1987, by Harold White's wife. Harold had been poisoned with arsenic by Donald Harvey and died several months later.

Glenn Whitaker, our family attorney, represented Mom in what became a joint lawsuit, filed along with the other families for varying settlements.

During our phone interview, I heard Glenn laughing in disgust and what can only be described as continued disbelief. He remembered Leo Breslin, who represented the county and Drake at the time, and "what was obviously an audacious and shameful ploy" by the lawyer to shield his clients from culpability: "Part of their argument was that these people were vegetative, had no life, and it was a blessing their lives were terminated. Terrible, but it did add some merit for lowering the settlement numbers."

Glenn added, "There were discussions (among the families' attorneys) of it all being settled at once," though he had protested, understanding that some of Harvey's crimes might stand out from others in the eyes of a judge or jury. Glenn felt strongly, "True that some of these victims were aged or didn't have potential for recovery, but not so for John Powell—he was young and starting to come back."

Again, it was good to hear that someone else understood this critical fact back then, however much the other side might have disavowed it. Speaking with Glenn was also the first time I'd realized that it certainly didn't hurt Drake to draw out these proceedings, while distancing themselves from Harvey's crimes and the county's mishandling. It also didn't hurt the county to later categorize Dad as an invalid in the class-action lawsuit. One might speculate that in cases of malpractice or wrongful death, the debilitated pay out less when dead than rehabbed patients would. Seems officials were banking on a court's conclusion that a comatose patient has no quality of life and no hope of recovery—that death may actually ease their burden.

Whatever the legal strategies at play, Glenn told me, "There was a great deal of pressure, after all the delays, to get the deal done and move on, and finally Patricia and everyone else agreed."

In short: heartbroken and exhausted, the families settled.

❖

WHAT STILL SEEMS OVERLOOKED is that Jan Taylor, the Drake Hospital administrator, a county employee, covered up concerns, allowing mass murder to go on undiscovered. He quelled complaints and directed his subordinates to do the same. Based on Taylor's actions alone, clearly, the county had some liability in these deaths. And they ran from it.

Repugnant, how inhumane this process was for the victims' families. Finishing high school at the time, I'm sure I didn't fully comprehend what was going on, and Mom didn't burden me with it.

Disappointed in the final result, Glenn, along with other attorneys, thought it was far too small of a settlement for the pain and suffering of the victims and their families. But, Glenn said, "Trying to prove that the hospital ultimately had responsibility for a guy who was committing murder there was tough. Not an easy case to prove—the medical examiner, she just made mistake after mistake, but in the end they were mistakes, so it was hard to prove. Collective wisdom was, take what we can get and get out."

Nearly three years after John Powell was poisoned, in late February 1990, plaintiffs and defendants agreed to a settlement: twenty-six victims' families would share a total of $2.3 million in damages, and the lawsuits were dismissed. If divided equally it wouldn't amount to $90,000 per family, before lawyer cuts.

No windfall, and certainly not enough for victims' families to live carefree. Still, Patricia Powell was able to close the book on a three-year nightmare. Ever generous, she gave thousands of her settlement share to other family members. After Glenn's attorney fees were paid, she made sure that John's sister, mother, daughters and son each had some of the money she'd been given, and she helped her immediate family as well. With the financial crisis of 2008 eventually forcing her to file for bankruptcy, Mom worked odd jobs, making do with a smaller life until we moved her in with us.

258 /MET THE END

Such a slap in the face to the families. Though Mom didn't receive anywhere near fair compensation for the loss of her recuperating, forty-four-year-old husband, other survivors received far less, and it remains a stain on the county's record to have forced further injury for so long, in what was certainly a concerted effort.

The Enquirer was remarkably quiet on the lawsuits, though other regional papers printed the ongoing story regularly and in detail. Without an altruistic attempt to make the families whole, or at least compensate for their ordeal in a sensitive or timely way, Hamilton County revealed what is sadly commonplace: a lack of accountability or amends by local government.

Paying their own attorneys the equivalent of what could have been resolved for survivors in early arbitration, prevailing heads in Hamilton County preferred to deny closure to grieving families, for over two-and-a-half years. The county chose the first stage of grief and remained there, missing the opportunity to apologize for their role in this travesty. Make no mistake, they played a role. County employees covered up reports of deaths, they excused and dismissed the actions of a killer at Drake Hospital for seven months.

How much were those lives worth?

The county determined, not too much. A lesson learned well in grief, the empty gesture.

The systemic and societal failures illustrated by this lawsuit go way beyond Hamilton County or Ohio, by the way. Nationally, our legal system has been hacked, allowing rampant disregard for altruism through the courts. On all sides, people without millions, without a legal education, and without connections pay the price of our dysfunctional legal system—none more than people of color. Judges are elected through biased campaign finance, which contribution limits cannot address. Huge class-action suits, armies of corporate attorneys, financial advantage, the constant plea deal and hushed settlements, all deny the faulted recompense for their losses or true liability for all parties. We've allowed robbers to run the system. Money rules the day, and poor, law-abiding folks rarely are rewarded. Courtroom strategy outweighs principle on the scales of justice.

This Drake settlement wasn't enough to care for our mother in her widowhood; it provided little safety net for our family's future healthcare expenses and therapies. Though she was able to take one year of classes at Mount St. Joseph College, the settlement didn't allow Mom to take a deserved break from work. She worked in real estate for a while right after Dad died, and sold Avon for thirty years after that. Making ends meet by cleaning houses and watching kids for her neighbors, she also carted boxes of books, cards and toiletries to create Premium Sales displays at supermarkets and department stores. Clipping her coupons, Patricia Powell worked hard for years to support her family—as she, and we, worked through our trauma.

24

absorb [ab-sawrb, -zawrb] *verb* (used with object)
1.   to suck up or drink in (a liquid); soak up
2.   to swallow up the identity or individuality of; incorporate
3.   to involve the full attention of; to engross or engage wholly
4.   to occupy or fill
5.   to take in without echo, recoil, or reflection

I N THE COURSE OF detailing this account, I conducted interviews
with key people for their perspective and context.

At my request, in April 2017, family members connected me to
Hamilton County Prosecutor Joe Deters. We had reacquainted at
these relatives' wedding seven years earlier, and he sincerely offered
help at that time, if ever I should find need. Offers are remembered,
and I reached out the week after Donald Harvey was killed. Deters
quickly called me back, eager to assist. Explaining my intentions
to finally write about the trauma of our family's experience, he
said he'd have his staff gather some documents that I had asked to
see. We met twice, and he kindly extended answers to my questions, provided access to read through any documentation that was
permitted through his office, and he offered his best wishes to my
family.

Joe is no stranger to the spotlight. Having secured a long career
with a string of notable cases, he has a strong and complicated
track record of prosecuting crime here in Cincinnati, where racism and justice have long been at odds. Plainly, Deter's had mixed
reviews. He defied expectations when, in 2015, he charged Ray
Tensing for murder in a case that received national attention, when
Tensing, a white police officer at the University of Cincinnati, shot

and killed Samuel DuBose, an unarmed Black man, during an off-campus traffic stop.

"Deters has historically been at odds with the Black community," Aaron Roco, an organizer with Black Lives Matter Cincinnati, told BuzzFeed News, July 2015. "We're no fans of Joseph Deters. We're happy with what he's done today, but that may be the only thing."

Sitting at a local coffee shop the first time we met, informally dressed, Joe looked tired. The Tensing verdict had ended in a hung jury, and the second trial date being set now settled over him like a dark cloud. Over coffee, he shared the weight he carried. As it turned out, that second trial was declared a mistrial only months later, that June of 2017, and Deters would be forced to drop the charges against Tensing.

He discussed the past, reflecting my dad's case back to me through the lens of his life's work. I quickly realized that thirty years and our own individualities and roles in the story stood between us. There was a disparity in perspectives on both the case and the timeline of events. It was not my intention to strongarm or dismantle; we both hold the truths we hold, and three decades is a long time to hold a narrative. In truth, I wanted to hear how Deters remembered the case, and so I listened, understanding how his own experience and expertise would expose, for him, a different view from mine. Deters was an assistant prosecutor at the time Harvey confessed to killing John Powell, and his boss and mentor was then Hamilton County Prosecutor Art Ney. Prosecutors push past doubt.

We small-talked for a while and then dug in a little further. He dropped his own seedy theories and unflattering points of view regarding WCPO reporter Pat Minarcin and defending attorney Bill Whalen, but I let those comments fall across the table, unanswered. Being in conversation regularly with men, my mind translated his man-speech, that hint of being bested flavoring his uncomplimentary thoughts and language. Joe has a harsh way of speaking at times, even saying himself he has no filter, but he was eager to help me, and I was grateful.

The second time we met, Deters' assistant scheduled for us to meet in his office. I had walked from home to his office building that warm day in April. His staff was exceedingly polite in greeting me. Sitting me in a large, windowless conference room, they provided me with everything I had requested—except, I then learned, I could not have access to the grand jury testimony or video recording from July 9, 1987, in accordance with state (rules vary by state) and federal law requiring they remain sealed until court ordered otherwise for public access.

Joe Deters walked in then, refreshed and in between meetings, wearing a suit when he shook my hand. He sat at the head of the table, and I positioned myself diagonally across from him in the first seat. With one hand on a stack of papers and manilla file folders, he leaned in and said, "Here is everything we have for your dad. My assistant removed anything that was too bad, and," he paused, "if it's any comfort, Harvey died a horrible death. They called us soon after it happened, and he was beaten terribly, so bad they didn't expect him to make it."

While I'm certain there are survivors who need that kind of assurance, to know that Harvey suffered a fate worse than death, I am simply not one of them. I cannot imagine the kinds of atrocities Deters has seen in his career—beyond awful, enough horror to desensitize him to violence or become more accustomed to its frequency. Though I didn't take comfort in his message, I recognized the intention of his sentiment, and nodded.

Restating that my dad's death saved lives, Joe stood to go; he had another appointment. But I admired and appreciated his kindness in sharing that truth. Again shaking his hand, I thanked him sincerely for his support, for gathering all the documentation laid out before me, as well as the use of his conference room. Prosecutor Joe Deters left me to do my research, offering his staff to assist me.

Getting to work, I laid out my notepad, pen in hand, and opened the first folder. Within half an hour, I had digested quite a bit of disturbing material. Both my dad's and Harvey's names were all over it: death reports and records, Harvey's confession, even the list Harvey had kept of his victims in a plastic bag, still here as evidence. It all caught up with me. My body pulsed. My heart rate rose. Recognizing the panic overtaking me there in the conference room, I felt heat chasing a chill up my chest and neck, spreading a sheen of sweat across my face, nerves standing on end, a leg bouncing, my whole body jittering. I kept running anxious hands through my hair, forcing myself to breathe. Taking a break, I drank some water, trying to remember why I was there, why I'd chosen to submit myself to this pain.

I had a plan. I had a need to write this story. And I would. Telling myself exactly that. Telling myself I would not be that easily deterred. Gut-wrenching information, difficult to read, while at the same time hard not to read. Not wanting to waste the time given, I sat up, growing impatient with myself, and worked to pull myself back together. Breathing deep in my nose, out my mouth, as I'd been taught so long ago, I willed my heart to slow its beat. Reminding myself this kind of reaction was to be expected, and that I needed to be professional, I stacked the documents neatly. Beginning again, I picked up my pen. Focusing on the order of the paperwork, reading, taking notes, wondering what else I might find or be able to use. Then, a soft knocking on the door, and the polite face of Joe Deter's administrative assistant peered in to ask if I needed anything. Looking at me, a quick sense told her that I needed more time. Suggesting I come find her whenever I was ready, she pulled the door quietly shut behind her.

Back to the task. I shook off my jitters, pressed palms down my legs, and dug in. Ludicrous, I knew, to be so bothered; this was going to be upsetting, I understood that going in. Hurt could come later, I told myself. Just focus for now. Reading these strangely impersonal, factual things about a loved one is bound to derail anyone, but I couldn't work from that mindset, so I kept reviewing a few folders, adding context, making frantic notes, until I'd consumed the final pages of information. I took a few photos on my smartphone to capture text I couldn't begin to decipher in one visit. Stacking them back to how I'd been given them, I stood and stretched. Grabbing my shoulder bag and the documents, another deep breath helped me open the door.

Leaving the conference room, I met Deters' administrative assistant at her desk. Accommodating as ever, she accepted my thanks and the stack from my outstretched hands, then asked me to wait at her desk while she safely locked the files away. Standing there, I looked down into the smiling face of Donald Harvey on the cover of Bill Whalen's book, *Defending Donald Harvey*, on top of her reading stack, at the edge of her desk. A few minutes later she returned to walk me out, and I entered the lift she had called up to the floor. We said goodbyes, and as the doors closed over my polite smile, my mood plummeted with the downward pull of the elevator. Miserable thoughts and fury raged inside me as I walked toward home, heated in the late afternoon sun.

I didn't know what to do with such an uncommon feeling for me. For decades, anger has not been my go-to emotion. I hadn't visited with it in quite a while.

Just then, Mom texted.

Had she sensed I might need to talk to her? But after quickly scanning and then re-reading her message, I realized this text was not about me or where'd I'd been. Abandoning my anger, I called her, anxious to hear what was going on. I did not reveal where I had just been. She then informed me that her biopsy result came back, positive. She had breast cancer.

Worry walked me home and weighed on my already heavy mind. I worked to keep my heartbeat steady amidst ruminations of all I'd read and reviewed, now blanketed with concern for Mom. Two hours and hundreds of documents floated through my mind. I'd made notes of pages of police records, court documents, recorded transcripts, hospital records, and the horrendous detailed timeline of my dad's last days and minutes on earth.

Harvey's confession for the murder of John Powell, for my dad, was full of cavernous holes unexplored by detectives in the moment. Hindsight lends perspective in ways unknown to the players then, but I couldn't escape the time machine I was now traveling in. My notes tracked all the moments when Harvey's responses went unchecked:

Miami river, or was it the Ohio river? The poison was dropped in which?
Questions circled.
Harvey said he loved my dad.
John Powell reminded him of his troubled relationship with his father.
He said John could not see, yet looked up to him pleading.
He said he thought John, long comatose, was such a loving man.
He said he worried for him and thought he was in a bad marriage.
He said that Pat Powell was a loving wife constantly at his side.
He said he was so worried about John, because he was so thin.
Autopsy report said John Powell was a healthy male of good nutrition.
His medical records have him at 151 pounds at death, much lost in the last two months.
He said he just gave him a little bit to ease his suffering.
He said he used enough cyanide to kill an army.
He said it was over quickly.
50 minutes later after the poison was administered, John Powell was still alive.

Everything Harvey said he knew about John Powell was a contradiction.

Donald Harvey had simply killed John Powell, killed my dad, because he wanted to kill. A liar, telling lies, to justify killing another human.

I turned into the gate of our condo, walked in the door, and my husband, knowing I was close to home, met me in the kitchen.

He asked if I was okay. I said I wasn't.

"It was a lot," I told him, as hot tears defiantly spilled down my cheeks. Even then I felt as if I didn't have the right to cry, having put myself in the position to have to deal with it. Damon reached out to hug me, but I couldn't be comforted.

"I'm aware that I asked for it," I told him.

Then I shared the one thing I'd specifically been digging for in those documents: a certainty that my dad had been poisoned and survived multiple times before he died. I walked away from Deters' office that afternoon with the conviction—only speculation and hearsay before now—that Dad had been poisoned several times. Such a strong man, John Powell had defied all odds, repeatedly. First by surviving that horrific motorcycle accident, surviving intensive surgery, coming out of a coma and surprising everyone by communicating and maneuvering around in a wheelchair. Defying multiple attempts on his life, John Powell's fortitude succumbed only after being given "enough to kill an army," a dose that even he could not defy.

The Donald Harvey/Drake case must have taught Joe Deters the worst and best to be found in criminals, from the heights of their intelligence to the depths of their malevolence. Deters stood out as the one attorney in the room in opposition to the plea arrangement Bill Whalen attempted to secure for his client, to save Harvey from death. Despite solid agreement among his more experienced colleagues, when the vote went around the room, Deters stood his ground, the only "no" vote for the plea deal. Obviously the bargain went forward, but the young assistant prosecutor showed he had a mind of his own. Given the early public attention, pressure on the county, the sheer number of victims murdered by one killer, a chilling grand jury account, and exhumations that turned a city sideways, this undoubtedly was, for Deters, a trial by fire.

His experience of being involved in this case certainly cemented his career. Deters has served Cincinnati, the state of Ohio, and Hamilton County since 1982, in the roles of assistant prosecuting attorney, Clerk of Courts, the State of Ohio's forty-fourth treasurer, and both the nineteenth and twenty-first Hamilton County prosecuting attorney, a role he's still serving in late 2022, a year after winning reelection against Judge Fanon Rucker.

We don't agree specifically on how things went down in 1987; prosecutors push past doubt; I understand and will expand on that. But Joe Deters was a key player who continues to be impacted by and attached to this case. His offers of help and thought for my family made him more personal to me, despite some of his viewpoints. I don't need to agree with someone to know they have a right to see things as they do. Joe has a narrative around this story that has served him, and though the facts do not entirely support it,

I can understand finding ways to cope with such an overwhelming case as this.

Not once, in any of our discussions, did I feel anything other than his concern for our family and a wish to ease any pain he could through his assistance. He was glad Harvey finally had gotten what he deserved, yes, but he was also adamant that Dad's death saved lives.

I WAS UNABLE TO MEET several other relevant players in this case. Bill Whalen, Harvey's defense attorney, died in 2012. For reasons still beyond my comprehension, he set off strong reactions in me. Aside from the courtroom that August of '87 and that victims' family meeting in the winter of '88, I'd stood next to Bill Whalen two other times.

On a dark winter evening during my senior year of high school, outside of the Mount St. Joseph college library, we both were waiting in the cold not ten feet from each other, looking for our respective rides. I was frozen, not by the chill in the air but by proximity: Whalen was an integral part of my traumatic past. Millions of thoughts and questions ran around my mind, bumping into each other, and yet, numb, I could not speak. We parted ways without more than a nod. He had no way of knowing whom he stood beside.

And then, around 2004, I'd been called for jury duty. In attendance each day for a week, so far my honest claims on the juror form of having being a family victim of murder had not released me. Seated on a bench, in an antechamber, about to enter the courtroom for voir dire, thinking how certain I was to be passed over given the circumstances of my Dad's death—at that moment, I saw Whalen walk into the room. Potential jurors likely sat beside me. I felt alone. He began speaking with the jury manager and a couple of other gentlemen directly in front of me. As he emerged through those doors, my heart nearly stopped, then raced as I heard his voice, saw him interact. He was there for about two minutes, taking no notice of me, though it felt far longer. Cemented to the seat, I was immobile. Concluding, he turned on his heel, pushing out through the same doors. When he left the room, I let out the breath I didn't realize I'd been holding. My stomach roiled; I went all over cold and clammy. With Whalen's exit, the jury clerk called attention, loudly announced that a plea deal had been struck and that we, the members of the jury pool, were immediately excused.

Every time I was near Bill Whalen, I became paralyzed by fear or apprehension. Panic during that first family meeting was the most severe, and now continued. Unable to put a precise finger on the cause, I can only imagine that because the defending attorney was so close to the killer who upended our world, I felt proximity to Harvey through him, a kind of nearness by proxy. For me, Whalen was an extension of Harvey, and whenever I saw him, I saw that other face sitting next to him in the courtroom.

When Whalen wrote his book *Defending Donald Harvey*, in 2005, my children were four and seven years old. Lover of words and books that I am, I often enjoy a trip to a bookstore (mostly independent stores on principle). Squatting in front of rows of books seated so neighborly on their shelves, I can never help buying a few. Wish I could buy the time to read them all. Immersing myself in their jackets, I'd determine if the author, cover art or storyline was the lure that hooked me.

In April of 2005, NPR revealed through my car radio that there was a book coming out from attorney Bill Whalen about his experience with the Harvey case. I was immediately on the line— but like any fish biting the bait, I was torn. My stomach contorted, knowing that to buy this book would put money in Whalen's pocket, and maybe benefit Harvey as well. I succumbed, by connection to this case; I needed to see something I myself had considered writing for so long.

The closest bookseller was a Barnes & Noble, and my sites were set. Walking into the store and up to the endcap shelf, I was confronted by a hundred replicas of the smiling face of my dad's murderer. I froze. Literally. There I stood in people's way. Physiological responses elicited in the past, whenever Bill Whalen was near, surfaced again in full force, and I could not make myself pick up that book. Paper, ink and glue held me at bay.

When I could finally move, I stepped aside. The kids were at school; I had a little time to work through this problem. With a spark of ingenuity, I picked up two other, benign books from a nearby shelf and sandwiched Whalen's book between them, thereby relieving me of touching it. As I write this, I fully understand how insane it sounds. I think we can all agree that we are not in our right minds all of the time. Books safely stacked in hand, I stuffed myself into a nearby reading chair and stared for a long time at the cover, the face, the title. *Defending Donald Harvey*.

Coaxing open a few pages with the other books and my shirt sleeve, I flipped toward where the victims' families were mentioned. Immediately I noticed Whalen had several points wrong in regards to my dad's condition, and from my mom's interrogation. Author Bill Whalen had not once called my mom to confirm any of his details. This, however, was his account, true to his own memory—subjective, like any memoir, though I cannot stress enough the importance of supporting research. Still, we're all human, the star witnesses to our own lives. Instinctively biased, tainted by time and experience, no two people would write the same account of any story, let alone this one.

Knowing I must look ridiculous, sitting in a bookstore with a book I couldn't touch and didn't want to need to read, I bit the bullet and decided to pay for the thing, so that I could flounder in the privacy of my own home. Carefully standing, I used the other two books in my hands to carry Whalen's curse and walked to the registers. Sliding the paperback volume onto that counter, I set my potholder books aside, and placed cash on the counter. The clerk slipped Whalen's book into a plastic Barnes & Noble bag... where it has remained ever since, stored away in its wrapping. I can honestly say that buying this book in 2005 is one of the oddest things I have ever done. Several times I have paused to consider actually reading it. As I write this, I have not.

Only when *Cincinnati Magazine* did an extensive piece on

Whalen's story in May of 2005 did I have more insight. Enough insight. That magazine article was lengthy and filled in a few details of interest, including the fact that Bill Whalen had helped Pat Minarcin with his investigative journalism on the Harvey case as best he felt he could. For that article being the first of several sources to later acknowledge that, I am grateful to Whalen.

Understanding that Bill Whalen was a good attorney and a decent man, I can see now that he figured out not only how to help his client avoid the death penalty; he also allowed a full accounting of his client's crimes. The State of Ohio appointed him for a case he couldn't have imagined would project him onto the national stage. Truly, I'm sorry for his family's loss, now that he's passed. I don't think for a minute that he would have purposely walked by me if I'd made myself known to him.

However, we can't always control what undoes us, and Whalen undid me. Hard to move past the relationship and correspondence Whalen kept with Harvey for years, until his death in 2012. Hard to know that he genuinely came to care for this killer, enough so that Harvey seemed the impetus to change his mind about the death penalty, as he indicated in an interview on a show by local CET (a local televised PBS affiliate), *Showcase* with Barbara Kellar.

Fast forward to the weeks after Harvey died from his wounds, late April of 2017. That same book cover upending me in a bookstore was staring up from the corner desk stack of Joe Deters' administrative assistant. She may have been reading up on the case and her boss's role in it. Not knowing the power it possessed over me, she asked me to wait there in order to lock her files away. Finding myself hovering awkwardly over the face of Dad's murderer, having just digested intimate details of his killings; finding myself in the office of the man who helped put him away for life, thinking how odd it was that I could not touch the book staring up at me, affirmed my decision not to.

Words and pictures are powerful things. Still, we have control over what is poured into our brains and psyches. The awareness that stalled me then propels me now, as my fingers fly over these keys.

25

stakeholder [steyk-hohl-der] *noun*
1. the holder of the stakes of a wager
2. a person or group that has an investment, share, or interest in
    something, as a business or industry
3. Law. a person holding money or property to which two or more
    persons make rival claims

O VER THE YEARS our family has been asked to participate in
several documentaries, TV episodes, interviews... endless
requests for newsworthy quotes about Dad's murder. Our usual
reaction has been to say "No, thank you," and think nothing more
about it. There are two notable exceptions. I'll recount one here, the
other later.

Mom was asked to participate in an investigative show called
Diagnosis: Unknown, fifteen years after Dad's death. She agreed to
return to the pain in order to share the lesser-known fact that her
husband, John, had been recovering when he was killed. Reading
journal entries from his hospitalization, she discussed the human
side of this story that, at the time, had yet to be told. Joe Deters,
homicide detective Bill Fletcher, and Drake nurses had also participated. When the episode aired in January 2004, we recorded
it from our TV on an old VHS tape. (In researching this book, I
re-discovered the *Diagnosis: Unknown* series on Amazon Video—
Mom participated in Season 2, Episode 3, "Death Shift"—but
at the time of this writing, the show is currently unavailable for
streaming.)

For that episode, Mom provided the very human element in

the story of investigators and their challenges. Reminiscing on camera about her husband, she was the soft side of a hard narrative. Nurses I hadn't seen in decades spoke on camera about how they had reached out to Pat Minarcin and cared deeply for my dad. Actors were cast to portray Mom, Dad and me in the story. Being the sibling most frequently at the hospital, nurses must have explained to those producers that one of Dad's children was a blonde teenager.

When a documentary or production team already has some of the most involved players among us already on board to assist in a project, we might look more closely at the angle the production company is coming from. *Diagnosis: Unknown* seemed to have a decent reputation for balancing murder investigation with family survivors in their episodes. We would not willingly participate in something that gives more notoriety to a killer, especially over that of the victim, their family, or the investigative team that was necessary to gain justice for the killing. This story circles us all, fades and returns, ad infinitum.

Connecting with others for this story I was writing, thirty-four years on, proved difficult at times. Frank Cleveland, Art Ney and Bill Whalen have all since passed away, along with homicide detectives Lawson and Camden. Others involved in the case were not as generous with their time as Joe Deters was, and some did not respond at all to my inquiries. A few folks graciously spoke to me even if they didn't feel they had much to offer. One source tried to make the history even darker than it was, and got carried away shaping it into their own story. Write it, I say.

I've not been able to connect with Detective Bill Fletcher, who has not responded to my attempts and networking through the documentary. I remember seeing him a time or two, early on, after Mom was no longer a suspect; he lived not far from our home. I heard him and Spec. Camden speak at a crime victims' support meeting on November 29, 1988. My diary shorthand recalls, "Homicide investigators talked. Very informative. Good officers. Don't like the way Pat Minarcin handles things."

Dr. Lee Lehman, the coroner who discovered Dad's cyanide

poisoning, did not return my calls. The other nurse's aide we really enjoyed, James Hale, a.k.a. "Big Daddy," I could not find, though he'd be a much older gentleman by now if indeed he is still alive.

Despite exhaustive efforts through nurse registries, online searches and social media avenues, I have been unable to locate nurse Sandra Huber. An unsung hero in this story, Huber's bravery in reaching outside the hospital to Pat Minarcin, was the step necessary to derive the best outcome from these events. From the thoughtful care she gave our dad, to the risk she took for her job, nurse Huber deserves some peace and recognition. As a participant in that *Diagnosis: Unknown* episode Mom was in, Huber shared her memories of her patient, John Powell, and after fifteen years revealed her role in stopping a serial killer.

Sandra Huber in *Diagnosis: Unknown*, Season 2, Episode 3, "Death Shift"

[22:14] "And we were really working diligently with him to try to get, get him to the point that he would be able to go home that, that would be a viable option for him, and he was reaching that goal little by little."

[23:13] "He would have one of these hemorrhaging episodes, and do great, come back all healthy, and then [a] while later he would have another one of these episodes, and the whole thing kept going in a cycle."

[24:11] "It was so unexpected. The feeling of seeing someone do what you never, never thought they'd do ever and how excited the family was because they were getting their dad back."

[31:15] "They did everything they could do to save him, and we knew that he wasn't gonna make it. You could just tell that he was slipping away little by little, and he knew that. And he was crying, he was such a fighter. The one thing that always stuck with me through that was watching him cry."

[44:01, referring to the difficulty of her first call to WCPO reporter Pat Minarcin] "Everything stopped and there was no other mention, no other investigation. We didn't hear anything. It doesn't take a brain surgeon to figure out that when you've given someone a list of names that you suspect died suspiciously, and it's not looked into, that there's a problem, and that's all we wanted, was somebody to listen."

THE COURAGE HUBER DISPLAYED in first reaching out to Minarcin still goes under-reported. Whistleblowers, whether on the job or after they've spoken up, are often under such duress and scrutiny, it is remarkable we hear from them at all. That a dedicated nurse such as Sandra Huber faced fear of losing her job for exposing wrongdoing within that health organization—her experience goes against healthcare's mission. How do we right our ships without a rudder or compass?

Reporters and the press, too, are often discredited, even demonized by some whose political and financial interests rely on an uninformed, distracted electorate. Granted, journalists are working under their own economic pressures; they can make mistakes, cut corners or go too far. Yet, what access to avenues of truth would we have without them?

The optimism within me wonders what the world would be like if all sides worked together for the greater good. I'm only repeating John Lennon's question. Picture a world where we don't disparage one another or mark territories in some turf war for valor or notoriety. If only we could value the significant and crucial roles each stakeholder plays in society.

As painful as it was to live through, my own story helped me understand the importance of things like attorney-client privilege, police protocols, the credibility of journalists maintaining anonymous sources, and other fundamentals of a free and fair system of justice. That system is still a work in progress, obviously, but we have to agree on a common goal. Public safety must be achieved, and at a fair price for our egos.

In her May 2009 *Showcase* interview with Bill Whalen, Barbara Kellar asks the attorney, "So you credit Pat Minarcin more than the public officials?"

Whalen says, "Oh yes," and goes on to talk about the other heroes in Harvey case, such as the Drake Hospital nurses and Coroner Lee Lehman.

In my own interviews, recent reports, and even in a more recent investigative documentary, the police and prosecutors seem to remember the series of events differently, out of the recorded chronological order and documentary evidence I remember and have affirmed. I can understand a desire to frame things in a way that doesn't reveal being caught unawares. And besides, this case took everyone by surprise—there was no real precedent, in Cincinnati or anywhere else (so far as history knows). Who could know how to handle such a monstrous scenario, without error? However, if an investigation was indeed still ongoing, somehow, secretly, after Police Chief Whalen had declared it closed, then wouldn't CPD be glad for the assistance of Minarcin's report, to put away a serial killer?

I'm reminded of a quote, sometimes credited to President Ronald Reagan (who supposedly kept it on display in the Oval Office), or to Harry Truman, but which I think goes back to Father William Strickland, a nineteenth-century Jesuit priest: "There is no limit to the amount of good you can do if you don't care who gets the credit."

For me, the saddest part of needing to reframe any of this story or to highlight more than was accomplished, is that it leaves no room to learn. We all must learn from this scenario. Overcoming it is pointless, unless we learn to do better next time. Trust that history will repeat; we must adapt.

Were things missed? Yes. Were things withheld? Yes. Was there a lack of cooperation? At times, yes. Was this the first serial killer any of us had happened upon, personally? Yes. Everyone involved in the Donald Harvey case did the best they could in real time. Truly. Homicide detectives did their job, and wanted to get a clean conviction. The reporter got the full story. The prosecutors' office pursued and followed a path that put Harvey away for life.

I have no doubt that certain truths were covered up in the interest of Hamilton County business. The commissioners said they were out of the loop, upset to learn about this string of killings at Drake Hospital from Minarcin's report. Certainly they would have known if a police investigation still had been underway in late spring of 1987—and if there was an active investigation, that officials had expressly ignored nurses' concerns. To save Drake, a county hospital, from scandal, the truth was suppressed for months. Someone chose to protect the hospital's reputation (and the careers of its leaders) over the well-being of its patients. My dad might still be alive had they listened. But he isn't, and we find ourselves here.

All the investigators, prosecutors and nurses, all have lived with the aftershocks Donald Harvey left in his wake. All of us were pro-foundly impacted. We are survivors of a horrific tragedy, and we are all imperfect humans deserving of compassion. Still, I can say this, though it will have zero impact on the results of the case: some actors in this story deserve more credit than others.

26

indicate [in-di-keyt] *verb* (used with object), in·di·cat·ed, in·di·cat·ing
1.   to be a sign of; betoken; evidence; show
2.   to point out or point to; direct attention to
3.   to show, as by measuring or recording; make known
4.   to state or express, especially briefly or in a general way; signal

ON AUGUST 25, 2017, Hurricane Harvey made the first of three landfalls, killing at least eight-eight people and devastating the lives of countless others. A third of Houston was covered in water when two feet of rain fell in twenty-four hours. Thirteen million people were affected, from Texas to Kentucky. Harvey was in the news constantly. Each time I see or hear that name, no matter which Harvey, momentarily, I'm held captive by my past. In this case it became a siren call to continue writing.

My youngest child had a teacher named Harvey Lewis at her start of school that same August. I'd met Harvey a few years before—a really incredible person, an astonishing professional athlete who, for over a decade, runs or car-free commutes to school every day. An inspiration to his students, he teaches government at the Cincinnati School for Creative and Performing Arts. He cared about my daughter's progress, and they really connected. I am thankful that he is my one positive "Harvey" association.

I began writing again, only to halt that winter, when my daughter's friends were cast in the high school play. We saw posters, saved the date, bought tickets, and heard all about rehearsals, through school communications and directly from her friends that January and February. In early March, 2018, to support the school and friends, we attended the performance. The play was *Harvey*.

Words flowed after that, until late May, when I again took a much-needed break. Around the beginning of June, 2018, Mom received a call from Craig Delaval, a producer at Shed Media interested in doing an investigative episode documentary about Donald Harvey's murders. She referred him to me.

The academic year had just ended, with my youngest officially a rising senior in high school. Meanwhile a lengthy renovation of our historic home was wrapping up, my family about to move in. A new puppy that winter proved more time-consuming than one remembers when really wanting a puppy. Between writing, working, volunteering, parenting, partnering and a social life, I was also the designer on the construction project of our home. Twice a day, I'd walk the two blocks from our condo downtown to the construction site giving input, creating solutions. At the time of Craig Delaval's call, most of my selections were complete, LEED and occupancy decisions remained, along with the very real task of boxing up our current life. Everything was in a state of disarray or flux. Humans live in moments of hustle or hibernation; this was not a restful time in my life.

When Craig called, a documentary was the last thing I had time for, and so I put him off for a while. He kept calling, leaving thoughtful messages. Finally I answered, asking him to explain his intent.

Multiple forces were bringing Dad's death into the public eye again. With my own book, a stop-and-go work in progress, amid all those Harvey-named reminders, and now this documentary... My family answered heaps of questions for my project, and overwhelmed me with support for my efforts.

We had been talking and sharing photos, stories, situations. Already considering what reopening this case through my writing might mean, we weren't sure about participating in another TV piece. Craig said he would send samples of his work, and he did. Discussing all aspects of this tragedy and of my efforts with my family, in the end we wondered if this TV episode might also help get out the story about Dad, the human piece often lost.

Another month of strong writing was stalled again by mid-June, 2018, due to the heavy activity of moving our family into a new house. Harvey Lewis, the high school government teacher/ultrarunner, often challenges himself with extreme races like the 135-mile Badwater through Death Valley. That summer, he had decided to conquer the Appalachian Trail, attempting a record-breaking run. We followed his journey all forty-nine days through that summer, posting encouragement as he completed 2,200 miles. Harvey's name was everywhere in Cincinnati news and social media; I couldn't escape it. Even more poignant, he was running the race with the support of his dad, who acted as Harvey's race crew-chief. We attended the premiere and party with Harvey for the release of their documentary, *Like Harvey Like Son*, which has won quite a few film awards.

Through those chaotic weeks, Craig was kind and patient. He said they already had Detective Fletcher, Joe Deters, Pat Minarcin and others on board, and really wanted our family to share Dad's story. We decided to participate.

Two months later, on August 22, 2018, our renovated historic house was set for filming. The night before, the director and a site crew member visited my house to get to know us, explore camera angles, and explain how the process would go. Mom, Heather, John and his wife Karie, and I sat on the patio and prepared.

Mom slept over in the room that was designed to be hers the following summer; in the morning we had coffee and dressed. She looked lovely in royal blue, her silvery white hair the only noticeable change since she was on camera fifteen years earlier. After my shower, I began to experience the same frustrating emotions I'd had on the night of Dad's funeral viewing, begrudgingly fixing my hair, fussing over the fit of clothes in my closet. Infuriating, "getting ready": I do far less of it now. Gads of time and effort expended on our physical selves could go into how we treat our inner selves, and each other.

I had laid out the three cuff bracelets I regularly wear that Dad had made of twisted metal, and wrapped them around my wrist to keep him with me that day.

John and Heather arrived early, looking fresh in nice clothes, faces rested but showing some trepidation. Then the team descended on our space: Tripods, lights, modifiers and microphones were set up around the kitchen, various filming sites for our individual interviews. Our home is an 1895 row house, built when Over-the-Rhine was one of the most densely populated neighborhoods in the country; spreading out for advantageous camera angles had not been part of the architect's plan, but the crew made it work. Moving together with care, the team was used to being on top of their photographed targets and each other. Home objects and belongings became props rearranged for best camera placement. At mid-morning, Damon left for work, promising to be back in the early afternoon. He hugged and kissed me, and wished us all well. While supportive, he wasn't sure if we should have agreed; he couldn't understand putting ourselves through it. It is hard to explain to anyone who didn't live it.

Heather had to work that afternoon, and so was filmed first. Extremely allergic to my cat, she spent much of the day on my patio or stoop, popping in and out to see what was happening with John and Mom's interviews. Lunch was served on the patio before Heather left. I was to be filmed last, so if anyone needed to leave, they could.

Exhibiting respect and kindness, the team revisited our loss with us. At one point Chris, the director, had to excuse himself as a wave of emotion hit while questioning Heather. Our memories were more easily shared with their humanity and professionalism. John was filmed next, and he represented us wonderfully. Chris eased him into comfort, and John spoke from his heart. Mom was situated so the late morning light glowed behind her. Her warmth and compassion came through on screen.

The cathartic process was in full force that day, a chance for our family to bond over loss in a positive way. Old photo albums were dug out. We turned pages and recounted stories of pictures we hadn't seen in ages.

Then I was positioned, in my rearranged dining room. Lighting discussions ensued, diffusers and angles adjusted, as I sat and waited for my interview. Strange, waiting to be filmed. I willed my mind to replay all the points I wanted to make, weighing words that might make any difference in my testimony to Dad. When the camera started rolling, I shared with Chris my hope that had spurred us to agree to take part in this production: that others would know the man whose death stopped a killer, and see his value as more than a victim.

Remembering the early days of my childhood with Dad wasn't difficult; Chris guided the conversation well. Once the camera is rolling, it's easier than you might think to forget you're being filmed. Determined to convey what most mattered, I stuck to facts as best I could, until my own storyline made me emotional. When Mom or Heather tears up, it's another Tuesday, but for me to cry, it takes a really good movie scene (ideally featuring a dog), a moving local theater or concert performance, or some other big emotional buildup. I had kept my deepest feelings locked down in writing much of this account—as if they were a barrier to the story, not a part of it. It shouldn't take an upheaval to express emotion, yet oftentimes it does. Unfounded, I always worried that my tears carried weakness, but without tears, this would be a story, not my story. Later, when I reread all that I'd written for this memoir, I cried for all the times I had not.

Still, for a while I couldn't spit out more than a few pages here and there, until another Harvey made the news, and from October 2018 to May 2019 occupied the consciousness of our society. Harvey Weinstein.

I could not make this stuff up.

REPEATEDLY REMINDED BY a name, not a common name, that has haunted me since April 1987, I was pushed to conquer what seemed an account I was destined to write. And so I continued.

The *License to Kill* docudrama was set to air on the Oxygen channel the next summer, July 20, 2019. The executive producer reached out to be sure we knew when it would run, conveying his hope that they captured our dad and family the way we'd intended upon agreeing to participate. Time constraints didn't allow my full family to be represented onscreen in the final cut, we were told; only Mom and myself were to be shown. This concerned me, with my siblings, and I went back and forth with Shed to see if there was a way to include us all. In the end they added extra content with my siblings that could be viewed online after the show. Though we wouldn't all be on-air as we'd expected for the program, we were assured of sensitivity around our involvement.

The day of the broadcast, we made a last-minute plan to have dinner together. Mom had fully moved in a couple weeks before, the long-term plan of her living with us carried out, and she and I invited John and Heather to the house before the program started. John and Karie were bringing LaRosa's pizza. Up until then I hadn't let anyone know about the show, other than my dear friend Lori, out of town, and two local friends, Patricia and Molly. Otherwise only my family knew, and it occurred to me that I might want to share this strange moment, that maybe I'd been remiss in not doing so. My friend Regina earlier that month had pointed out how I withhold, how I don't "dish" easily, so I figured I'd try to learn from that personal feedback. An hour before the program I texted Karena and four other friends, explaining what was happening.

My family made small talk, poured drinks, prepared paper plates and ourselves to see if Oxygen's *License to Kill* series would be able to convey the part of our family's story that we'd hoped to share. None of us had ever watched this particular investigative show. We crowded near the television.

In the end, "Killing Everything" (*License to Kill* Season 1, Episode 5) attempted too much. Too complicated a tale was packed into forty-two minutes, with commercials filling the rest of the hour. Host Dr. Terry Dubrow opens the show in a hospital setting, his white lab coat (he's a plastic surgeon) and weighted cadence over-explaining what's in store: His opening line dramatically states, "In some cases, there are those with a deranged mind and a license to kill." Background music lays over the opening scene, a flatlining beep accompanying the show's title page, fading to black before the episode officially begins.

Dubrow's narration begins with Drake Hospital, setting the stage in 1986 when Harvey was hired, disclosing how haunting the case remains to the city and to the Powell family. A photo of little John and me fills the screen, we kids wrapped on either side of Dad on an amusement park bench. I must have been five or six. A cymbal clash shimmies the scene into wide-angle drone footage of the Cincinnati skyline as a soft piano highlights the footprint of Music Hall and Over-the-Rhine across the frame. Then we see Dad's handsome face in closeup from another old snapshot, Mom's soft voice layered over it; then we see her speaking, mentioning how she and John met each other as parents and how much she loved Dad's smile. My own voice and face then fill the screen, and suddenly I'm outside myself talking about Dad's cool Harley motorcycle, the one he had when I met him, and how he was a stable force in our family. It's odd to hear your own voice and see your own face on video; this kind of footage, versus the now commonplace self-filmed TikTok video, rarely matches anyone's idea of themselves. Heat rose in my face at seeing myself, flushed with vain embarrassment—the camera really does add ten pounds. Sensitive to my siblings who would not appear, though, I quickly moved through my own annoyance.

As the program goes on, Pat Minarcin's familiar voice precedes him onto the screen, his white hair describing the number of years I'd not seen him. Next we heard from Bill Fletcher, lead investigating homicide detective on the Harvey case. He had aged well, looking like a mildly greying version of the man I remembered. When Fletcher says that the police originally focused on Patricia Powell as a suspect, with the supposed motive being that our medical insurance was running out, and Dad's lengthy convalescence was draining the family finances—we all, out loud, simultaneously scoffed. Bill Whalen, Harvey's attorney, had said the same thing in his book, *Defending Donald Harvey*, and on the Barbara Kellar show. As I've mentioned, GE had excellent employee benefits.

Also, not a well-known fact: after a nurse visited Drake and saw how well Dad was recovering, Metropolitan Insurance had extended a million-dollar policy for his continued rehabilitation. Any thorough investigation would have revealed that fact, negating that motive.

Back and forth camera shots went between Mom, Minarcin and myself, as Dad's death, and the beginning of the investigation following Dad's autopsy, were explained. Actors for Mom and myself moved in vignettes across descriptions of Dad's hospitalization and death. Fletcher and Minarcin are talking about their roles and motivations in the investigation.

Jarring commercials for local car sales and pharmaceuticals intruded, as we sat on the edge of our seats for a story we knew too well. During breaks we would breathe, talk to each other about discrepancies, then shift quickly back into the experience as the show restarted.

Detective Fletcher brazenly states in the episode that he had lied to Pat Minarcin when asked about an ongoing investigation. Minarcin is saying, "Get the story, get it right. Stop a horrid injustice from occurring. I did what journalists are supposed to do."

Next Fletcher is on camera saying, "Then Pat Minarcin said, 'What are you doing, are you looking at more deaths?' and I said 'No.' I lied to him, because we didn't know if there's some other people involved in this. We didn't know if Harvey was acting alone, or could be other nurses, but the investigation was still going on, still interviewing. Then worked on a lot of background on Donald Harvey and trying to find if there's any other victims." Fletcher fades.

Dr. Dubrow pops back into view: "At this point in the investigation, police were still working on the theory that there may have been other victims." Dubrow can only know what he's been told; this doctor is essentially an actor, reading a script. But it isn't truthful.

Let me recap again: On June 12, Police Chief Whalen sent a letter to administrator Taylor at Drake, assuring him the case was closed. Nurses' statements, and other documentation uncovered in my research, do not support that claim of a continued investigation. How was it that from March 7, when Dad died, to June 23, when Minarcin aired his report, that only one person had the facts to suggest more deaths in the case? No matter how much work homicide did to secure Harvey's conviction for Dad's murder, for more than four months—even with Harvey's own confession hinting he'd killed others, on top of his alarming history and hospital staff concerns—the investigation had halted. Background might have turned up Harvey's confession the last time he was in police custody, in 1975. Nurses, silenced at work, were waiting; they had not been approached and had not been interviewed further by police. This is the exact reason they reached out to Minarcin a month after John Powell's death.

Dubrow says, "While police were continuing their covert investigation, journalist Pat Minarcin interviewed Donald Harvey's coworkers for a story that would implicate Donald Harvey in multiple murders." I am left to assume that Shed was told a covert investigation had been ongoing; so covert, I might add, that no one, not even the Chief of Police, Drake Administration or trustees, Hamilton County Commissioners or even the prosecutors' office knew about it.

Then there's the familiar, well-aged face of Hamilton County Prosecutor Joe Deters, appearing almost impressed by Harvey's astonishing recollection of his crimes. Deters is talking about the grand jury testimony, saying the proceedings started, "Maybe like 7:30 in the morning, and we ended up maybe 9 o'clock at night." Then Deters says, "It was incre—" but stops mid-word, choosing "unbelievable" instead. Seems to me, in that moment, with a flash of empathy, Deters considered how Harvey's victims—people often seen as unremarkable—might take a term like "incredible," attached to a killer's résumé.

As the docudrama continues, we watch portions of the long-ago leaked video from Harvey's grand jury testimony on July 9, 1987. Speaking of Harvey's numerous murder attempts, including that of his own partner, Deters said, "The magnitude of it was so… disturbing. He was gay, and his boyfriend ran a hair salon, and they would have dinner parties, and Harvey was jealous of, like, the girls that worked at the salon, and he'd poison them. Didn't kill them, but he had different types of things—I think he had HIV virus that he dumped on a salad. He had lovers outside of his relationship that he killed, he was using arsenic on his boyfriend…. Carl is lucky he's not dead. He was just an evil guy."

Referring to Harvey, Deters says, "He was just killing everything."

This is where the show's producers got their episode title.

Assistant prosecutor Terry Gaines appears next, saying how troubling the grand jury testimony was then and that to this day he is still deeply affected by that case: "At the time I was listening to it, it didn't affect me nearly as much as it did, like, the next day. I was very emotional about it. I shook it off and went to the office, but when I really thought about it, it bothered me. It still does."

Pat Minarcin was also featured in the *License to Kill* episode, recalling questions he had back in April of 1987 about only one death being investigated. He described when the Drake Hospital nurses approached him, how he dropped everything to hear their stories of being silenced by their superiors for seven months prior to John Powell's murder. Eight nurses agreed to meet with him after scores of anonymous phone calls, risking their jobs to set the record straight. He then describes the most painful fact: that Harvey told him that his victims knew they were going to die. Harvey would tell them before or as he was killing them.

What must have been so broken in Harvey that he needed to break others so brutally? What level of fear lives with the sick anticipation of waiting to die with no means to protect yourself?

Another victim's family member, introduced in the episode and now a magistrate, lost her grandmother to Harvey's poisoning. She speaks of her love for her grandmother, and of her grandfather's dedication, how he spent every day with his wife at Drake. She shares the difficulty of discovery when her dad told her about the evil man who had killed her grandma. We know too well the wish she makes, hoping her grandmother didn't know she was being poisoned.

Minarcin goes on to share pieces of his Lucasville, Ohio prison interview with Harvey, after his conviction—old footage of Minarcin's back, the camera angle on Harvey sitting on the other side of plexiglass with a phone receiver to his ear. The reporter says to Harvey, "You know you're going to die in prison?" Harvey quickly responds, "Yes." Minarcin says again, "Sooner or later you are going to die in here." With his blank gaze and gentle Kentucky drawl, Harvey responds, "Well none of us have a guarantee of tomorrow, do we?"

Eerie.

I'd never seen that footage. To hear Harvey recite a fundamental tenet of a well-intentioned life, felt off-kilter. How could anything Harvey said be trusted? A whole lot of people were guaranteed tomorrows before he met them.

In the episode's closing moments, Dubrow reminded viewers of the justice Harvey was served by dying in prison, fatally beaten after serving thirty years.

Relieved it was over, my family and I let out a collective sigh. Karie knew a lot through John but said it was very different to see and hear it in full detail. While she felt better informed, she was all the more hurt for John and all of us. We talked after the program about the harsh reality of seeing Dad's face next to Harvey's again. We had hoped to see more of one and less of the other.

Mom, who onscreen had looked lovely and strong in that royal blue blouse, was able to share that Dad had been recovering prior to his death, which was the most important detail to us. License to Kill was no more or less than we knew it would be: an intriguing if somewhat pulpy show about killers and investigators, specifically describing techniques for uncovering murderers. Plenty of people are drawn to such shows—likely because they haven't lived it.

Shed attempted to balance the show with family perspectives and the human cost of Harvey's crimes, as best they could. Additional web content uploaded after the show aired offered a bit more time with our family and the investigators, for curious viewers. Shed had accomplished their goal and some of ours, with photos of our family and Dad filling the screen, warmth and humanity provided in those moments. Still, it made me realize how much has to be left out of a TV program, and how much more important it was for me to write this story myself.

The amount of time we had to look at Harvey's cold stare or hear his voice as he recounted his murders was a struggle at the time of our viewing, but one we were prepared for. Shouldered together, not merely victims, my family have become testaments to ourselves and others for moving through trauma without breaking.

THROUGH MY DEAR FRIEND Tim, I found a channel for contacting the head of the prosecutor's Municipal Court Division in 1987, Terry Gaines, and reached out in a hand-written, stamped letter. I realize what a rarity that is for me now to put pen to paper, with the keys of a laptop so swift to capture and deliver my thoughts. He phoned me on November 2, 2020, the day he received it.

Gaines introduced himself and said that yes, of course, he would answer my questions. I was at once excited and nervous to hear from him and thanked him for the call, grateful he'd agreed to take the time to discuss the case with me, grateful I had answered my phone. Reaching into the junk drawer nearby, I grabbed a notepad and pen and began scribbling as we spoke.

"So you had some questions about Donald Harvey? It's over thirty years ago, but I can answer some of your questions," Gaines offered.

I told him I was actually more interested in his perspective, having gone through it from that side of things. Mentioning that I saw him on that Oxygen channel show last summer, I told him it stuck with me how haunted he still seemed.

"Thinking back, at the time, I had some emotional difficulty. That number of elderly people. And your father. And your father was not elderly."

Nodding from my side of the phone, silent acknowledgement.

Terry Gaines went on, "A nurse, I think there was a nurse—I

have a recollection that a nurse said that your dad did not want Donald Harvey around him." This did not surprise me, but pained me nonetheless. He thought for a moment, then said, "Bottom line. I was not at all upset with how Harvey died, that he was beaten in his cell. If there is anyone who so richly deserved to die that way, he did."

Again, though I couldn't agree, I understood his sentiment.

"But yes," he continued. "It was, overall, very traumatic. We all had difficulty with it. We wanted to seek the death penalty in the very worst way, but the facts were such that we knew we weren't going to prove anything without Donald's testimony." Regret tinged his words. "Sitting in my living room, I remember one morning just feeling terrible, just full of emotion. At that time, I was not a particularly emotional person. You felt sorry for the families, you empathize with their suffering. But I was traumatized."

I could feel that through the phone.

"Crime and punishment. You see the crime, and seek the punishment, that was our job." This stone-cold certainty in a prosecutor, I have discerned, must be a requirement for that line of work—but Gaines' voice, coming through the receiver, was pensive: "I did have some difficulty because of the sheer numbers.

"After the trial with the twenty-three others"—Gaines, thoughtfully, reserved a special number for my dad among the twenty-four victims killed at Drake—"Donald Harvey came back to us and said he had more. Four to six more victims to report to us. So we went and took that information and prosecuted him. About a year later he came back again. Went up to Lucasville where he was, and his attorney, Bill Whalen was there. I read him his rights. I said, Donald, I don't have to remind you that we have a written agreement, a plea agreement with you, and if we think that you are lying or catch you in a lie, then we can seek the death penalty. Donald looked at me and said he wanted some time with his attorney. When we came back in, Bill Whalen said "my client has nothing further to say."

I was sensing how well Terry had gotten to know Harvey when he said, "See, he was trying to get into the *Guinness Book of World*

Records."

We both breathed through this additional, almost ludicrous proof of Harvey's deep sociopathy.

"You know," I said, "going through this, I can see that it affects people on all sides. From here it is more about healing. It changes the view and spins things much differently." I could hear him agreeing with an "mmm-hmm."

"Your timing is perfect," I went on. "I held out hope that I'd hear from you. I've been writing this story for a long time, it has been part of my healing, and I've spoken with Pat Minarcin and Daisy Key and Joe Deters, and I was hoping to have the chance to speak with you."

"Have you talked to anybody else? Did you talk with the psychiatrist who tested Harvey? The Waynesville psychiatrist?" Gaines asked me.

Just then someone knocked on my door, and I balanced my notepad with the phone to answer the door and receive a package. It was my friend Felicia, delivering a Fanon Rucker yard sign—it was election season, and Rucker, a local attorney and municipal court judge endorsed by the Democrats, was running (unsuccessfully, as I've said) to unseat Joe Deters as Hamilton County Prosecutor.

I apologized to Terry that "someone was at my door, handing me something, and we were trying to be careful and distant." After all, we were in a pandemic, my hands were full, I didn't have a mask on, and I had to rebound from being handed Deters' opponent's campaign sign in the middle of this call.

"Yes," Terry said, "I understand that—good to be careful, I am too, I am closer to eighty than I care to be."

"Absolutely!" I said, "My mother lives with us, and we are trying to be very careful."

That awkwardness managed, we went on with the small talk. He told me that he enjoyed cooking, and cycling on the Little Miami bike trail, and that he's been retired for twenty-one years from the Prosecutor's office, retired ten years from everything. We exchanged email and mobile contacts. I shared again how this book has been a way of healing, and though it is very personal, that if anything I went through might help others, I'd achieve my goal. Then, remembering our conversation before the door interrupted, I asked, "You mentioned this psychiatrist. Were you there, did you speak with him or anyone else?"

Gaines said, "I was there in the office when he gave his verbal report. I remember his comment to me. Joe Deters, Art Ney were there. Dr. Tennay said, 'Donald is not sick in the sense we use the word. If you see a three-hundred-pound man with a cold, he's not just sick, but also has a weight issue; that is someone who is sick. Donald's problem is that he has no superego. No conscience. He could do anything he wanted, and with impunity. He is defective; that superego, he doesn't have it, missing that part of his psyche.'"

Then Gaines said, "That stuck with me. He (Harvey) knew right from wrong; he just didn't care."

"Yes, I had read that," I told him. "I have read all the documents that my research found and that Joe Deters was able to supply, I even have the grand jury testimony. I got it through a public records search at CPD (Cincinnati Police Department)."

"You have that? They gave you that?" he asked, clearly stunned.

"I do. Probably because the grand jury video has been released and circulated for so long," I suggested.

"Well, that is probably right. When I was there, the grand jury was sacrosanct. I guess it is different these days."

As we were wrapping up our conversation, he said to call if I had other questions, and he wished my family well. I thanked him for that, and for agreeing to talk with me. His final thoughts came at a cost—a reflection back on his career and the lack of any true resolution, and a warning to me, perhaps: "Homicide. When I ever asked why... There is never a rational reason for an irrational act. Never a reason leading to harm and hurt. People try to rationalize it, and I just don't think you can."

Scribbling, my hand hurting, I could sense the weight of Terry's words.

"Homicide is that way. You expect someone old to not wake up. Homicide takes someone at an early age, and I've seen a lot over my years, but I never found a way to figure out a reason. I've had that feeling for over thirty years."

❖

WHILE PARTICIPATING IN the *License to Kill* episode, I reconnected with Pat Minarcin in January of 2019. Through correspondence, we discovered a shared interest in writing and research, and I was grateful to have found someone else as willing as I was to dig deep into the details of this case, willing to share the weight of both the shovel and the shit.

Minarcin has wished for me to find peace through this process, sharing a Hemingway quote, from his short story, "Fathers and Sons," in a 1933 collection titled *Winner Take Nothing*: "If he wrote it, he could get rid of it. He had gotten rid of so many things by writing."

Responding to Minarcin, I wrote, "Without a doubt, Hemingway fought his demons on the page, laying them flat to better conquer them. Of course that is also what this process is for me. I was always meant to write this story. Now I am and I will."

In a phone interview with Pat Minarcin on March 5, 2019, I asked the reporter what he specifically knew about Dad's death and multiple poisonings. Minarcin clearly recounted what he knew: "I already suspected that John knew beforehand. The nurses told me John had been transferred twice back to University because he got pneumonia, and in retrospect they thought he might have been poisoned then. So I asked Harvey in the Lucasville [prison] interview if he'd poisoned John previously, and he said yes. I asked why; he shrugged, then said, 'Why not?' He felt sorry for John, he insisted, and he believed, he said, that John wanted him to do it 'to end his suffering.' But then he added that John had seen him kill another patient in the same room, and he couldn't let John live."

Dad knew exactly what was happening to him, and who was doing it. Harvey admitted to Minarcin repeated poisonings of John Powell. Frequent and sudden unexplained trips to University

Hospital, and the symptoms he experienced the last six weeks of his life, are further evidence of the repeated trauma John Powell suffered at the hands of a psychopathic killer.

As Terry Gaines said, grand jury testimony is often sealed; however, this complete document was made available to me in a public records request that spring of 2019. I have in my possession, and can accurately recount, the horrible details transcribed on paper, of the more than twelve hours of video testimony that Donald Harvey provided to the grand jury and prosecutors in his plea deal to avoid the death penalty.

The morning I picked the heavy stack up, I stared at its rubber-banded weight in the passenger seat next to me—enough weight to set off the seatbelt alarm, blaring to strap in. When I drove home, immediately I went to my room and situated myself in the comfort of my bed. I sifted through the reams of paper, a page at a time, digesting my disgust. I did not leave my bedroom for the next twelve hours. Damon didn't disturb me, though halfway through, brought me tea and something to eat.

July 2019 marked the 70th anniversary of WCPO-TV in Cincinnati. Deters, Minarcin and others were repeatedly named in retrospectives, in regards to the case that brought both shock and notoriety to this city. Strange to revisit this story now, with this award-winning journalist, steeped as I've become in this case and its specifics. I asked Minarcin directly about his take on these recent attentions, including the media interviews, the case itself, and the differing takes and timing discrepancies still noticeable in the documentary we'd all just contributed to.

Minarcin said, "I took pressure, a lot of it, from the prosecutors, and the police department, with the exception of homicide." He then credited the work the homicide team was doing, and went on to say, "I will note that Deters recently said I aired that first report without any evidence. That is untrue, and he knew it when he said it—by then Bill Whalen's book was out. And Fletcher said at the same time he lied to throw me off the scent, which is also untrue. I never talked to Fletcher. I find it peculiar that after all this time, two such high-ranking officials would continue to defend the indefensible with untruths. That's a hallmark of coverups."

Pat Minarcin also agreed to describe for me, here, his memory of that first night we all met: "I remember your mom's tears that Sunday night when I told her about your dad's murder—and also that the hospital could have prevented it. She said she wasn't surprised; we'd been troubling her for weeks, asking for pictures and documents, and she said she was half-expecting what I came to say. Then she asked if I would tell you kids, and your tears came next, and I saw John Jr.'s jaw clench and his face darken, then Heather's bewilderment. And too, I remember the atmosphere in the family room, the sense that despite the sorrow I'd brought, something of your dad was still there, and everyone seemed to resolve themselves to shoulder the news and carry on. When I left, I had an awful sense that I'd just dropped an enormous bomb on all of you, flattening you again—first your dad's death, and now this. But it was essential, I thought; you all deserved to hear the truth from me, and I had to tell you. I've worried about it ever since."

In September of 2019, a producer from FOX19 Cincinnati left a voicemail I actually didn't realize was on my phone for a couple weeks, requesting an interview with my family. It mattered little; I probably wouldn't have given a comment after having participated in the TV episode. FOX-19 did secure interviews with both Deters and Minarcin about what they remembered from the case and that time.

In a forty-two-minute phone interview, Minarcin gave a detailed account of the story as it unfolded, including the struggle of the nurses when they first anonymously called and shared their concerns. He also describes Bill Whalen, "a heroic figure to his imagination," who, bound by attorney-client privilege, encouraged the reporter to "Keep digging." Pat discussed patients and staff involved, who came to be known as "Minarcin's Army," crediting the numerous people involved in the investigation that he conducted alongside the WCPO team. Minarcin noted a meticulous process for airing the report, ensuring facts, pertinent materials and experts were in place, remembering how the station reached out to Patricia Powell for photos and documentation. The former anchor then shared that immediately after the story broke, the county surprisingly focused an investigation on Minarcin himself.

In sharp contrast, and in a seven-minute onscreen video, Joe Deters begins by describing the Channel 9 efforts and states, "they had concocted this bullcrap story," alluding to his interpretation of Bill Whalen having given Harvey's confessions to WCPO. When the interviewer asked Deters, about Harvey as a killer, "Did he watch them die?" Deters remarked that, "No, he would always do it (kill or poison someone) at the end of his shift and then leave. That's what he'd do."

Deters' kind intentions and sincere offers of help aside, hearing this interview cemented what had become obvious to me: that time has erased, for Joe Deters, some relevant facts of this case. Harvey was typically the one who would find the patient dead, alerting staff to a decline or demise—hence the reason nurses named him "The Angel of Death." This title was bestowed due to what nurses at the time thought was a strange coincidence of Harvey's being present when a patient died. Harvey poisoned John Powell at the start of his shift on March 7, 1987. In that same FOX19 interview, Deters described Harvey, in comparison to the four other serial killers he prosecuted in his career, as more of a "hands-off killer."

In Deters' own experience, Harvey may not have caused the outward-appearing physically violent deaths of other killers he'd prosecuted; Harvey didn't use guns or clubs. Yet Deters' interpretation doesn't accurately explain Harvey. Instead, it simplifies the various drawn-out, painful methods by which he operated.

Harvey killed most of his patients and friends by poison. His victims ingested it in beverages or food he'd prepared and handed to them or inserted into their gastro tubes. He also killed by other means: suffocation, using plastic or a pillow over faces, wire to obstruct bowels or other organs. He'd drift in and out of their presence on a long shift, observing how his victims suffered, and knowing why. Harvey revealed to his immobile patients that he was killing them, and in some cases, repeatedly attempted to do so. A gunshot from across a room is more "hands-off."

All along I'd been puzzled about the timelines, perceptions

and responses I couldn't line up, by my accounting, from the many people in this story. This messy enigma is a large part of why I wrote this book, holding true to the promise I made to Harvey and myself at sixteen: to find everything out that I could about this case, to better understand.

Of course, like Terry Gaines, a retired prosecutor closing in on eighty, I'll never really understand. But a few things have become clearer during this process. For one: a lot of discrepancies come down to ego. We "know" what we need to know, to be okay with ourselves. Also clear: Neither Minarcin nor Deters hold affection for each other.

Facts now in hand and laid out, I have whatever understanding I'm ever going to have about this case, and its players. And I use the term players here in more of the dramatic solitary sense, as we certainly cannot describe them as a team.

27

survive[ser-vahyv]
verb (used without object), sur·vived, sur·viv·ing
1. to remain alive after the death of someone, the cessation of
   something, or the occurrence of some event; continue to live
2. to remain or continue in existence or use
3. to get along or remain healthy, happy, and unaffected in spite
   of some occurrence

EXIT NUMBER 13 for Shepherd Lane on I-75 North still makes
me uneasy. Every time I pass the site of Dad's motorcycle accident, that horrible scene plays out in my mind. I can't help but see
him wrecked and damaged there. For years I avoided driving that
section of highway, accessing northern routes circuitously. Again,
we can't always help how we are affected.

Once, during my last year in college, I was driving my Honda
Civic north to Bowling Green, Ohio, from Cincinnati—my path
often took me there, and I had no alternative but to drive I-75. A
hot sunny day heated past rush hour, traffic was humming along,
slowed by minor construction. Wheels were rolling me closer to
that dreaded exit as lanes narrowed with cones and markers. Without a shoulder in the far left lane, my car hugged close against the
concrete median, streaming past. Late afternoon sun warmed my
left shoulder to discomfort.

Out of nowhere, a tire blew out boisterously on the eigh-
teen-wheeler just ahead, one lane over to my right. A slash of black
rubber flung from under the truck and landed with a thud, thick
across my entire windshield, blocking all forward vision. Danger

screamed from all sides. No shoulder to pull into, I was closed in between a semi-truck working to slow down on my right, cars directly in front of me and a concrete median on my left side, higher than my car door. Tasting panic even now, I recall those tires swerving, slowing and rolling back past my passenger window, the blurry gray concrete wall moving fast and immediately forward to my left. Impossible scenario. At Dad's exit? Was I meant to die here?

Miracle. I did not ram into the car in front of me. Slowing the car by pulse braking, I thought to switch on my wipers. After a few swipes the shredded tire began to dislodge, flinging from my car to the roadway, my window cleared to see the sign just as I passed Exit 13.

With obstruction and calamity behind in my rear-view mirror, the road opened before me. Adrenalin shook my arms and sped my heart to an uncomfortable pace, driving past the General Electric plant that sprawled across a quarter mile. My chest ached, a cold sweat broke on the back of my neck, and nausea rose in me. The car kept driving itself as I continued the next few miles, heart rate slowing, hands steadying as I realized immense gratitude for being alive.

Terrifying seconds that felt like an eternity. Keen in mind, after all this time, a reel of fine details is painted there. Thankfully Exit 13 didn't bring more devastation to my family. Reverence and caution accompany me there now, but I consider a drive past that exit to be a sign of my own strength and no longer avoid it.

In the summer of 2019, construction began on that dreaded exit. Entire sections of highway and even the exit itself have since been rebuilt, wider, with lanes rerouted—an unrecognizable road all but erasing the accident site where we all started down this path.

I'm often pulled back to the beginning of this story, the first pages of which are written in the messages of bedside journals. Tangible hands recall a truth that until now, few outside our family knew: the possibility of an alternative reality, no longer in reach.

11-17-86

[Dad scribbles on page]
John Powell
Smile [in print]
John Powell [in cursive]

11-17-86

John,
You were very responsive with nodding and moving fingers — You also
scribbled with a pen. The nurses are even commenting on your progress.
We'll be back soon.
Love
Pat & your son John

December 4, 1987 evening

Dad,
Hey I've heard how great you've been doing. In a wheelchair now and
everything.
I also heard about the speech therapist. That's great. Everyone is so hap-
py to see you come this far but I know you've got a lot farther to go. Don't
give up. I know it won't be easy but we are all here for you. We all love
you so much, and all that love has helped bring you to the point you're at
now and it will carry you further.
Keep up the (hard) good work.
(Silly face drawn) — funny huh?
Love you,
Holly

I VISIT WITH POSSIBILITY now and again. Not too often. Reality
is the healthier place to live. For years I thought I would die when I
was forty-four, the same age as when Dad died. Regularly I lived in

fear and woke up scared. Three years after Dad died, an insensitive person who was very close to me in college told me to "grow up" when I shared my fear with him after an awful nightmare.

Well, I have grown. Thankfully I have been given the time to do so. Grief tends to feast alone. Love shares the bounty of her table. What I've learned by remembering a person lost to us, is that love stays with us when we share their story. "Good" does come from revisiting all this "Bad," linked by need to experience each other. Memories long sunk have risen to the surface. Little things forgotten, images clipped and faded, are filling in, returning to me as small gifts.

Visions of the naps Dad took in the afternoon on our living room floor, like a cat in the sun—that ugly, mustard-yellow carpet flattened warm beneath him. Mom, piping mad when Dad cut down her pine tree in the backyard, not realizing its importance. Recalling how Dad took his bourbon with water, drinking from his favorite Igloo-brand insulated tumbler, staining the ivory lining with his favorite Kentucky liquor. Giddy, the first time he saw the ocean in St. Augustine, Florida. No swimsuit of his own, he wore white cut-off jean shorts that became a beacon to me when I drifted too far out to sea on our family vacation, guiding my salt-stung eyes and exhausted arms back to shore.

The way Dad loved animals, like we all do now, is a strong connection. I remember him carefully bottle-feeding and bathing the baby raccoons we'd rescued in our chimney flue, letting them climb on his head and shoulders. I can still see what rescuing and having his first dog meant to him, my own pup sees that meaning in my eyes.

One sunny evening has returned, when Dad rode me on his bike to the Gold Circle (an early version of a Target store) and bought me a very cool pair of green-tinted sunglasses that wrapped around my face, for our future motorcycle rides. He purchased a matching reddish rose-colored pair for himself, and we rode home smiling beneath them.

A childhood memory emerged: being squeezed onto a crowded wedding reception dance floor, Dad and Mom slowly dancing nearby and me hearing him singing into her ear, "So put me on a highway, and show me a sign, and take it to the limit, one more time."

John brought Dad's sky-blue wool sweater vest to me last Thanksgiving—iconic John Powell, a cursive "JP" embroidered on the right chest, dressing him in photos like the framed portrait that hangs on our wall, always a perfect fit over a wide-necked collar. That woolen classic now resides in a drawer with cedar chips. Someday I will wear it, but the time isn't now. I struggle to let go of certain items of clothing, things of his I realize I'll never wear. They all end up with me for some reason—everyone knows to pass them by me before discarding. There's a sensitivity towards me from my family that I cling to. I am the perfect packrat for such items. Cloth sweat-caps Dad wore to fit under his motorcycle and welding helmets are housed here, hung on doorknobs in my studio and adorning coat hooks in my home. The bulky, heavy, tan-canvas Carhartt overalls, with his Sharpie marker-stained "JP" logo, also moved in with me this past holiday season, when my brother John discovered it cleaning out a storage area in his house. Dad's blue suede brush-popper suit jacket quietly lives with my brother now.

Silly, the things we hold onto, the things that keep a loved one here when they are gone. Tokens, talismans, reminders that unlock memories to return a loved one to us. There's comfort in wearing the jewelry he made: Dad's silver cuffs band together on my wrist most days, the polished heart-shaped stone necklace I save for special. The belt buckle he made for me on display in my office. That striated orange and yellowed gemstone, sunset in a circle, stares at me from my bookshelf while I write, trimmed with sterling detail, Holly, carved into the shining rim at the bottom.

The thought I put behind these items isn't prolonged or pained; it simply feels better to keep them near. I'm not a hoarder (says every hoarder), I keep it contained. Plastic bins are labeled and stored in the cellar, and the rest I keep in places I will feel them. Their placement serves as a live-action storage trunk, my own reality and its evidence. These things occurred. Some folks don't want or need reminders of loved ones lost, and I get that. Reminders can bring sadness into an otherwise undisturbed day. My treasures provide a positive way for me to stay grounded. This is how I function, and that is, after all, what this story is about.

Happiness, I have realized, is a choice I get to make, to create and experience joy despite trauma. Thankfully, that joy balances out some of the hard times we faced. A band I like, Wilco, on their latest album *Cruel Country*, has a song that resonates, called "A Lifetime to Find." Philosopher and songwriter Jeff Tweedy writes, "It takes a lifetime to find, the life like the life we had in mind." Each day, I come closer. We didn't have a long life with Dad, yet he was and has remained a deep part of my life. I can be grateful for the time we were granted. We each count ourselves fortunate to share so much time with Mom.

As kids, she would take each of us on a special day trip into downtown Cincinnati. Mom made us feel special to be a part of this city, bringing us by bus or car into the heart of Cincinnati; she'd recount jobs and lunch counters that rounded out her young adult life. Now it's my turn to give some of that joy back to her. She and her cats are downtowners now, and with both of Mom's knees replaced, we plan to have some fun. We celebrated her seventy-ninth birthday in quarantine with a family video call, and were able to host an outdoor event with balloons and sunflower covered masks for her eightieth. Her eighty-first, another gift to us, just passed with a brunch downtown and a tea party at my sister's house.

During those early COVID-19 months, with shelter-in-place, she watched her church online, attended group video calls. We watched my friend Molly's video happy hours, binged our favorite shows on TV, and put together several jigsaw puzzles. Now that we are through the worst of the pandemic—we hope—are fully vaccinated and can get out, Mom takes daily walks around the park and talks about the adorable dogs she sees there. Meeting her friends for lunch or church, she is out and about. We have coffee, help each other out around the house, and walk to lunch. We have set aside a monthly date just for us. Lovers of green things, we water and pinch dead flowers off our plants and get in a little outdoor patio time. John stops by, or Heather meets us for lunch. My sister Jen lives in New England now, far from the desert. We keep in good touch with plenty of text humor and photos of her first grandbaby.

Having Mom home just feels right. She is my husband Damon's biggest fan, and we enjoy the wonderful dinners he creates. We feel so thankful she moved in the summer before the pandemic hit, and can ensure her care here amidst any future health crisis. This remarkable, independent woman, the kindest I know, has earned some lightness of being.

Fran and I talk regularly. When I let her read this manuscript, she mailed me a notecard that simply said, "You nailed it!" We talked later; she feels it is a worthy account, and it felt good to do justice to Fran and Joe's steadfast friendship to my parents. Fran and Mom meet up regularly, for walks in the park or a nice lunch. With visits picnic-style or in my kitchen, both tables offer ginger ale for Fran, a beer or donuts for Joe. We share this life, births and deaths and all the celebrations in between, and Joe and Fran still hold claim on Suesz hill.

Heather, too, deserves her share of relaxation. An extremely dedicated healthcare worker, my beautiful sister works the long late shift at a local hospital, facing fears of her own daily. She recently moved into a home she happily shares with her fiancé, not far from where we all used to spend summer day camp as kids. She's a loving mother who would do anything she could for her three accomplished grown children. A great do-it-yourselfer, Heather is crafty and resourceful on a small budget, and she is discovering Mom's love of flowers and planting. She is also, by far, the biggest Cincinnati Bengals fan I know! My sister has a humble heart, coupled with the rowdiest spectator presence. Dad would have enjoyed her continued sports enthusiasm. Down-to-earth and caring, my big sister always sees the best in others, and is so much stronger than she knows.

John and his family live in the house we three grew up in: The house Dad left his mark on now feels his son's hand. How separate my brother must have felt, after Dad died, living as the lone male in a world of women—but I think it has served him well. Principled and kind, "Little John" is a sensitive, thoughtful person with an acute attention to detail. His mannerisms are so reminiscent of Dad, of a once Bigger John. A loving partner to his wife, Karie, and a caring father to four of my wonderful nieces and nephews, he's fulfilling his role as a family man. I'm so grateful for our relationship, the mutual reliance we have built. His deep perspective is one I truly value. If I need anything, he will be there. He owns his own company and has remarkable precision as an artisan and skilled craftsman. That quiet shield he wears, similar to his father's, can't hide the wheels turning behind. John would make his dad extremely proud.

AS FOR THAT SELF-CENTERED teen, the girl who robbed herself and her parents of even an ounce of the joy they each deserved, forgiveness has been the hardest thing to offer myself. We hurt each other in this life, intentionally or not, yet we are also capable of mending. Blaming others is easy, and at times right, when things go wrong, when terrible things happen to us. But trapping ourselves inside thoughts and cycles of blame yields negativity. One bad fight turns into a bad day spiraling out of control into a bad week or month. Anger sucks away at this fleeting life.

I won't live there. Feeling truest to myself when I respond with grace, restraint, empathy and love, that includes loving myself. Through each smile and tear, this entire journey, this education, each mistake, every choice, all my broken and built-up bits have created the person I am today, and I am a good person. No one is perfect, and if I have hurt you in the passage of my life, I sincerely ask your pardon. My choices have always reflected the best I knew or could accomplish at the time. I will get the chance to try again with any tomorrows I am allotted.

Through this entire process, from Dad entering our lives until today, I have declared clemency for myself. As Confucius says, *The more you know yourself, the more you forgive yourself.* Knowing the best and worst we humans hold inside has only solidified, for me, the necessary balance in all things.

Mom in her wisdom often says, "I take the bitter with the sweet." She knows that both lie within each of us, and one cannot be had without the other. Her example, as a person who loves every living thing and especially us, unconditionally, is a treasure. So is my sister's smile, even when her heart is hurting, and my brother's life spent building rather than destroying.

Personally, I'm most proud to have fought for and found joy. My cultivated mindset, I do not take for granted. The daily quest I've accepted to uncover love and light in each face I meet, in every moment given, brings optimism. I allow hope, that daring proposition, to fill me with the enticing, unpredictable risk of living.

To survive trauma through toilsome exploration of self is not only revealing, it is freeing. To fully understand my role at each stage of life, to know who and where I have been, who I am and was to others, allows forgiveness and grace, informing who I want to become. Selfishly I crave a life without regret, so yes, I have forgiven those that brought me low in life, including myself, and have finally made peace with the unchangeable actions of Donald Harvey as they affected my life.

Through Dad's shortened days I've learned to sincerely value each of mine. With immense gratitude I walk this world with the man I love, in equal partnership, having raised two brilliant, creative children. Having Mom's good health and the wealth of a loyal family is what I think Dad would love the most.

Through this telling I've fulfilled a promise to myself. I've discovered a deeper love for my city. I've tapped into the interconnected nature of things. My ripple, my mark, has impact, as does yours. And so we walk. Me, with faithful friends, purpose, passion, empty pages to fill and stories to share. Casting light on my shadows, I've lived to tell new beginnings. And I fear the endings far less.

Gallery

Al, baby Dick, Patricia and Kay Myers, 1945

John Powell in 1945, Sedamsville

John Powell, c. 1951

Birthday celebration: Patricia, Heather, Holly, John, 1977

John Powell with arms around John and Holly, Kings Island, 1976

Myers Family dinner table, 1977: John, Patricia, Holly, Lori,
Al, Robert, Heather, Kay

John and Patricia
New Year's Eve,
1977

Holly, John, Patricia, Little John, wedding day, August 23, 1979

John Powell, birthday celebration, around 1981

*Wedding family photo, Oak Hills Methodist Church, with kids and
witnesses Trish Ninos and Mike Sweeney; August 23, 1979*

Wedding cake cut on Shafer Avenue, Holly, Patricia and John

*Al Myers,
Patricia and
John,
wedding day,
Aug 23, 1979*

Family photo, 1980

Dad (JP) with Holly, 1981

John Powell with four raccoon rescues, 1980

Below: John and Patricia, ready to hit the road

Joe and Fran Suesz with Patricia and John Powell, 1982

John, Patricia, John, Holly, 1983

John Powell and a friendly squirrel, 1986

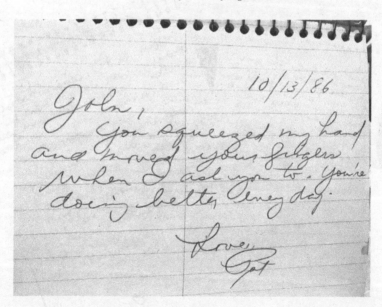

Hospital journal entry Patricia left for her husband, October 13, 1986

Hospital journal entries
by Holly, November 1986
to January 1987

Dad
I came in today and you were wide awake. You look alot better. Mom and I brushed your hair. You looked straight at us. It snowed yesterday and its really cold out. Thanksgiving is coming up. Sorry you can't spend it with us in Illinois, but how about coming home for Christmas, huh? Well I'll be back. Get Better.

Love,
Holly

11-15

John's
Visitors

Please Leave a note.

Dad,
You were really tired and depressed tonight so we didn't get alot of response out of you. You said you weren't looking forward to therapy but its good for you. Don't give up!

I love you,
Holly

12-27

Dad,
Mom and I came up today and ya were wide awake. We talked to you alot and you moved around alot. Ya started lifting yourself up in bed. You're getting restless. You said you didn't want a T.V. so it wouldn't bug you. I made a joke about "ya getting addicted to soaps" and you laughed. You are really restless. Well see ya later!
Happy New Year
We love you,
Holly
+
Pat

1-1-87

Patricia, Heather, Holly, John in Hamilton County courtroom, August 1987

The Cincinnati Post front page April 6, 1987

Holly Brians at Sawyer Point, Cincinnati Riverfront, 1989

Jack Brians and Holly Brians Ragusa, November 2014

Patricia Powell, Holly, Heather and John with Shed Media crew during filming of License to Kill *episode, August 2018*

Above: Patricia Powell with John, Heather and Holly, rooftop of Ragusa home in Over-the-Rhine, August 2018

Right: Patricia Powell during filming of License to Kill episode

Joe and Fran Suesz with John and The Cincinnati Enquirer, *1985*

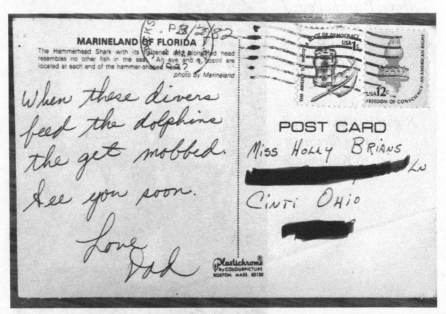

Postcard John sent to Holly from Florida, 1982

Afterword

IF YOU HAVE GONE THROUGH something traumatic, please find
the strength to seek out any help necessary to carry the burden.
Move beyond anger, get sad, get strong, question yourself, learn
who you want to be. Dig deep and find out how you can move
away from powerlessness to find purpose. Revel in the love or innocence you miss. Recognize hatred in your thoughts and deeds as
your own. Capitulate to vulnerability, your truth lies there. Above
all, forgive yourself for the roles you played so you may find peace.

Thoughts on Healthcare Now

DANIEL DRAKE MEMORIAL HOSPITAL has transformed. That
tainted facility lost credibility and dedicated professionals when
Donald Harvey and improper management took its toll there.
Purchased in 1989 by UC Health, the forty-two-acre property now
houses a post-op, rehabilitation treatment facility in the rebranded
Daniel Drake Center for Post-Acute Care. Necessary outpatient
care and skilled nursing, transitional and long-term care facilities
are offered at three different satellite branches, broadening the
reach of consistent patient care under the confines of illness or accident. I hope Daniel Drake persists in his medical legacy and that
his namesake overcomes.

Rehabilitative care requires patient and thoughtful caregivers—lifesavers to patients and family. As we have seen during this
pandemic, skilled hands are often the last someone will hold. Rely-

ing on professional caregivers for family care, I encourage us all to recognize these heroes walking among us. My gratitude extends to each of them for their skill in caring for others, for the amount of patience, bravery and endurance one must possess to accomplish it.

Please accept that we may still bother you with requests to comfort our loved one when we can't. You'll face daughters over-explaining situations to knowledgeable nurses and doctors, feeling she knows better about her mother. You won't be aware of her reasons for anxiety, the hidden stress felt by family, because one of you has the same coloring and size as the orderly who killed her father. We are all walking this road together, and I thank you for all the patience and dignity you extend.

In Gratitude

WITH CEASELESS GRATITUDE I recognize the love of my life, my equal, my soulmate, Damon. You are the fulcrum underpinning our beautiful life; your unwavering belief in me as a person and a writer has traveled steady under our nearly 10,000 moons. Despite exhaustive attempts, words cannot express the appreciation I have for the force and fortitude of you and all you bring to our life. To our incredible offspring, Nillin and Deej, two of my favorite reasons for being, thank you each for the music, art and imagination you bring to our world, for the lessons you've provided, for seasons weathered, songs sung and for your love, patience and continued belief in my ability to put one word in front of the other.

Indebted for life to my benevolent mother, Patricia Ann Powell, who with zeal supported my/our story from first concept. Thank you for the compassionate example set daily, for unconditional love, for sharing your strength. I love you so dearly. To my true-blue brother, John R. Powell, thank you for your hand in our world—I am forever grateful for and honored to have your love and trust. To my lovely sister Heather L. Abrams, thank you for a lifetime of knowing your tender heart, your spunk and spirit. A thousand thanks for your support, I treasure you, and your smile in my life. My dear sister Jennifer LeFavor, thank you for the thought, care, laughter and love you bring.

To Julie Coppens, my sagacious, journalistic editor, surely you know what your scholarship, cleverness and candor mean to this book, and to me.

Sincerest thanks to the family, friends and involved parties who cooperated, shared information, stories and showed kindness and support. Fran, we are indeed most fortunate. Lorri and Tina Powell, we share a dad and a story. Thank you for your early kindness and support. Barb Hodges for your pain. Lori Gresham for looking through the mirrored life we share in truth and for your devotion to late bloomers. For lifelong friendship that feels like family, Holly Earley. Lynn Meyers, the next ice cream is on me. Lissa Levin, stay bitchin! Kim Walden, for your unwavering depth of friendship and for an early read. Kim Miller for your friendship, a million things to thank you for and a midpoint read. Elizabeth Yarris, for understanding the tangle of family, for your love and a middle read. Bethany Vondran, for being real and beautiful and for a middle read. My Sista Christine, I adore you. For Big-Bird and Jail-Bird, Karena Garriques. For laughs and wine time, Regina Yearout. In appreciation to Dr. Julia King, truth and timing are everything. Glenn Whitaker, Esq. enjoy retirement. For looking through a different lens, thank you, Joe Deters. For all the hard work, Cincinnati Homicide Squad 1987. Dr. Lee Lehman, for your training and that nose. My first agent, Emmy Nordstrom Higdon, thanks for the education. Writers need community— thankful to be baked into a warm batch of Ohio word creators, crafters and lovers.

For the monthly feasts of words, my poetry and haiku group, and for writers' workshops at The Mercantile Library. For crossing borders in spirit with The Well and OnBeing Project and for holding space to share in the Ohio Poetry Association.

My wonderful grandparents, I was so lucky to have you. Jack Brians, you are remembered, and I thank you for my life. To the entirety of my family, good hearts all, the Myers and extended family, the Vetters and extended, the Wassermans, LeFavor/Wetzel family. With love Dona and Jerry and The Van Asdale Family Singers, the wide Ragusa family, Elizabeth Yarris, Fogliettis, Signores, Roses, Meehans, Travis, Borges, Halletts, Richter and Rich family, et al., I am grateful to be kin. And to my furry family, Chess and Whiskey, much love and thanks for keeping me company while writing.

I possess the colossal fortune of friendship in Lori Gresham and Hugo Gervais and family, Ana and Jeff Vissing, Kim Miller and Eugene Chung, Joe Hoffecker and Yvette Simpson and TSCJ, Kim and Shane Walden, Cate Dean, Trevor Kroeger, Molly Wellmann, Peter and Helga Vogt, Ron and Karena Garriques, Bethany and Jim Vondran, Regina and Keith Yearout, Lynn and all Sprafkas, Debbie and Tom Finn, Amanda and Cristian Pietoso, Annique and Tom Link, Andrew and Becky Moore, Dave and Lisa O'Brien, Doreen and Annabel Stanley, Jacob Matheney and the Jones Family, Tara Byrd, Rachel Stone, Jennifer Zvokel, Kristy Davis and Mitch Mustain, Mary and Al Bunker, Andrea Frieder, Emma Heines, Andrea Scheiber, WES—Patricia Bittner and Andre Bilokur, Thea Tjepkema and John Morris Russell. Tim Cagle and Rick Kammerer, Malinda McReynolds, Roy Jones, Michelle and Chris Abernathy, the Manley-Wick and Gastenveld families, Amanda Cawdrey, Ford Clark, Sam Kerns, Rhonda Shires, Jacquie Wells, Fran Bailey and Scott Feldman. For all my favorite OTR restaurants, haunts and drinkeries and for so many wonderful friends and hard-workers in my SCPA, FMH, CAA and ETC communities. My cup overflows with even more beautiful humans… I adore you all and appreciate your support in my endeavors. To Mom's lovely friends—true blessings all.

For moments of kindness, thanks to Sherry Wurster Gregor, Jennifer Bachler (1971-2019), Michelle Beacock Dooley and Carrie Charrington.

For my go-to soundtrack of sanity during this project: Deej, Stevie Nicks, Brandi Carlisle, Joni Mitchell, Sam Cooke, Edith Piaf, Otis Redding, Classical, Tedeschi Trucks Band and Wilco.

To each and every author who gave me a tough bit to chew on, or a soft place to land. For every writing teacher I've been fortunate enough to aim to please, know that I appreciate your talents, especially as they enable young writers to express themselves more fully. You've each marked me indelibly. Mrs. Gibbons at OHHS, Ms. B at SCPA, Ms. Murphy at MMHS.

To all the Harvey survivors out there, I hope you are all well and have found your peace. POMC—keep up the hard and important work. Adolescent care workers, don't stop giving of yourselves for them; you are the difference. Health-care professionals, your dedication means the world to more than your patient.

To Cincinnati, my hometown, together we went through this. Thanks for becoming my ideal home.

Pouring my soul on the page—a lifetime

- HBR

Endnotes by Chapter

Personal journals and public record documentation quoted throughout. Any other articles or attributions are mentioned in text.

1

Over-the-Rhine Foundation: References for German immigration, Rhine River
The Farmers' Almanac
Cincinnati Public Library online sources

7

Ohio History Central: Cincinnati, Hamilton County, Daniel Drake
Greater Cincinnati Police Museum: Chronological history of CPD 1800-
Ohio Attorney General website
Find a Grave website, City infirmary, Cemetery
Newspapers.com image from *The Cincinnati Enquirer,* Feb. 13, 1995, A5
Newspapers.com image from *The Cincinnati Enquirer,* Oct. 6, 1976,
    Drake Hospital, C1

8

Slate: "Who Said it First," article by Jack Shafer, August 2010
Cornell Law: Freedom of expression, speech and press
*The Enquirer/*Cincinnati.com: "Our History: Adapted over long history,"
    by Jeff Suess, April 2019
Xavier University Library: Documents on Moses Dawson Biography
Biographical Guide of the United States Congress, James Faran, 1808-1892
Spring Grove Cemetery history
New World Encyclopedia: E.W. Scripps
Encyclopedia Britannica: Copperhead, political faction
*The Enquirer/*Cincinnati.com: Lincoln assassination
Newspapers.com image from The Cincinnati Enquirer, Dec. 17, 1987,
    Drake Hospital, A10
Cincinnati Business Courier, "Cincinnati Enquirer cuts arts reporter," by
    Tom Demeropolis, Sept. 19, 2017
WKSU: NPR's *All Things Considered,* "Job cuts Gannett," Aug. 6, 2019
History.com: United States Constitution, Freedom of the Press

Pulitzer Prize 2018, *The Cincinnati Enquirer* Staff for distinguished reporting

12

Cincinnati Police Department: public record request materials
Newspapers.com image from *The Cincinnati Enquirer,* "Poison Suspect,"
   April 10, 1987, A1

13

American Association for the Advancement of Science: "Eureka alert,
   Forensic/Cyanide Peer reviewed," Feb. 2012, Sam Houston State University
Newspapers.com image from *The Cincinnati Enquirer,* Aug. 19, 1987,
   "Wrongful Deaths - Guilty Pleas," by Camilla Warrick, "Killer Deformed," by
   David Wells, A8
Cincinnati Magazine: "Angel of Death Asks for Mercy," by William Whalen and
   Bruce Martin
Peabody Awards: profile on WCPO Drake Hospital Investigation
Cincinnati Business Courier, "After 18 years, lawyer gives scoop on Donald
   Harvey," by Dan Monk, May 2, 2005

14

Newspapers.com image from *The Cincinnati Enquirer,* June 24, 1987, Drake, A11
CPD public records request: Psychological consultant's sample material,
   Dr. Lippert, p. 5
WCPO: "From the Vault: 'Angel of Death' case was unlike anything ever seen
   in the Tri-state," posted on WCPO online March 30, 2017, and updated
   May 4, 2019, fourth video 1:35-1:45
FOX News: Crime Vault "Raw interview with Hamilton County Prosecutor
   Joe Deters on Donald Harvey," Sept. 19, 2019
Newspapers.com image from *The Cincinnati Enquirer,* June 25, 1987, Drake, D1

15

WCPO: "From the Vault: 'Angel of Death' case was unlike anything ever seen in
   the Tri-state," posted on WCPO online, March 30, 2017
Rights and permission obtained through WCPO, Photo credit Cincinnati.com
Fox News: "'He just liked killing': Donald Harvey convicted of 37 murders," by
   Jason Scott, Sept. 23, 2019
Newspapers.com image from Associated Press, *Sioux City Journal*: "Harvey's
   lawyer doesn't know if client will admit to more murders," Aug. 23, 1987, A8
Harvard Health Publishing, Harvard Health School: "Adverse childhood experi
   ences, in particular, are linked to chronic health conditions," Feb. 12, 2021

16

Police Statement of Joseph Suesz

Variety Magazine digital news, March 29, 2020, "Tiger King," by Todd Spangler

Last Podcast On the Left

United Nations 2019 edition data

Serial Killer Shop online, documentaries

Internet Movie Database, IMDB.com

Centers for Disease Control: statistics for COVID-19

17

Newspapers.com image from *The Cincinnati Enquirer*, "Funding for Millcreek Psychiatric Center," Nov. 25, 1971, pg. 34

Newspapers.com image from *The Cincinnati Enquirer*, Ad for Nursing Director, April 4, 1987

TouringOhio.com: Showboat Majestic

18

Exodus 14, *King James Bible*

Biblegateway.com: The Red Sea Crossing

IsraelBibleCenter.com: Red Sea/Reed Sea

19

Parents of Murdered Children, pomc.org

20

WCPO: "From the Vault: 'Angel of Death' case was unlike anything ever seen in the Tri-state," posted on WCPO online March 30, 2017

21

Personal letter to Donald Harvey

Letter sent by Patricia Powell to Drake Memorial Hospital shortly after March 7, 1987

22

Radford University, Department of Psychology: "Donald Harvey," by Elizabeth Sellers, Pannill Hedgecock, Melissa Georges, Fall 2005

Newspapers.com image from *The Cincinnati Enquirer*, "Wrongful Deaths," by David Wells, Camilla Warrick, "Exhumations," Aug. 19, 1987

FBI.gov Statistics: Serial Murder Journal, "Federal Probation"

Volume 44, Issue 3, "Profiles in Terror - The Serial Murderer," R.M. Holmes

National Center for the Anaylysis of Violent Crime: NCJRS abstract

Academic assessment, "Angel of Death," Dr. Lippert

Clay County News, "I was with the Angel of Death," by Col. T.C. Sizemore, March 13, 2013

Murderpedia.org: Harvey

23

Newspapers.com image from *The Cincinnati Enquirer*, "Drake Workers Struggle," by Elizabeth Neus, Aug. 20, 1987, C section

Newspapers.com image from *The Courier Journal* (Louisville), Aug. 10, 1989, Associated Press report, "Drake Denies Killings"

Newspapers.com image from *The Messenger-Inquirer*, "Families of Harvey victims frustrated," Associated Press, Oct 29, 1989, 7B

Newspapers.com image from *The Dayton Daily News*, "Hamilton County braces for lawsuits," by Doug McInnis Aug. 20, 1987 pg. 8

24

Buzzfeed.com: "This Prosecutor took Cincinnati's Black community by surprise after charging a police officer with murder," by David Mack, July 29, 2015

WVXU: "Arthur M. Ney Jr., dead at age 88, prosecuted high profile cases," by Howard Wilkinson, May 12, 2015

WLWT: "Deters one-on-one with WLWT: 'I don't have good filter. I tend to say what I think,'" Sept. 24, 2015

Law.com legal dictionary

Newspapers.com image from *The Cincinnati Enquirer*, "Defense Attorney: 'crossed aisle,'" by Peggy Lane, Aug. 23, 1987, A12

Cincinnati Magazine: "Angel of Death Asks for Mercy," by William Whalen and Bruce Martin, excerpt

25

Amazon Video: *Diagnosis Unknown*, Season 2, Episode 3, "Death Shift," originally released in 2003

IMDB.com

WCET-TV: *Showcase* with Barbara Kellar, Season 7, Episode 2, interview with Bill Whalen

26

Irunfar.com: Badwater 135 Race Results 2021

WCPO: "Harvey Lewis Finishes Appalachian Trail in Less than 50 Days," by WCPO staff, June 29, 2019

Like Harvey Like Son documentary

BBC.com: Harvey Weinstein, Oct. 5, 2017

Oxygen Channel: *License to Kill*, Season 1, Episode 5

WCPO: "70th Anniversary famous faces through the year," by Evan Millward, June 25, 2019

WVXU: "WCPO plans long 70th Birthday Celebration," by John Kieswetter, July 17, 2019

FOX19: "Crime Vault: Raw Interview with Pat Minarcin," Sept. 19, 2019

FOX19: "Crime Vault: Raw Interview with Joe Deters," Sept. 19, 2019

Additional Historical References

Beltmag.com: "2020 Vision: Cincinnati's West End Displacement," by Cailin Pitt, March 23, 2020

Cincinnati Magazine: "Lost City - Kenyon Barr Queensgate, 25,737 people lived in West End when the city razed to ground," by Alyssa Konerman, Feb. 10, 2017

Cincinnati Business Courier: "Fork in the Road - Central Parkway could get a new life," by Chris Wetterich, Nov. 25, 2021

❖

About the Author

Holly Brians Ragusa (she/her/hers) is an interdisciplinary writer, speaker and community activist based in Cincinnati. Author of MET THE END (Nov 2022), DYING TO KNOW MYSELF IN TIME and INVERSE; IN-FORMED THOUGHTS BY AN UNFIT POET (2023), she serves a range of nonprofits and lives in historic Over-the-Rhine, sharing space with her husband, mother, three cats, one dog, and (sometimes) two grown children. Her passions also include moon-gazing, seeking meaning, and mustard.

www.hollybriansragusa.com